INSIGHTS

Comprehension Strategies: Responding to Literature

READING AS THINKING

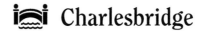 Charlesbridge

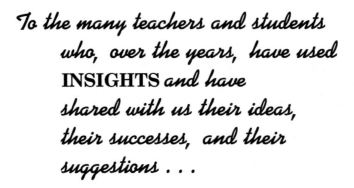

To the many teachers and students
    who, over the years, have used
    INSIGHTS *and have*
    shared with us their ideas,
    their successes, and their
    suggestions . . .

And to all those
    who will in the future take
    the strategies presented
    here and make them an
    integral part of their own
    approach to reading . . .

We dedicate this edition of
INSIGHTS: Reading as Thinking

Send permission requests to: Charlesbridge Publishing, 85 Main Street, Watertown, Massachusetts 02472.

Printed in the United States of America.

ISBN: 1-57091-065-0

10 9 8 7 6 5 4 3 2 1

CONTENTS

Yellow Level — Kindergarten

Comprehension Strategies

Phonics in Context

Red Level — Grade 1

Comprehension Strategies

Phonics in Context

Green Level — Grade 2

Comprehension Strategies

Phonics in Context

Orange Level — Grade 3

Comprehension Strategies

Content Area Strategies

Blue Level — Grade 4

Comprehension Strategies

Content Area Strategies

Tan Level — Grade 5

Comprehension Strategies

Content Area Strategies

Gold Level — Grade 6

Comprehension Strategies:
Responding to Literature

Strategies for
Reading with a Purpose

Purple Level — Grade 7

Comprehension Strategies:
Responding to Literature

Strategies for
Reading with a Purpose

Silver Level — Grade 8

Comprehension Strategies:
Responding to Literature

Strategies for
Reading with a Purpose

AN OVERVIEW OF **INSIGHTS**: *READING AS THINKING*

Through the *INSIGHTS* series, students develop effective, flexible reading strategies. They learn to adjust reading for different purposes and different types of text.

Specific critical-thinking strategies are essential to the reading required by content-area texts and library resources. *INSIGHTS: Comprehension Strategies: Responding to Literature* helps students develop the clarity of thought that is necessary to appreciate and respond successfully to readings in mathematics, science, and social studies. Used with *INSIGHTS: Strategies for Reading with a Purpose*, and literature appropriate for your students' needs and interests, this program empowers students to learn from books.

The goal of *INSIGHTS: Comprehension Strategies: Responding to Literature* is to enhance self-direction and learning efficiency in content-area studies. Each unit is designed to integrate critical thinking strategies across the curriculum. Metacognition is incorporated through thinking journals and discussion in cooperative-learning groups.

The structure of *INSIGHTS* promotes learning for all students. Lessons present information and structure responses using a variety of modalities. Alternate lessons and assessments help teachers plan appropriate guidance, remediation, and extension.

Direct Instruction

Demonstration guidelines, prompts, explanations, and discussion questions are provided.

Literature

A variety of titles and teaching methods are supplied to allow for consideration of different reading levels and interests.

Activities

Guidelines are provided for teacher-directed and cooperative learning activities, which include a variety of modes for instruction and response.

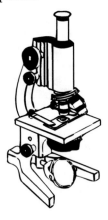

TEACHER MANUAL

❏ **INTEGRATING SEQUENCES OUT OF ORDER**

After students have read the strategy for integrating sequences, discuss the concept of *flashbacks*. Ask the students to suggest recent movies or books that use flashbacks. Tell students it is helpful to visualize the events and mentally note whether the events are occurring in the present or in the past.

Investigation A: IDENTIFYING THE SEQUENCE

Have volunteers read the passage. Remind students to pay attention to the signal words that tell them whether the events are occurring in the present or in the past. Check that students have circled all the words. Go over the sequence chart when they are done.

Answer Key
Paragraph 1, circle: Before, As, back, early, After, finally
Paragraph 2, circle: Suddenly, interrupted, early, Prior to, then, throughout, back to the present, final

Sequence Chart
Events in the Dressing Room
  2. about her early days of competition.
  3. There is a knock on her door and a warning.
  4. She thinks about early days again.
  6. Latisha looks in mirror; tells herself she can do it.

Events in Early Days of Training
  2. with parents about grades.
  3. Received consent to train intensively.
  4. Latisha believed in herself.

One strategy would be to number the events in the correct order. However, this requires marking your text. If you cannot make marks in a book, you may mentally note to yourself the correct order of events.

In the following passage, two sets of events are occurring: the events in the present and the events in the past. This is a literary device called a *flashback* that you will find in books and movies.

 A: IDENTIFYING THE SEQUENCE

❏ Read the following paragraphs and circle all the sequence signal words.
  • Complete the sequence chart that follows the passage.

Before the Match

Before Latisha could face that huge crowd of excited tennis fans, she just had to have a few moments by herself to think. As Latisha tied her hair back to keep it out of her face, her thoughts strayed back to her early days of competition. After arguments with her parents about the need to keep up her grades, she finally received their consent to go into intensive training.

Suddenly, Latisha's thoughts were interrupted by a knock on the door; a voice told her that she had only a few moments more. Latisha's thoughts traveled again to those early days. Prior to her decision to go into training, Latisha had little self-confidence, but her coach, Mrs. Chen, urged her to keep trying. There were so many mistakes then; but Mrs. Chen would always say, "The only failure is not to learn from mistakes, Latisha." That thought had kept her going throughout her training period, until she believed in herself. The two-minute warning buzzer forced her back to the present; she took one final look in the mirror and thought, "You're on, Latisha. You've got what it takes."

Sequence Chart

Events in the Dressing Room	Events in Early Days of Training
1. Latisha awaits match.	1a. Many mistakes in early training
2. She thinks_____	1b. No self-confidence
_____	1c. Mrs. Chen encouraged her.
3. _____	2. Argued_____
4. _____	3. _____
5. The last warning sounds.	_____
6. _____	4. _____

INSIGHTS: Reading as Thinking ©
Charlesbridge Publishing • (800) 225-3214   UNIT 5 – Comprehending Complex Information **159**

Curriculum Connection

Language Arts: Flashbacks.
Charting the events in the flashback with a parallel chart for the current events is quite useful in grasping the concept of flashback in literature. Choose a novel involving sequences that are chronologically out of order and have the class construct a sequence chart.

238 *Strategy Lesson 3 – Making Sequence Charts*   UNIT 5: Comprehending Complex Information

Assessment

Assessment and Re-assessment of student performance is a natural and integral part of each unit. Students complete a self-evaluation in each unit so they will take responsibility for their learning.

The Teacher Manual that accompanies each student book offers research-based and classroom-tested instruction, with a variety of options to accommodate individual teaching and learning styles.

Comparing Information

COMPARING INFORMATION

You have been applying a strategy for understanding complex sequential information: making a sequence chart for events given out of chronological order. In this lesson, you will use a strategy for understanding complex comparative information and putting it into a form that is easier to understand and to remember.

 COMPARING SUBJECTS AND ATTRIBUTES

Have you ever compared two movies or the personalities of two friends? Have you ever compared the plots in two or more books? If you have, then you are comparing *subjects* and their *attributes*, that is, their characteristics or features. The subject may be two or more persons, two or more places, two or more things, or two or more events. Attributes are usually given in the predicate. Note that compound predicates usually mean compound attributes.

 Example

Ingrid decided to work for the Park Department during the summer. The Park Department assigned her to help people put away their sailboats in special racks for storage. To do the job requires knowing the sizes and special features of each type of boat that is stored. Consequently, the Park Department gives each employee who does this job a description of each boat and a short quiz before the job begins. Here are some of the things Ingrid had to learn.

A (Catamaran) has no keel and only one sail. (It) is very heavy and is stored on the bottom shelf. The (Lightning) is the next heaviest and is stored on the second shelf. (It) has a large keel that must be raised and two sails. The (Sunfish) is a lightweight, single-sail boat and is stored on the top shelf. (It) has a medium-sized keel that can be removed for storage.

Explanation

The topic in the example above is sailboats. You know this because the subject in every sentence of the second paragraph is the name of a sailboat or a pronoun that stands for one. Thus, the passage is a description of two or more things. The subjects, which identify the names of the sailboats, are circled. The verbs are underlined because they give you a clue to the number and location of the attributes, or characteristics, of each sailboat.

160   UNIT 5 – Comprehending Complex Information   INSIGHTS: *Reading as Thinking* © Charlesbridge Publishing • (800) 225-3214

Have the class read the first paragraph. Ask students to raise any questions they have about charting sequential events. Explain that in this lesson, they will use charts to organize complex comparative information. Point out that comparisons can be made for both similarities and differences.

❑ **COMPARING SUBJECTS AND ATTRIBUTES**

Have the students read the introductory paragraph. Give examples of two characters from a popular movie and ask students to describe several features of each character. Point out that the two characters are *subjects* and their features are *attributes*.

Ask the students to read the Example describing the attributes of different sailboats. Have the class read the Explanation. Discuss the clues regarding the number and location of the attributes that are provided by the underlined verbs.

Strategy Lessons

Cognitive strategies are presented through "thinking aloud" teaching structures, graphic organizers, and clearly demonstrated processes.

Writing

Journal and creative writing activities allow students to use concepts and apply strategies.

Curriculum Connections

Each unit includes activities for linking unit concepts to specific math, science, social studies, writing, or art lessons.

STRUCTURE: *INSIGHTS* is designed to maximize achievement for all students. Its organization allows the teacher to preview each unit and review its purpose and objectives with the class. The teacher models the strategy to be learned and guides students as they apply it to different types of text. Unit assessments include criteria for mastery. If the concepts in the unit are not mastered in the initial presentation, the teacher is provided with alternate activities and re-assessments.

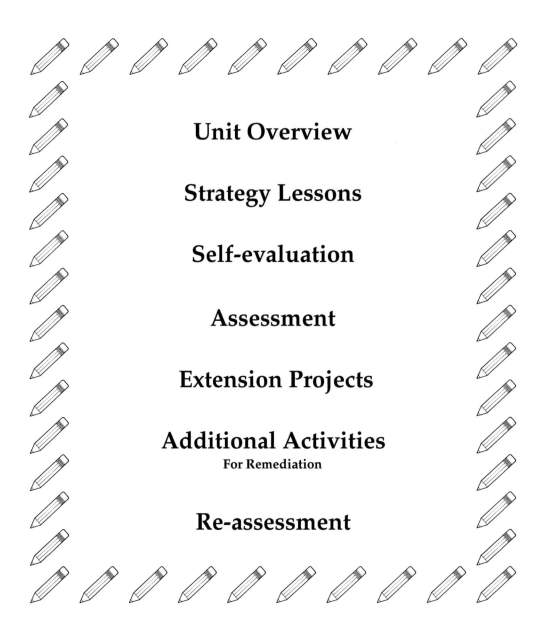

Unit Overview

Strategy Lessons

Self-evaluation

Assessment

Extension Projects

Additional Activities
For Remediation

Re-assessment

UNIT 1
Using Context Clues

Learning Objectives

In this unit the student will infer the meaning of unfamiliar words by

- analyzing sentences containing words in a series
- analyzing sentences containing words linked by meaning associations, "go-togethers"
- using sentence context to determine appropriate meanings of words with multiple meanings
- analyzing unknown words into base words and suffixes to infer word meanings
- using context to confirm meaning inferred from word analysis

Lesson 1: Using the context of words in a series to infer meaning
Lesson 2: Using a substitution strategy
Lesson 3: Analyzing associations as context clues
Lesson 4: Using context clues to determine the meanings of multiple-meaning words and words with misleading roots
Lesson 5: Using context clues in longer passages
Assessment: Blackline Master Pages 28-29
    Extension: Context clue crossword
    Remediation: Additional Activities on Blackline Master Pages 34-39
Re-assessment: Blackline Master Pages 41-42

Purpose of this Unit

In this unit, thinking strategies help students to be active readers. Actively reading means constantly using creativity, logic, and analysis to get the most out of a story or passage. Good authors let their readers meet them halfway, so reading is exciting and challenging, not boring and passive.

Activating Prior Knowledge

Before beginning the unit, ask the students what they do when they see a word they do not understand. Some students will say that they look up the word in a dictionary. Others will say that they try to figure out the meaning from the information in the sentence. Explain that this unit focuses on specific strategies for deriving the meaning of new words.

Prerequisites and Introduction

❏ WHAT IS CONTEXT?

Have students read the introduction. Ask if they have ever read a new word in a book, looked it up in a dictionary, and still not been sure of its meaning. Ask why a dictionary alone might not answer their question. Point out that most words have more than one meaning, and we look at the context to decide which meaning is most appropriate.

❏ WORDS IN LISTS

Have students read the Example. Have a volunteer read the Explanation aloud.

Explain that using context clues is like doing detective work. The reader examines the surrounding clues and uses them to piece together the meaning of the unfamiliar word.

PREREQUISITES AND INTRODUCTION

If you can find the meaning of an unfamiliar word from the sentence context, then you do not need to look up the word in a dictionary.

■ WHAT IS CONTEXT?

Sometimes you hear or read a word you do not understand. One way to find out what the word means is to look it up in a dictionary. But what if you do not have a dictionary handy or you do not want to stop reading? What do you do then?

Sometimes you can understand the new word because it is included in a list or group of words that you do know. The words you know become the context of the new word. They help you to infer the meaning of the new word. (*Infer* means to find out the meaning by reasoning.)

■ WORDS IN LISTS

Ada and Tom saw a sign in the supermarket. Here is the sign.

 Example

> Sale on Jams and Jellies
>
> apple   strawberry
> peach   cherry
> quince   grape

 Explanation

Tom asked, "What does *quince* mean?"

Ada thought, "Apples, peaches, strawberries, cherries, and grapes are kinds of fruit. So, a quince must be a kind of fruit, too."

Ada understood the word *quince* because she understood the other words in the group. The context told her the meaning of the new word.

INSIGHTS: Reading as Thinking ©
Charlesbridge Publishing • (800) 225-3214

UNIT 1 – Using Context Clues   1

★ Example

Feeding Times		
lions	—	11:00 AM
tigers	—	11:00 AM
cougars	—	11:20 AM
lynxes	—	11:30 AM

☆ **Explanation**

Sara and Carlos went to the zoo. They saw this sign.

Sara asked, "What is a *lynx*?" (Help Carlos complete his inference.) Carlos thought, "Lions, tigers, and cougars are *animals*. They are very big cats. So, a lynx must be _____ ."

Carlos understood the word *lynx* because he understood the other words in the group; these words are the *context* for *lynx*. Carlos *inferred* the meaning of *lynx* from its context.

 Investigation A: WORD MEANINGS FROM LISTS

In each of the following lists, one word is underlined. Your task is to infer the meaning of the underlined word from its context.

❏ Read all the words in the list.
 • *Think:* To what group do all the things named in the list belong?
 • Write the name of the group on the line in the *Think* statement.
 • Complete the inference sentence that explains the underlined word.

1. Langston Hughes
 Beverly Cleary
 Charles Dickens
 <u>Virginia Hamilton</u>

 Think: Langston Hughes, Beverly Cleary, and Charles Dickens are all ___authors___ .

 Inference: Virginia Hamilton must be the name of a famous _____ .

2. puppies
 <u>goslings</u>
 cubs
 chicks
 kittens

 Think: Puppies, cubs, chicks, and kittens are all _____ .

 Inference: A gosling must be a _____ .

INSIGHTS: *Reading as Thinking* ©
Charlesbridge Publishing • (800) 225-3214

 ### Literature Connection

Encourage students to read poems by Langston Hughes such as "Harlem," or Charles Dickens's *Great Expectations, Oliver Twist,* and *A Tale of Two Cities,* Virginia Hamilton's *The People Could Fly* and *Sweet Whispers, Brother Rush.* Students may be more familiar with Beverly Cleary, the author of the *Ramona* books.

Have students read the Example. Tell them to complete Carlos's inference. ("So, a lynx must be a big cat.") Point out that "a dangerous animal" and "an animal in the zoo" are not correct, because they could be made more specific. There are many kinds of animals in the zoo, and there are many kinds of dangerous animals. Inferring that a lynx is a big cat gives Carlos a much better idea of what lynxes are.

Ask students to define the word *context* in their own words. (the text that surrounds a word and that can shed light on its meaning; the environment in which something exists)

Investigation A: WORD MEANINGS FROM LISTS

Have students read the instructions. To model the thinking process, use the first list to infer who Virginia Hamilton is. Ask, **What do the words have in common?** (They are all names of famous authors.) Tell the students to write the name of the group to complete the *Think* statement. Ask, **What can we infer from this?** (that Virginia Hamilton must be the name of a famous author) This is the characteristic that she shares with the other members of the group.

Answer Key
 1. authors, author
 2. young animals, young animal

Investigation A: WORD MEANINGS FROM LISTS
continued

Have students write the names of the groups and complete the inference statements for items 3-9. Review the students' responses and discuss the logic of any other groupings they suggest.

Answer Key

3. Running, hopping, and walking are kinds of movement or action; sprinting must be a kind of movement or action.

4. Anger, pride, and sadness are emotions or feelings; adoration must be a kind of emotion or feeling.

5. Spanish, Russian, English, Italian, and Chinese are languages or nationalities; Latvian must be the name of a language or nationality.

6. Squares, circles, and triangles are all shapes; a trapezoid must be a shape.

7. Guitars, pianos, and drums are musical instruments; zithers must be musical instruments.

8. Kennedy, Lincoln, and Washington have all served as Presidents of the United States; Woodrow Wilson must be the name of a President of the United States.

9. Blue, yellow, and green are all colors; fuchsia must be a color.

---

3. running
   hopping
   walking
   <u>sprinting</u>

   Think: Running, hopping, and walking are kinds of

   _____ .

   Inference: Sprinting must be a kind of _____ .

4. <u>adoration</u>
   anger
   pride
   sadness

   Think: Anger, pride, and sadness are _____ .

   Inference: Adoration must be a kind of _____ .

5. Spanish
   Russian
   English
   Italian
   <u>Latvian</u>
   Chinese

   Think: Spanish, Russian, English, Italian, and Chinese

   are _____ .

   Inference: Latvian must be the name of a _____

   _____ .

6. square
   circle
   triangle
   <u>trapezoid</u>

   Think: Squares, circles, and triangles are all _____ .

   Inference: A trapezoid must be a _____ .

7. guitars
   pianos
   drums
   <u>zithers</u>

   Think: Guitars, _____ , _____ ,

   and _____ are _____ .

   Inference: Zithers must be _____ .

8. <u>Woodrow Wilson</u>
   John F. Kennedy
   Abraham Lincoln
   George Washington

   Think: Kennedy, Lincoln, and Washington have all

   served as _____

   _____ .

   Inference: <u>Woodrow Wilson</u> _____

   _____ .

9. blue
   <u>fuchsia</u>
   yellow
   green

   Think: Blue, yellow, and green are all _____ .

   Inference: <u>Fuchsia</u> _____ .

INSIGHTS: Reading as Thinking ©
Charlesbridge Publishing • (800) 225-3214

☐ LISTS IN SENTENCES

Lists often appear as groups of words in sentences. All of the *Think* sentences in the previous exercise had lists in them. Lists or groups of words in sentences give you clues to the meaning of any word you do not know in the group. They are the context of the new word.

Investigation **A**: INFERRING MEANING FROM SENTENCE CONTEXT

☐ Read each sentence carefully and pay attention to the underlined word.
  • Circle the words in each sentence that help you infer the meaning of the underlined word. They will be words that belong to a group.
  • Complete the sentence that explains the underlined word.

1. Sports lovers in England like to play tennis, soccer, and <u>rugby</u>, but they do not play baseball.

   Inference: Rugby is _____ .

2. Lizzy really likes spinach, lettuce, and cabbage, but her mother cannot make her eat <u>chard</u>.

   Think: Spinach, _____ , and _____ are

   all _____ . So chard

   must be a _____ .

   Inference: Chard is _____ .

3. During the gold rush of 1849, prospectors (people digging for gold) were <u>venturesome</u>, brave, and daring.

   Inference: Venturesome describes people who are _____ .

4. The teenagers left the concert singing, <u>chanting</u>, and humming to themselves.

   Inference: Chanting is a kind of _____ .

INSIGHTS: Reading as Thinking ©
Charlesbridge Publishing • (800) 225-3214

☐ LISTS IN SENTENCES

Now students read sentences that contain lists of words. They decide which words in the sentence belong in the same group as the underlined word. These words – or context clues – can help a reader infer meaning.

Investigation A: INFERRING MEANING FROM SENTENCE CONTEXT

Use the first sentence to model the strategy. Ask, **To what group of words does rugby belong?** (tennis, soccer, and baseball) **What do these words have in common?** (They are names of ball games.) **Therefore, what do we know about rugby?** (It must be a type of ball game.)

Have students complete items 2-4 independently.

Answer Key

1. Circle: tennis, soccer, baseball.
   Inference: a ball game
2. Circle: spinach, lettuce, cabbage.
   Think: lettuce, cabbage, green leafy vegetables, green leafy vegetable.
   Inference: a green leafy vegetable
3. Circle: brave, daring.
   Inference: risk-taking
4. Circle: singing, humming.
   Inference: sound, noise made by children, music made by the human voice.

Investigation A: INFERRING MEANING FROM SENTENCE CONTEXT *continued*

Students infer meaning from lists in sentences 5-10. Discuss students' answers. Ask how they decided which words to circle. You might ask, **For sentence 9, why didn't you circle** *meal, After, eating,* **or** *children*? Elicit the idea that in the sentence, *drowsy, quiet,* and *lethargic* all describe the children after the meal. They are related words, so the reader can ask what they all have in common. (They all mean sleepy, tired, or slow moving.)

Answer Key

5. Circle: nests, houses; *Inference*: a type of shelter, a kind of house used by animals
6. Circle: limp, stumble; *Inference*: move with difficulty
7. Circle: blow, toss; *Inference*: move forcibly, disturb, lift with a sudden motion
8. Circle: grasshoppers, beetles; *Inference*: insect, bug
9. Circle: drowsy, quiet; *Inference*: sleepy or tired, slow moving
10. Circle: trunks, suitcase; *Inference*: a type of luggage or baggage

5. Young birds are in their nests, small animals are in their <u>burrows</u>, and children are in their houses.

   Inference: Burrows are _____.

6. Coming up the hill, the tired hikers began to limp, stumble, and <u>falter</u>.

   Inference: To falter is to_____.

7. To our alarm, the wind began to blow, toss, and <u>buffet</u> our small boat.

   Inference: To buffet is to _____.

8. The grasshoppers, beetles, and <u>locusts</u> were humming and buzzing in the grass.

   Inference: Locusts are a kind of _____.

9. After eating the large meal, the children were drowsy, quiet, and <u>lethargic</u>.

   Inference: To be lethargic is to be _____.

10. The trunks, <u>valise</u>, and suitcase were loaded onto the train.

    Inference: A valise is _____.

INSIGHTS: Reading as Thinking ©
Charlesbridge Publishing • (800) 225-3214

2 Using Sentence Context

USING SENTENCE CONTEXT

You have seen that you can infer the meaning of a new word in a sentence from the other words in its group or list. These other words are the context of the word. Sometimes it is helpful to try out different words to explain the meaning of the new word. Remember to read carefully for context clues, and be aware of how each word choice fits in the context.

Example

Carlos had to choose the word or phrase that best explained the underlined word in this sentence: The grasshoppers, beetles, and <u>locusts</u> were humming and buzzing in the grass.

Carlos had to choose from:

a. apples   b. a kind of insect   c. birds   d. sticks

Explanation
Carlos thought, "I know what grasshoppers and beetles are. They are insects. So locusts must be a kind of insect."

Could they be apples? No, because an apple is not an insect. Could

they be birds? _____ , because a bird is _____ an insect. Could

they be sticks? _____ , because a stick is _____ an insect.

Example

The flowers in the store were blue, yellow, <u>crimson</u>, and orange.

a. sweet   b. tall   c. red   d. ugly

Explanation

1. Blue, yellow, and orange are colors. So crimson must be a color, too.

2. *Ask yourself:* Could *crimson* mean sweet? No, because sweet is not a color. Could *crimson* mean tall? No, tall is not a color.

    Could *crimson* mean ugly? _____

    _____ .

    Could *crimson* mean red? Yes, because red is a color that flowers often are, and it is not already named in the sentence.

Have students read the introduction. In this lesson they will use a substitution strategy to infer the meanings of words.

Discuss the two Examples, asking the questions in the Explanation of different students. Explain that the question-answer process is just one way to try out different words in a given context.

Investigation A: TRYING OUT WORD MEANINGS

Ask students to read the instructions and use the thinking process to infer the meaning of the underlined word in each sentence.

Answer Key
1. a. vegetables, No, No
2. b. leaders, not, not
3. a. a water sport, No, No
4. jewels, precious stones, c. blue jewels, No, No

Investigation **A**: TRYING OUT WORD MEANINGS

❑ Read each sentence. Pay attention to the context of the underlined words.
- Complete the *Think* statement.
- Answer the questions about each answer choice.
- Circle the letter of the answer choice that best explains the underlined word.

1. You can make good soup out of leftover meat, potatoes, and <u>legumes</u>.

   Think: Meat and potatoes are kinds of food. So legumes are _____ .

   a. vegetables   b. forks   c. pencils

   Ask yourself: Could legumes be forks? _____ , because forks are not kinds of food.

   Could legumes be pencils? _____ , because pencils are not kinds of food.

2. A special person at the White House takes care of the foreign presidents, kings, and <u>prime ministers</u> who come to visit our president.

   Think: Presidents and kings are leaders. So prime ministers are _____ .

   a. frogs   b. leaders   c. vegetables

   Ask yourself: Could prime ministers be frogs? No, because frogs are ____ leaders.

   Could prime ministers be vegetables? No, because vegetables are _____ leaders.

3. My grandmother enjoys swimming, sailing, and <u>snorkeling</u>.

   Think: Swimming and sailing are water sports. So snorkeling is _____ .

   a. a water sport   b. modern dance   c. animals

   Ask yourself: Could snorkeling be dance?____ Could snorkeling be animals? ____

4. The queen wore diamonds, rubies, and <u>sapphires</u>.

   Think: Diamonds and rubies are _____ . So sapphires are _____ .

   a. celery   b. chairs   c. blue jewels

   Ask yourself: Could sapphires be celery? _____ Could sapphires be chairs?_____

INSIGHTS: Reading as Thinking ©
Charlesbridge Publishing • (800) 225-3214

UNIT 1 – Using Context Clues   **7**

---

5. Miners used to look for gold and silver, but now they look for uranium and <u>molybdenum</u>.

   Think: Gold, silver, and uranium are _____ .

        So molybdenum must be _____ .

   a. food   b. a song bird   c. a rare mineral

6. Fish, water snakes, and <u>crustaceans</u> were hiding in the waving seaweed.

   Think: Fish and water snakes are _____ .

        So crustaceans must be _____ .

   a. sea animals   b. eagles   c. chocolates

7. The baby cried, screamed, and <u>caterwauled</u> until his mother picked him up.

   a. smiled sweetly   b. made unhappy sounds   c. looked surprised

8. Jennifer likes to draw her pictures in pencil and then fill in the colors with paints or <u>pastels</u>.

   a. chickens   b. love   c. soft crayons

9. Measles, chicken pox, and <u>roseola</u> are children's diseases; adults almost never have them.

   a. nose colds   b. cancer   c. kind of German measles

10. In Alaska, Ted's favorite winter sports are ice hockey, skating, and <u>curling</u>.

   a. game played on ice   b. baseball   c. outdoor tennis

> Now you should be ready for more difficult words. Remember to find the words that belong in a group. Ask yourself what these words have in common. Keeping this in mind, choose a definition for the underlined word. Be sure you consider each of the choices.

Investigation A: TRYING OUT WORD MEANINGS *continued*

Have students try out word meanings for items 5 through 10. Discuss their answers.

The thinking process should progressively become more intuitive and automatic. To demonstrate this, ask volunteers to describe the thinking process behind questions 1, 5, and 10. Ask students if their method of trying out words changed.

Answer Key

  5. precious or valuable minerals, c. a rare mineral
  6. sea animals, a. sea animals
  7. b. made unhappy sounds
  8. c. soft crayons
  9. c. kind of German measles
10. a. game played on ice

 ## Curriculum Connection

Math: On the chalkboard, write a math problem with one factor missing. Provide several answer choices. For example, you might write:

$$18 - \underline{\hspace{1cm}} + 1 = 15$$

  a. 3   b. 7   c. 2   d. 4

Ask students to determine the answer by substituting each of the 4 choices into the equation. Ask a volunteer to show how *d* is the correct answer and *a, b,* and *c* are incorrect. Point out that this is the same strategy they have employed in choosing word meanings from a series of choices.

Investigation B: INFERRING MEANING

Explain that while students may have been familiar with the underlined words in the previous sentences, the underlined words on this page are less common. They will have to rely more on sentence context to infer the meaning of each word.

After students have inferred the meaning of the words, discuss their answers. Discuss why authors use unusual and rich words. (to spice up their writing or convey complex ideas)

Answer Key

1. colors, d. red-brown
2. ways things taste,
   c. slightly spicy
3. b. pleasant
4. a. killer
5. a. gasoline
6. b. valleys
7. b. mocking
8. a. bad-tempered
9. c. a goose
10. d. unbelievable

Investigation **B**: **INFERRING MEANING**

❏ Read each sentence. Pay attention to the context of the underlined word.
  • Circle the letter of the answer that best explains or defines the underlined word.

1. I like horses that are white, gray, or <u>roan</u>.
   Think: White and gray are _____ . So roan must mean _____ .
   a. large   b. fast   c. young   d. red-brown

2. Some people like their fruit sweet, some like it <u>piquant</u>, and some like it spicy.
   Think: Sweet and spicy are _____ . So piquant must mean _____ .
   a. red   b. big   c. slightly spicy   d. hard

3. When you ask him for a favor, his response is warm, kind, and <u>amiable</u>.
   a. angry   b. pleasant   c. cold   d. unhappy

4. The people shouted, "Murderer! <u>Assassin</u>! Someone has shot President Lincoln!
   a. killer   b. dancer   c. office worker   d. farmer

5. Coal, wood, and <u>petroleum</u> are good sources of energy.
   a. gasoline   b. metal   c. minnows   d. paint

6. In the spring, mountain goats come down into the canyons, river beds, and <u>ravines</u> in search of food.
   a. peaks   b. valleys   c. houses   d. city

7. The pitcher was upset by the teasing, taunting, <u>derisive</u> remarks of the crowd.
   a. kind   b. mocking   c. happy   d. fast

8. The old mule was <u>cantankerous</u>, stubborn, and unfriendly.
   a. bad-tempered   b. kind   c. humorous   d. smart

9. The barnyard at the farm was full of pigs, chickens, and a <u>gander</u> eating corn.
   a. a tiger   b. a bear   c. a goose   d. an elephant

10. The acrobat performed tricks that were wonderful, unusual, and <u>phenomenal</u>.
    a. friendly   b. average   c. boring   d. unbelievable

Analyzing Word Associations

Strategy Lesson **3**

ANALYZING WORD ASSOCIATIONS

❑ GO-TOGETHERS

Often the context of a new word in a sentence is not a group of words like those you have been learning about. The context is often **go-togethers** — words or phrases that are part of the same mental picture the sentence creates. Here is a sentence you read earlier.

The barnyard at the farm was full of pigs, chickens, and a gander eating corn.

This sentence creates a picture in your mind similar to the one below.

The question mark represents a gander. What barnyard animal could a gander be?

Here are some things that might go in this same picture, and some things that do not go in the picture. Check off the things that could be in the picture.

1. _yes_____ grass   6. _____ a pail someone forgot

2. _____ bushes   7. _____ a frog

3. _____ a skyscraper   8. _____ a duck

4. _____ a fence   9. _____ a lion

5. _____ a watchtower 10. _____ a factory

INSIGHTS: Reading as Thinking ©
Charlesbridge Publishing • (800) 225-3214

❑ GO-TOGETHERS

Have students read the introductory paragraph about groups of words which are in the same category.

Explain that words go together in different ways. Ask students to examine the picture and read the list of things that might or might not go in the picture. Tell them to write *yes* beside the things that go in the picture and *no* beside the things that would be out of place.

Answer Key

1. yes	5. no	8. yes
2. yes	6. yes	9. no
3. no	7. yes	10. no
4. yes		

Write the following sentence on the board:

Inside the tent, there were mosquitoes, sleeping bags, backpacks, and gorp.

Explain that to figure out why these words are all in the same group, the students might make a mental picture. Ask the students to visualize the scene and describe it. Have them explain how the words go together. (They are all things that can be found on a camping trip.) *Gorp* must be something people take on camping trips. It is trail mix. In a paragraph, additional clues might help the reader infer an exact meaning for *gorp*.

❏ GO-TOGETHERS AS CONTEXT CLUES

Have volunteers read the two Examples and Explanations aloud. Encourage students to visualize the scene described in each sentence. Ask volunteers to describe their visualizations and discuss any differences.

Write a third example on the board:

Corine carefully slid the vegetables into the bubbling pot of *ratatouille*.

> a. paint   c. salad
> b. soup   d. steam

Tell students to visualize the sentence. Ask three different students to describe their mental pictures. Discuss how the pictures helped the students infer the same meaning even though the pictures differed from each other.

▣ GO-TOGETHERS AS CONTEXT CLUES

Often you can understand a new word in a sentence because you understand the words with which it is grouped. You understand its context, and the context helps you infer the meaning of the word.

Example

Cassy was <u>irate</u> as she slammed the door, shook her fist, and ran down the steps shouting at the sky.

Explanation

Visualize this scene. What can *irate* mean? It must go together with slamming doors and shouting at the sky. You can infer that someone who does these things is angry. Inference: *Irate* must mean *angry*. If you understand the other words in a group, then you really can understand a new word in a sentence. Sometimes it helps to try out different words in place of the new word.

Example

You cannot <u>subsist</u> in the desert without plenty of water and some shade.
a. read signs   b. eat apples   c. wear clothes   d. stay alive

Explanation

1. Visualize a desert scene. What can *subsist* mean? It must be something you need water and shade to do.

2. *Ask yourself:* Could *subsist* mean to read signs? No, because reading signs does not go together with water and shade. You do not need water and shade to read signs.

   Could *subsist* mean to eat apples? No, because eating apples does not go together with water and shade. You do not need water and shade to eat apples.

   Could *subsist* mean to wear clothes? (You answer.) _____ because wearing clothes _____ go together with water and shade. You do _____ need water and shade to wear clothes.

3. *Inference: Subsist* must mean to stay alive. You do need water and shade to stay alive in a desert.

INSIGHTS: Reading as Thinking ©
Charlesbridge Publishing • (800) 225-3214

Investigation A: INFERRING MEANING FROM GO-TOGETHERS

Investigation A: INFERRING MEANING FROM GO-TOGETHERS

❑ Read each sentence. Pay attention to the context of the underlined word.
  • Complete the *Think* statement and answer the questions.
  • Circle the letter of the answer choice that best explains the underlined word.

1. The iron railing was <u>corroded</u> and all its paint was peeling off.

   a. beautiful   b. broken to pieces   c. rusty

   Think: Corroded goes together with *all its paint was peeling off.*
     Does *beautiful* go together with peeling paint? _____
     Does *broken to pieces* go together with peeling paint? _____
     because something which is peeling is not necessarily broken.
     Does *rusty* go together with peeling paint? _____
     because when paint peels off an iron railing, the railing does rust.

2. Some people from city hall are trying to find a good <u>site</u> for a housing development.

   a. place   b. tree   c. book

   Think: Site goes together with *housing development* and *find.*
     Does *tree* go together with finding a housing development?_____
     Do you need to find a good tree to have a housing development? _____
     Does *book* go together with finding a housing development?_____
     Do you need to find a good book to have a housing development? _____
     Does *place* go together with finding a housing development?_____ ,
     because you do need to find a good place to have a housing development.

3. Joel felt nothing but <u>contempt</u> for the people who threw trash on the beach.

   a. love   b. envy   c. disgust

   Think: Contempt goes together with *felt,* and *threw trash on the beach.*

Investigation A: INFERRING MEANING FROM GO-TOGETHERS

Have students read the instructions. Tell them they will now infer meaning from go-togethers – words or phrases that are part of the same mental picture.

Ask students to visualize an iron railing with peeling paint. Is such a railing likely to be beautiful, broken to pieces, or rusty? Discuss the thinking process outlined for the first sentence.

Have students infer the meaning of each word from go-togethers in its sentence. Suggest that students can infer meaning by asking focused questions, substituting words, or visualizing.

Answer Key
   1. c. rusty
   2. a. place
   3. c. disgust

Investigation A: INFERRING MEANING FROM GO-TOGETHERS *continued*

Have the students infer the meaning of the underlined words in the remaining sentences.

Discuss students' answers. For each sentence, ask volunteers which words they used as go-togethers. What kinds of questions did they ask themselves?

Answer Key

4. b. money; *Think*: albums, tennis balls, and comic books
5. car, empty lot for a week, b. left forever
6. from your heart and around and back to your heart, a. goes around
7. c. very happy
8. a. get the meaning of
9. b. choose

---

4. Victoria spent all her <u>income</u> for the week on albums, tennis balls, and comic books.

   a. energy   b. money   c. losses

   Think: <u>Income</u> goes together with <u>spent</u> and _____ . Does *energy* go together with *spending on albums, tennis balls, and comic books?* _____ . Do you use a week's energy to buy albums and tennis balls? _____ . Does *losses* go together with spending on albums and tennis balls? _____ . Does *money* go together with spending on albums and tennis balls? _____ , because you need money to buy albums.

5. The car had been in the empty lot for a week; the children decided it had been <u>abandoned</u> by its owner.

   Think: *Abandoned* goes together with _____ .

   a. chopped into bits   b. left forever   c. thrown in the lake

6. Did you know that your blood <u>circulates</u> through your body, running out from your heart and around and back to your heart?

   Think: *Circulates* goes together with *blood, running,* and _____ .

   a. goes around   b. stands still   c. dries up

7. When Rita learned that she had won the first prize, she was <u>elated</u>.

   a. very sad   b. angry with herself   c. very happy

8. Larry was able to <u>decipher</u> the message, even though the handwriting was messy.

   a. get the meaning of   b. scramble the meaning of   c. hide the parts of

9. There were so many kinds of basketball shoes at the store that Ivan did not know which to <u>select</u>.

   a. wear   b. choose   c. drink

INSIGHTS: Reading as Thinking ©
Charlesbridge Publishing • (800) 225-3214   **UNIT 1 – Using Context Clues**   **13**

Investigation B: VISUALIZING CHOICES

❑ Read the sentence and visualize the picture it creates.
- *Think:* What words go together with the underlined word?
- *Ask Yourself:* Which answer choice goes with the picture the sentence creates?
- Circle the letter of the answer choice that best explains the underlined word.

1. A peal of thunder sounded out, shaking the bushes and frightening the birds.
   a. loud sound   b. nice smell   c. whisper   d. moment

2. Tanya was afraid that having her tooth pulled would be excruciating.
   a. easy   b. fun   c. painful   d. exciting

3. She reimbursed his money when he returned the sweater to the store.
   a. thought about   b. slid   c. paid back   d. threw away

4. In the fall, you can see many wild ducks flying through the sky as they migrate from the cold of Canada to the warmth of Florida.
   a. dig   b. swim   c. hiked   d. travel

5. Patrick could not tell whether the man coming down the street was Mr. Ryan or a policeman because in the fog, nothing was distinct.
   a. clear   b. unusual   c. tired   d. tasty

6. When Olga sprayed the antiseptic on her cut, it killed all the germs.
   a. medicine   b. candy   c. paper   d. sweater

7. Emile brings his mother leaves that fall off the trees in the park because his mother likes foliage better than flowers.
   a. coffee   b. leaves   c. fire hydrants   d. ponds

8. High winds caused the flight to be cancelled due to inclement weather.
   a. mild   b. harsh   c. known   d. usual

9. The diver plunged into the deep water, splashing lots of foam.
   a. threw herself   b. touched her toe   c. eased   d. looked

10. The sword-swallower performed his amazing feat.
    a. friendly hand shake   b. ballet   c. desk   d. daring act

INSIGHTS: Reading as Thinking ©
Charlesbridge Publishing • (800) 225-3214

Investigation B: VISUALIZING CHOICES

Students will make a mental picture for each sentence on this page and choose the answer that goes with the mental picture. Ask several volunteers to describe their mental pictures for the same item. Discuss whether or not their answer choices were the same.

Put together a list of challenging words that can be clearly visualized. Have each student choose a word and look up its definition. Tell students to visualize their word and draw a picture of their visualization. Have students exchange pictures and infer the meaning of the words from the illustrations.

The words may be from a unit you will teach later in the year, or from a historical setting of a book the class will read. The following is an example list from a novel set during the Revolutionary War.

wick	shawl
breeches	mantle
sleigh	canopy
cradle	spindle
harness	latch
musket	powder horn
andirons	kettle
cauldron	trough
yoke	sconce
loft	

Answer Key

1. a. loud sound	6. a. medicine
2. c. painful	7. b. leaves
3. c. paid back	8. b. harsh
4. d. travel	9. a. threw herself
5. a. clear	10. d. daring act

Words with Several Meanings

Ask the class to generate a list of words that can have more than one meaning. Have them look around the room for ideas such as chair, ruler, table, or light. List their words on the board. For each word, write two sentences that require students to infer different meanings. For example, for the word *chair*, you might write:

1. She sat on the red chair.
2. The president will chair the meeting.

For the word *light*, you might write:

1. Turn off the light because Mom is sleeping.
2. The bag is so light, I can carry it easily with one hand.

Elicit the idea that context is critical for defining multiple-meaning words.

Have students read the Example and Explanation.

WORDS WITH SEVERAL MEANINGS

You can use context clues to infer the meaning of unfamiliar words. You can also use the context-clues strategy with multiple-meaning words.

There are many words that have more than one meaning.

 Example

Sphere can mean a three-dimensional shape like a globe. Sphere can mean a field or range of influence.

How can you tell which meaning the word has in a sentence? The context (the go-togethers) will tell you what the word means. Circle your choice for the meaning in the sentence below.

1. The politician's sphere of influence included many powerful senators.

   a. area

   b. a three-dimensional round shape

2. She made a sphere for her geometry project.

   a. area

   b. a three-dimensional round shape

 Explanation

If you circled 1a. and 2b., you used the context to infer the meaning of a word that fit the context. When you look up a new word in the dictionary and find that the dictionary entry includes several meanings, you have to find the meaning that makes sense in the context. You can try out each one to see which meaning goes with your mental picture and with the clues in the text.

INSIGHTS: Reading as Thinking ©
Charlesbridge Publishing • (800) 225-3214

Investigation A: WORDS WITH MORE THAN ONE MEANING

❑ Read each sentence and the answer choices.
- Circle the words that go together with the underlined word. These are the context words; they give you an idea of what the underlined word means.
- Circle the letter of the choice that best explains the underlined word.

1. Because she gets good grades, people think that Nellie is very <u>bright</u>.
   - a. well lit
   - b. smart
2. Don't <u>spring</u> at me that way from behind the tree!
   - a. jump
   - b. season after winter
3. My friend, Alex, can <u>train</u> any dog to do all kinds of tricks.
   - a. teach
   - b. an engine pulling some cars
4. Since I do not know how the disagreement started, I cannot <u>draw</u> any conclusions about whom to blame.
   - a. make pictures
   - b. come to

 ANALYZING WORD PARTS AND CONTEXT

Often in your reading, you will find an unfamiliar word that seems to have a root word or base word that you know. Analyzing words to find the prefix, suffix, and root is a good strategy, but be careful. Use the context clues to check out the meaning in the sentence.

 Example

Marilyn found this sentence in a book: If you know Spanish, you will find it relatively easy to learn French. She did not understand the word *relatively*, so she decided to try to figure out its meaning by analyzing the word parts.

Explanation
Marilyn thought, "The root of *relatively* must be *relative*. A relative is someone in your family." Marilyn then asked herself, "Does *family member* go together with *easy to learn French*?" Marilyn read her twin sister, Evelyn, the sentence and asked her what *relatively* meant. Evelyn said, "I'll give you three choices. You just have to figure out which one it is." These are the choices she gave.

   a. mother and father   b. comparatively   c. lately

Marilyn substituted each one in the sentence. What answer choice did Marilyn make? _____

INSIGHTS: *Reading as Thinking* ©
Charlesbridge Publishing • (800) 225-3214

Answer Key
1. circle: good grades
   b. smart
2. circle: from behind the tree
   a. jump
3. circle: dog, tricks
   a. teach
4. circle: conclusions
   b. come to

Investigation A: WORDS WITH MORE THAN ONE MEANING

Students infer the correct meaning from the given context.

Have the students write a sentence for each of the other meanings. Tell them to include context clues.

❑ ANALYZING WORD PARTS AND CONTEXT

Write the following words on the chalkboard and ask volunteers to circle the root word and underline the prefix or suffix.

personal   computer
recyclable   underestimate
television   Internet

Point out that analyzing a word by dividing it into its parts can be a useful strategy. Sometimes, however, it can be misleading. Write the following words on the board:

halyard (root is not *yard*)
apiary (root is not *ape*)
lamprey (root is not *lamp*)

These words seem to have familiar root words. Have students look up one of these words to find its real root.

Explain that if students' word part analysis does not make sense in the context of the sentence, they need to test the definition against the context clues to check if it goes together with the other words in the sentence.

Investigation A: WORKING WITH LOOK-ALIKE ROOTS

Explain to the students that the underlined words may be tricky because they contain root words or base words that appear familiar. Ask students to look carefully at the context to determine the best definition for each word.

Model the thinking process with the first sentence. Ask students, **What root word in** *rappelled* **seems familiar?** (rap) **The choices include some meanings of** *rap,* **but do they make sense in this context?** Substitute choices *b* and *c* for the word. **Does it make sense for the climbers to hit with a hammer or knock on a door?** (no) **Does it make sense for them to descend using a rope down the cliff?** (yes) **What context clues help you figure this out?** (*climbers, down, cliff*) **Rappel means to descend using a rope.**

Have the students infer the meanings of the words in sentences 2-9 independently. Discuss their answers and any look-alike roots.

Answer Key
1. a. descended using a rope
2. a. shook
3. c. part
4. b. went with
5. a. supplies
6. c. just
7. b. people
8. a. broad statements
9. a. survey of people's ideas

Investigation **A** : WORKING WITH LOOK-ALIKE ROOTS

❑ Read each sentence. Pay attention to the context of the underlined word.
   • Ask yourself if each answer choice makes sense with the context.
   • Circle the letter of the answer choice that best explains the underlined word.

1. The climbers <u>rappelled</u> down the cliff.
   a. descended using a rope   b. hit with a hammer   c. knocked on a door

2. His heavy footsteps <u>jarred</u> the table so that the milk spilled.
   a. shook   b. put in a container   c. covered

3. Jerry's <u>role</u> in the play was that of the butler.
   a. wheel   b. piece of bread   c. part

4. Faye <u>accompanied</u> her brother to the dentist's office.
   a. described   b. went with   c. gave business to

5. Our country has many natural <u>resources</u>, such as coal, oil, wood, and iron.
   a. supplies   b. books   c. beginnings

6. We missed the bus and arrived at the movie <u>barely</u> in time.
   a. without any clothes   b. like wild animals   c. just

7. Some <u>inhabitants</u> of the Atlas Mountains still live in caves, like prehistoric humans.
   a. customs   b. people   c. plants

8. Cecily says people from Seattle are better than anybody else; I say it is silly to make <u>generalizations</u> like that.
   a. broad statements   b. army personnel   c. questions

9. A woman came to our house and asked us a lot of questions; she said she was taking a <u>poll</u>.
   a. survey of people's ideas   b. stick   c. person from Poland

INSIGHTS: Reading as Thinking ©
Charlesbridge Publishing • (800) 225-3214

10. Mr. Soo <u>upbraided</u> his puppy for chewing up his slippers.
    a. praised   b. scolded   c. combed

11. The sight of the injured bear cub aroused great <u>pathos</u> in the group of campers.
    a. direction   b. pity   c. amusement

12. In his oil painting, Max used a <u>pigment</u> that gave the sunset a soft, rosy glow.
    a. ball-point pen   b. football   c. coloring

13. Flora carefully <u>soldered</u> the link of her broken bracelet with heated metal.
    a. sold   b. joined   c. ruined

14. Space shuttle members have to <u>supplement</u> their food intake with vitamins.
    a. add to   b. digest   c. exercise

15. Harry was <u>ravenous</u> after spending two days without food.
    a. bird-like   b. extremely hungry c. bored

16. Benjamin Franklin published a <u>treatise</u> on electricity in Philadelphia in 1751.
    a. scholarly paper b. candy   c. recipe

17. Walruses, seals, and polar bears are all <u>denizens</u> of the Arctic.
    a. rooms   b. caves   c. natives

18. Iron has many <u>properties</u> that make it useful to people.
    a. supports   b. qualities   c. owners

19. Ari is so <u>apathetic</u> that he just sits around all day and won't participate.
    a. energetic   b. uninterested   c. on the road

20. Ashley was <u>engaged</u> in a conversation with Hernando when the teacher entered the room.
    a. agreeing to marry   b. involved   c. measured

Investigation A: WORKING WITH LOOK-ALIKE ROOTS
continued

Have students choose the meaning that best explains the underlined words in sentences 10-20. Then, have students discuss their answers, pointing out the traps they had to avoid.

Answer Key
10. b. scolded
11. b. pity
12. c. coloring
13. b. joined
14. a. add to
15. b. extremely hungry
16. a. scholarly paper
17. c. natives
18. b. qualities
19. b. uninterested
20. b. involved

Investigation B: MIXED CONTEXT CLUES

Ask students to list some of the strategies they have used in this unit to infer the meaning of an unfamiliar word. Write the following strategies on the board:

Look for groups of words.

Try out different words.

Look for go-together clues.

Visualize.

Don't be fooled by multiple-meaning words or misleading roots.

Explain to students that each sentence may require them to use a different strategy. After they have defined the 10 words, have volunteers explain the strategy or strategies they used to define each word.

Answer Key
1. c. looked
2. a. riddles
3. a. matched
4. d. strong
5. c. fell apart
6. d. passed
7. b. help
8. a. contagious
9. b. disaster
10. a. noisy

Investigation **B**: MIXED CONTEXT CLUES

❑ Read each sentence and look for groups of words and go-together clues. Don't be fooled by multiple-meaning words or misleading roots.
   • Circle the letter of the answer choice that best defines or explains the underlined word.

1. Mario <u>peered</u> carefully around the corner to see if the bully had gone.
   a. backed   b. wrote   c. looked   d. whistled

2. Lena had a book full of puzzles, <u>conundrums</u>, and guessing games.
   a. riddles   b. cars   c. instruments   d. candy

3. Our shorts and T-shirts <u>corresponded</u> perfectly to the weather.
   a. matched   b. wrote letters   c. protected   d. talked back

4. The heat of the fire was so <u>intense</u> that it melted the pot.
   a. cold   b. weak   c. anxious   d. strong

5. During the earthquake, a big office building <u>disintegrated</u>, covering the streets with bricks, plaster, broken glass, and pieces of furniture.
   a. joined   b. became friendly   c. fell apart   d. shook a little bit

6. After many years had <u>elapsed</u>, Paula's grandmother remembered where she had buried the gold.
   a. been forgotten   b. sat on her lap   c. climbed trees   d. passed

7. Eating the right foods will <u>enable</u> you to grow up strong.
   a. stop   b. help   c. hurt   d. kill

8. We are afraid that this kind of flu is very <u>infectious</u>.
   a. contagious   b. purple   c. sweet   d. tall

9. It was a real <u>debacle</u> when the snakes escaped from their cages and we couldn't find them.
   a. argument   b. disaster   c. bakery   d. weakness

10. The classroom filled with <u>boisterous</u> laughter when the teacher told a funny joke.
   a. noisy   b. pretty   c. staring   d. musical

INSIGHTS: Reading as Thinking ©
Charlesbridge Publishing • (800) 225-3214

UNIT 1 – Using Context Clues   **19**

Reading Between the Lines

READING BETWEEN THE LINES

In this unit you have used context clues to infer the meaning of unfamiliar words. You can use the context clues strategies whenever you read. Making inferences from clues in the text is the basis of understanding what you read. This is called "reading between the lines" because it is inferring information that is not directly stated.

Example

a. He was very worried about his _____ .

What words would make sense in this sentence? Try to think of at least five. _____

Explanation

There are many words that would make sense in the sentence. Now read the sentence that comes before sentence **a.**

Henry looked all over the neighborhood.

When you put the two sentences together, some of the words you wrote may no longer fit the context clues. Look back at the words that you thought might fit in sentence **a.** Eliminate any items from your list that Henry would not have looked for all over the neighborhood. Now look at the sentence that comes after sentence **a.**

Henry looked all over the neighborhood. He was very worried about his _____ . She had promised to be home an hour ago.

Now you have more clues. *She* might apply to a puppy or a sister, but would not apply to a brother. *Promised to be home* would apply only to a person, since a pet would not be able to speak. Therefore, the word *sister* would complete the meaning of the passage. To make the inference you added the context clues in the sentences before and after the inference to complete the meaning of the paragraph.

Investigation **A**: MAKING INFERENCES FROM CONTEXT

❑ Read the passage and the five choices in the margin for each missing word.
  • Use the context clues to infer which of the choices in the margin makes the most sense in the passage.
  • Circle the letter of the best choice, and reread the paragraph to be sure it makes sense.

INSIGHTS: Reading as Thinking ©
Charlesbridge Publishing • (800) 225-3214

Have students read the introduction and Example. Ask them to generate at least five words that would make sense in the sentence. Write the list on the chalkboard. They might suggest words such as the following:

grades	sister	team
puppy	brother	recital
test	health	

Point out that many words would make sense in the sentence.

Have students read the Explanation. Ask them to mark a line through the words that no longer fit the context. Have them look at the sentence that comes after sentence *a.* Ask what they did to make the inference. Elicit the idea that they used the context clues in the sentences that came before and after sentence *a.* Then they made the inference that was needed to complete the meaning of the paragraph.

Investigation A: MAKING INFERENCES FROM CONTEXT

Tell students that, in each of the following passages, certain words have been taken out and replaced by a number. That number also appears to the right of the passage, along with five words.

Investigation A: MAKING INFERENCES FROM CONTEXT
continued

Discuss the first paragraph in Passage 1 as an example. Read the paragraph aloud, stopping after the sentence with the first missing word. Ask, **Which word is the best choice here? Each word makes sense in the sentence, but only one makes sense in the context of the paragraph.** (joined) Tell students to look for context clues that come before and after the sentence with the missing word. Ask a volunteer to explain the context clues he or she used to find the missing word. (Europe and Asia are not separate land masses; therefore, they must be joined.)

Have students find the best choice for the second missing word. (continents) Ask how they knew that the author was referring to continents. (The author contrasts "others" with Europe and Asia, which are continents.)

Have students complete the remaining three paragraphs independently and discuss their answers.

Answer Key
1. a. joined
2. e. continents
3. b. huge
4. a. difficult
5. c. cold
6. c. few
7. a. areas

Passage 1

There are seven continents: Africa, Antarctica, Asia, Australia, Europe, North America, and South America. Europe and Asia are not separate land masses. They are __1__ as one land mass. They do not have any bodies of water separating them. All the other __2__ are nearly surrounded by oceans. Russia is part of both the European and Asian continents.

Europe is a small continent with a very large population. Three reasons Europe's population is so __3__ follow. They are its moderate climate, available resources, and good farming land. On the other hand, there is Australia. It is a small continent with a small population. Australia's interior, the bush country, is very dry. For this reason, it is __4__ to farm. Since not much food can be grown, the continent cannot support many people.

Antarctica is the continent located near the frigid South Pole. Its climate is extremely __5__. The continent is almost completely covered by ice all year. There is no agriculture. As a result, very __6__ people live there.

Asia is a large continent with a large population. Although it has a lot of land, many areas have unfavorable farming conditions. Much of the land in Asia is mountainous, too cold, too dry, or too tropical for farming or ranching. Most of the people, therefore, are crowded together in a few __7__. In these places, conditions are more favorable for farming.

1. a. joined
   b. separated
   c. split
   d. divided
   e. given

2. a. islands
   b. countries
   c. bodies
   d. kinds
   e. continents

3. a. stable
   b. huge
   c. important
   d. tiny
   e. unstable

4. a. difficult
   b. easy
   c. pleasant
   d. necessary
   e. illegal

5. a. sunny
   b. warm
   c. cold
   d. rainy
   e. fine

6. a. many
   b. young
   c. few
   d. lovely
   e. ancient

7. a. areas
   b. ships
   c. houses
   d. mountains
   e. prisons

INSIGHTS: Reading as Thinking ©
Charlesbridge Publishing • (800) 225-3214

Passage 2

The mass of air surrounding the earth is called the atmosphere. The atmosphere is made up of __1__ principal layers. The layers are named the troposphere, the stratosphere, the mesosphere, the ionosphere, and the exosphere. Each layer is described below.

The troposphere is the lowest layer of the atmosphere. It is the layer __2__ to the earth. Almost all weather conditions, such as clouds and storms, occur in the troposphere because almost all of the water vapor in the air is located in this layer.

The stratosphere is the layer above the troposphere. It extends __3__ from the troposphere. It may reach a height of twenty miles above the earth. In the stratosphere the air is much thinner, and few weather conditions occur here because the stratosphere is clear and cloudless.

Above the stratosphere is the mesosphere. It extends to a height of fifty miles. A special form of oxygen called ozone is found in the __4__. The ozone in this layer absorbs most of the ultraviolet rays that come from the sun. Ozone protects people on earth from the sun. Without this substance, people might be severely __5__. The ozone is the air conditioner for our planet.

The fourth layer, the ionosphere, extends from the top of the mesosphere to a height of about 400 to 500 miles. Scientists have found a way to use the charged ions in the ionosphere. __6__ figured out that radio waves can bounce off ions in the ionosphere and land back on a different part of the earth. This makes long-distance radio communication possible.

The highest layer is the exosphere. It extends thousands of miles beyond the ionosphere. It becomes __7__ the higher it goes. It doesn't end at a particular height, it just blends into outer space. There is almost no air up in the exosphere.

1. a. many
   b. two
   c. three
   d. four
   e. five

2. a. given
   b. nearest
   c. sent
   d. attached
   e. similar

3. a. upward
   b. downward
   c. across
   d. widely
   e. inward

4. a. mesosphere
   b. stratosphere
   c. atmosphere
   d. oxygen
   e. clouds

5. a. punished
   b. frozen
   c. dizzy
   d. burned
   e. ill

6. a. We
   b. You
   c. Others
   d. They
   e. He

7. a. darker
   b. prettier
   c. heavier
   d. faster
   e. thinner

INSIGHTS: Reading as Thinking ©
Charlesbridge Publishing • (800) 225-3214

Investigation A: MAKING INFERENCES FROM CONTEXT
continued

Have students read Passage 2 and supply the missing words. Discuss the context clues for each of their answers.

Answer Key
1. e. five
2. b. nearest
3. a. upward
4. a. mesosphere
5. d. burned
6. d. They
7. e. thinner

 Curriculum Connection

Social Studies: Substitute Wording Have each student write a mini-story of one or two paragraphs about an historical event or person. Have the student erase several important words (nouns, verbs, and adjectives) for which there are context clues.

Ask students to exchange stories. Have the students supply the missing words by using their own knowledge of history and the context clues. The completed story should make as much sense as the original.

Investigation A: MAKING INFERENCES FROM CONTEXT
continued

Have the students read Passage 3 and identify the missing words.

Answer Key
1. c. forms
2. e. Beneath
3. d. Rocks
4. a. larger
5. c. categorized
6. b. high
7. e. rise

Curriculum Connection

Science/Social Studies: As the students read a chapter in a science or social studies text, ask them to make a list of important terms or new words. Have the students infer the meanings from context and write each definition. Discuss the words as a class. Then assign certain words for students to look up in a dictionary or glossary. Ask them to evaluate the accuracy of their inferences.

Passage 3

Geologists examine the earth and its layers. The outside of the earth is called the crust. The crust is a layer of rock that is mostly granite and basalt. The top of it __1__ the earth's continents. The lower part of the crust is the ocean floor. Beneath the crust is the mantle, or middle layer. The mantle goes down to a depth of 1,800 miles. __2__ the mantle is the core, or third layer. It goes down to about 2,200 miles, to the center of the earth.

The earth's crust is made up mostly of great masses of rock. Rocks are almost always made of two or more minerals. A mineral is a substance found in nature that is not made of animal or plant material. __3__ come in all shapes, sizes, and colors. Their appearance depends on what minerals are in them. Most of the rocks you see are small pieces that have broken off from a __4__ mass.

Many forces of nature are at work breaking the rocks down into soil. There are hundreds of types of rocks. They can be __5__, however. The three main classes of rocks are igneous, metamorphic, and sedimentary. Igneous rocks are formed when molten (melted) materials cool in or below the earth's crust. Inside the earth's crust, the earth's materials become molten. This event occurs because of the extremely __6__ temperatures. This heat is thought to be caused by radioactive substances and pressures inside the earth's core. This melted rock does not always stay in the core. Sometimes it can __7__. Molten material comes to the surface of the earth during volcanic action.

1. a. covers
   b. pushes
   c. forms
   d. resembles
   e. washes

2. a. Above
   b. Around
   c. In
   d. Over
   e. Beneath

3. a. People
   b. Crusts
   c. Animals
   d. Rocks
   e. Plants

4. a. larger
   b. real
   c. dark
   d. colorful
   e. smashed

5. a. weighed
   b. valuable
   c. categorized
   d. found
   e. heavy

6. a. low
   b. high
   c. varied
   d. variable
   e. cold

7. a. run
   b. combine
   c. fall
   d. melt
   e. rise

INSIGHTS: Reading as Thinking ©
Charlesbridge Publishing • (800) 225-3214

UNIT 1 – Using Context Clues   **23**

Passage 4

Much of the earth is made up of minerals. Minerals are materials naturally found in the __1__ crust. Rocks are made of combinations of minerals, as are metals and many jewels. Minerals are solid. They are not made by humans. They occur __2__. They do not come from living matter either, as some rocks do.

Atoms are the building blocks of minerals. A few minerals, such as gold, silver, and diamonds, are made of single atom types. __3__, however, are made from combinations of elements. These combinations are what you see when you find a rock on the ground.

In 1822, Freidrich Mohs (moz), a German scientist, devised a way to scale minerals. He ranked them according to their hardness. A rating of 10 was extremely __4__. Mohs used a scratch test to determine the hardness. On his scale, any mineral that can scratch another mineral is the harder of the two. Calcite, for example, scratches both gypsum and talc. It is, therefore, __5__ than both. This scratch test is a fairly simple way to tell hard from soft minerals.

Talc is a soft, soapy-feeling mineral. It is __6__ up to make talcum powder. It is so soft that it is easily scratched by a fingernail. Calcite is a glossy looking soft mineral. It is used to make limestone, chalk, and marble. It can be __7__ by a copper penny, but not by a fingernail. It is, therefore, harder than talc. A diamond is the hardest mineral of all.

1. a. moon's
   b. sun's
   c. earth's
   d. rock's
   e. atmosphere's

2. a. alone
   b. naturally
   c. simply
   d. beautifully
   e. early

3. a. None
   b. Few
   c. Most
   d. All
   e. Two

4. a. wild
   b. unusual
   c. hard
   d. weird
   e. valuable

5. a. smoother
   b. rougher
   c. softer
   d. larger
   e. harder

6. a. ground
   b. dug
   c. covered
   d. boiled
   e. worked

7. a. hurt
   b. scratched
   c. decorated
   d. pushed
   e. held

INSIGHTS: Reading as Thinking ©
Charlesbridge Publishing • (800) 225-3214

Investigation A: MAKING INFERENCES FROM CONTEXT
continued

Have students read Passage 4 and use the context clues to identify the missing words. Discuss their answers and the strategies they used to arrive at them.

Answer Key
1. c. earth's
2. b. naturally
3. c. Most
4. c. hard
5. e. harder
6. a. ground
7. b. scratched

 Literature Connection

Students who have enjoyed reading about geography, meteorology, and geology in these passages might also enjoy the following biographies of scientists and inventors:

Inventors by Martin Sandler

Niels Bohr: Gentle Genius of Denmark by Ray Spangenburg and Diane K. Moser

Lewis Howard Latimer by Glennette Tilley Turner

American Astronomers: Searchers and Wonderers by Carole Ann Camp

American Environmental Heroes by Phyllis Stanley

Self-evaluation

❏ STUDENT SELF-EVALUATION

Have the students complete the Self-evaluation. Encourage them to use the Self-evaluation to identify areas in which they need further preparation. Discuss any areas of concern with students before conducting the unit Assessment.

 Curriculum Connection

Grammar: Mad Libs are funny stories that are made up by putting together parts of sentences with no context clues.

1. Instruct students to choose partners so that each student is paired with someone who has not read her or his story from the Curriculum Connection on page 23.

2. The student tells the new partner what type of word is needed, but does not give any context clues.
   For example: Once upon a time, there was a _____ who lived in the _____ .
   Student 1 might ask for a word that describes a person, a word that tells what a person does, the name of a place, and so on.

3. The first student uses the new words to complete the story.

4. Then it is student 2's chance to ask for words.

5. Have students read some of their stories to the class. Elicit the idea that if we didn't use context clues, our writing and speech would be very odd!

This is an excellent way to review the parts of speech using the stu-

dents' own words and sentences. Have students label each deleted word with its part of speech.

Also, point out that another strategy to figure out a word's meaning from context is syntax. How does the word operate within the sentence? This is a strategy that is especially useful for multiple-meaning words that are both nouns and verbs.

Self-evaluation

1. What strategies did you learn?

   _____

   _____

2. What part of the unit was easiest?

   _____

   _____

3. What part of the unit was the most difficult? Why?

   _____

   _____

4. When can you use the unit strategy?

   _____

   _____

   _____

5. Write one question you think should be on a test of this unit.

   _____

   _____

   _____

6. Circle the number that shows how much you learned in this unit.

1	2	3	4	5	6	7	8	9	10
DIDN'T LEARN		LEARNED A LITTLE		LEARNED SOME		LEARNED MOST		LEARNED ALL	

INSIGHTS: Reading as Thinking ©
Charlesbridge Publishing • (800) 225-3214

Assessment

The assessment is used as a diagnostic tool to provide feedback on the learner's progress. A student's performance is rated against a predetermined level of mastery.

Blackline
Master Pages
28-29

Hand out copies of Blackline Master Pages 28 and 29. Ask the students to read the instructions carefully.

Collect, score, and record the Assessments before returning them and discussing them with the students.

Answers for Blackline Master Page 28
1. b. thorns
2. c. shortened
3. b. exploding
4. a. piled up
5. c. looked closely at
6. d. supplies
7. c. demonstration of support
8. b. picky
9. b. distracted
10. a. aware

Answers for Blackline Master Page 29
1. c. Many
2. d. vitamins
3. e. They
4. b. diet
5. b. fruit
6. c. cause
7. d. prevent

❏ Scoring

Score 1 point for each correct answer.

Mastery Level: 14 out of a possible 17 points.

 Conditional Knowledge

Ask students what good readers do while reading. Elicit that they constantly visualize and make predictions and inferences as they read. They analyze each new sentence for new information and alter their inferences as needed.

Discuss with the students when they would infer an unknown word's meaning from context. Students might suggest situations such as the following: reading a book, reading a newspaper or a magazine, watching the news on TV, watching a movie, or exploring the Internet. Discuss the importance of using context clues for accurate communication. Ask why people object when their remarks are "taken out of context." Elicit examples of this kind of miscommunication.

Assessment

❏ Part 1 - Context Clues in Sentences

- Read each sentence.
- Circle the letter of the answer choice that best defines the underlined word.

1. When he hiked through the woods, Leroy tore his new shirt on brush and <u>brambles</u>.

   a. deep pools   b. thorns   c. paths   d. fields

2. A long story can sometimes be <u>condensed</u> into a few sentences.

   a. felt   b. pleaded   c. shortened   d. answered

3. When school let out, the students began hurrying through the doors, and the school building looked like an <u>erupting</u> volcano.

   a. silent   b. exploding   c. frozen   d. tall

4. So much snow <u>accumulated</u> in the streets that no traffic could get through.

   a. piled up   b. froze   c. happened   d. disappeared

5. The raccoon <u>examined</u> the crumb carefully before popping it into its mouth.

   a. disliked   b. ate   c. looked closely at   d. threw far away

6. When Rita and Soon Li went camping, they took a tent, sleeping bags, water, a medicine kit, and other <u>provisions</u>.

   a. proofs   b. answers   c. useless things   d. supplies

7. The team received an <u>ovation</u> from its fans, who clapped and cheered throughout the game.

   a. trophy   b. letter   c. demonstration of support   d. ticket

8. He is so <u>fastidious</u> that he changes his shirt if the smallest spot is on it.

   a. pretty   b. picky   c. fast   d. unclean

9. The baby reached for the knife, but Brian <u>diverted</u> her by handing her a balloon.

   a. liked   b. distracted   c. distanced   d. sent home

10. When Rashid took Emily's coat by mistake, he was not <u>conscious</u> of what he was doing.

    a. aware   b. proud   c. tired   d. trained

❏ Part 2 - Context Clues in a Passage

- For each missing word, circle the letter in front of the word that makes the most sense in the passage.

Before the mid-1700s, sailors who went on long sea voyages often became ill from a disease called scurvy. __1__ of these sailors died. For example, the famous explorer Vasco da Gama lost half of his crew to this disease on one of da Gama's first voyages. Scurvy was a horrifying illness.

No one knew what caused the disease. At the time, people knew very little about nutrition. They did not know about the need for certain __2__ . Lacking in modern techniques, scientists of the day had to rely on observation. __3__ must have wondered why the diseases affected mainly sailors. Doctors noticed also that sailors did not eat the same foods as people who stayed on land. One thing was very different about the sailors' __4__ . They did not eat any fruits when they were at sea.

In 1747, a Scottish surgeon began to investigate the connection between scurvy and what sailors ate. He hoped that by giving them __5__ , the disease might be cured or prevented. He treated patients who had scurvy by giving them lemons and oranges. Many patients recovered. This experiment proved that lack of fruits was the __6__ of scurvy. At last, an answer to the puzzle had been found!

In 1795, the British Navy began to distribute lime juice to its sailors, as a way of keeping them from contracting scurvy. They found that the lime juice did __7__ the disease. This is why British sailors are still sometimes called "Limeys." Today we know that it is the vitamin C in fruit that keeps people from contracting scurvy.

1. a. Few
   b. All
   c. Many
   d. None
   e. One

2. a. clothing
   b. weather
   c. exercises
   d. vitamins
   e. records

3. a. He
   b. You
   c. She
   d. Sailors
   e. They

4. a. homes
   b. diet
   c. ships
   d. clothing
   e. hair

5. a. hope
   b. fruit
   c. meat
   d. milk
   e. shots

6. a. result
   b. benefit
   c. cause
   d. enemy
   e. meaning

7. a. cause
   b. encourage
   c. worsen
   d. prevent
   e. alter

Extension

The Extension is a crossword puzzle. Students supply the missing word in each sentence to complete the puzzle.

Curriculum Connection

Literature and language: Hand out copies of the poem "Jabberwocky" from Lewis Carroll's *Through the Looking-Glass*. Explain that Carroll (or C.L. Dodgson) was a 19th-century professor of mathematics. He delighted in logic puzzles and brain teasers and filled his beloved *Alice* books with them. "Jabberwocky" is one example of Carroll's "nonsense poetry," in which he makes up words and uses them as if they were real. This requires the reader to rely on context clues and imagination.

Have the students examine the first, third, fifth, and sixth stanzas of "Jabberwocky" and choose their favorite. For the stanza, ask students to make a list of made-up words and use the context clues to determine each word's probable meaning.

Students may be interested in knowing that certain words of Carroll's, like *chortle* (a portmanteau word meaning to chuckle and snort), can now be found in the dictionary.

Extension

Use the context clues to do the crossword puzzle. (Hint: 42 across is an abbreviation; 47 across and 54 down are prefixes; 53 across and 4 down are suffixes.)

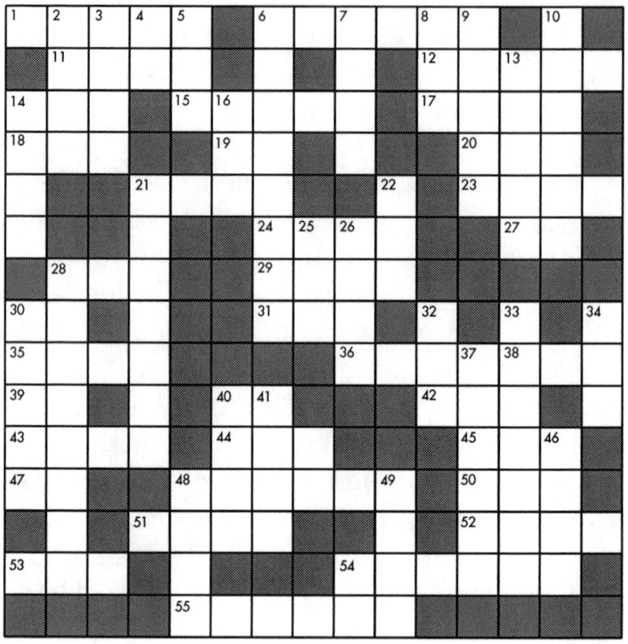

[crossword puzzle grid]

Across

1. Mr. Gove _____ for the Democratic candidate in the election.
6. They _____ some extra money by mowing lawns.
11. The day was _____ cold: the temperature was below freezing.
12. After the game, the _____ shook hands with the winner.
14. Edith said, "_____ , I'd be happy to come to your party."
15. A frog is a fly's natural _____ .
17. The new dress _____ her perfectly.
18. They went to the _____ museum to look at all the paintings.
19. They climbed _____ to the top of the mountain.
20. Brad refused to attend the movie, saying he would _____ attend anything so ridiculous.
21. She and her twin brother _____ received bicycles for their birthday.
23. My grandfather, who loves dogs, raises sleek and speedy _____ hounds.

INSIGHTS: Reading as Thinking © Charlesbridge Publishing • (800) 225-3214

---

24. Chung refused help, saying that he was perfectly _____ to carry the desk upstairs by himself.
27. His name was Edward, but his friends called him _____ .
28. Her mother would not _____ her stay out after 10:00 PM.
29. For many people, the lunch hour begins at _____ and ends at 1:00 PM.
30. For her birthday, Lehani's father took her _____ the circus.
31. I was _____ busy doing my homework to help with dinner.
35. They _____ on the school bus every day.
36. The bank robbers drove their getaway car through many _____ lights.
39. The baby was as pretty _____ a picture in her new dress.
40. Our parents took ____ to the zoo on Sunday.
42. The _____ (Royal Air Force) defended Britain during World War II. (abbreviation)
43. The computer would ____ access to anyone without a proper password.
44. The whaling boats went to _____ and returned a week later.
45. Everyone attended the parade: _____ women, and children.
47. Their lives were _____dangered by the hurricane. (prefix)
48. "Neither a borrower nor a _____ be," wrote Shakespeare.
50. After buying a skateboard, an album, and a concert ticket, Joe had only _____ dime left.
51. The cowhands rounded up the ____ of cattle.
52. Ella bought a _____ car because she could not afford a new one.
53. On hot summer days the family sits on the porch and drinks lemon_____ . (suffix)
54. When the teacher asked a question, several students _____ their hands.
55. At 8:00, he ____ out the door to catch the bus.

Down

2. She turned the sheet of paper _____ and wrote on the back.
3. Inez felt terrible when she failed the _____ .
4. Pia was small, but her best friend was even small_____ . (suffix)

5. The color of her blouse was so faded that she decided to _____ it a new color.
6. At the circus the clown rode a horse, a camel, and an _____ .
7. The _____ of morning sunshine made him happy to be alive.
8. A gnome, an imp, and an _____ are all imaginary creatures.
9. He was _____ his household chores when his wife came home from work.
10. After a good night's sleep Ramon felt well _____ .
13. Her mother sent her to the _____ to buy groceries.
14. Virginia took out her ___ and began to knit.
16. Squirrels like to eat _____s and seeds.
21. The car's _____ was dead so Shosanna took it to the station to be recharged.
22. Same as 45 across.
25. At Halloween, the neighborhood is full of little goblins shouting "Trick or Treat" and "_____"!
26. The burglar escaped with a bag of _____ .
28. When Ms. Santiago _____ her grip on the leash, her poodle pulled away and ran down the street.
30. "I'll _____ you six baseball cards for your frog," the little boy said to his friend.
32. The gymnast's hands slipped from the_____.
33. Our football team's defensive squad is good, but their _____ is better.
34. In some card games, the _____ is both the high and low card.
37. The _____ movie star was mobbed every time she went outside.
40. A person who uses something is called a ____ .
41. Zolton decided to _____ flowers to his girl friend for Valentine's Day.
46. The family was in _____ of a new car when the old one broke down.
48. The scout promised to _____ the settlers to safety.
49. In school you learn to _____ , write, and do arithmetic.
54. The teacher asked the students to _____edit their papers. (prefix)

Below are the answers to the crossword puzzle.

Crossword Answers

Across	Down
1. voted	2. over
6. earned	3. test
11. very	4. er
12. loser	5. dye
14. Yes	6. elephant
15. enemy	7. rays
17. fits	8. elf
18. art	9. doing
19. up	10. rested
20. not	13. store
21. both	14. yarn
23. grey	16. nut
24. able	21. battery
27. Ed	22. men
28. let	25. Boo
29. noon	26. loot
30. to	28. loosened
31. too	30. trade
35. rode	32. bar
36. traffic	33. offense
39. as	34. ace
40. us	37. famous
42. RAF	40. user
43. deny	41. send
44. sea	46. need
45. men	48. lead
47. en	49. read
48. lender	54. re
50. one	
51. herd	
52. used	
53. ade	
54. raised	
55. dashed	

Additional Activities

The Additional Activities are designed as the remediation for those students who did not achieve mastery on the Assessment.

❏ WAYS OF GOING TOGETHER: GROUPS

Blackline
Master Pages
34-35

Hand out copies of Blackline Master Pages 34-35. In the unit students found lists or groups of words in sentences to help infer the meaning of an unknown word. Here they are given groups of words and supply the missing words. Review the Example and Explanation on Blackline Master Page 34. Discuss with students how they can try out the words given in the Explanation to make the correct choice.

❏ WORDS THAT GO TOGETHER

Help the students complete the first two sentences and then do the remaining sentences independently. If students have difficulty, help them brainstorm possible responses.

❏ NAME THE GROUP

Explain that to complete the group, students will need to think about the words in each sentence and decide to what category they belong. Read aloud the *Think* statement for the first sentence. Ask volunteers to explain how they would describe the group in each of the remaining sentences.

Answers for Blackline Master Page 35

WORDS THAT GO TOGETHER
1. hopscotch
2. squirrels, porcupines, skunks, or any small animal
3. pizza, macaroni, spumoni, or any Italian food
4. water, or moisture
5. drums, trombones, flutes, or any portable band instrument

NAME THE GROUP
1. cheese
2. musical instrument
3. sport
4. shelter, house, or building
5. sea bird or bird

❏ WAYS OF GOING TOGETHER: PICTURES

Blackline
Master Page
36

Hand out copies of Blackline Master Page 36 and read aloud the Example and Explanation. Explain that visualizing is another way of finding words that can be grouped together.

❏ GO-TOGETHERS

Discuss with the students the picture created by the first sentence. Have them complete the last four sentences and discuss the mental pictures they made. If students have difficulty visualizing any of these situations, suggest other sentences in which you know the settings are familiar to the students.

Answers for Blackline Master Page 36

2. ached, were often tired
3. dogs

4. screwdriver
5. worried, anxious, concerned

❏ THE CONTEXT OF NEW WORDS

Blackline
Master Pages
37-38

Hand out copies of Blackline Master Pages 37-38. Have students read the paragraphs about context.

❏ CONTEXT CLUES

Explain that students can use both kinds of context clues — mental pictures and lists — to define the underlined words. Demonstrate the thinking process you would follow in the first sentence, using the chart on Blackline Master Page 38 as a guide. Tell students to follow a similar strategy for the rest of the sentences.

Answers for Blackline Master Page 37

1. a. capable of being seen
2. b. digs
3. a. faced

4. b. carelessness
5. c. kind

❏ CHECK YOURSELF

Review the chart with the students. After they check their answers, have them explain why each choice is best.

❏ READING BETWEEN THE LINES

Blackline
Master Page
39

Hand out copies of Blackline Master Page 39. Read aloud the instructions. Have students read the passage. Discuss which word best completes the second sentence. Discuss why *c* is the best choice in the context of the paragraph. Have students choose the best words to complete the rest of the passage, providing help as necessary.

Answers for Blackline Master Page 39

1. c. them
2. b. eat
3. a. ice
4. e. common

5. d. fresh
6. a. dinner
7. e. fastest

What do you do when you come to a word you do not know, and a dictionary is not available? If you met a silent stranger with some of your friends, you might ask your friends who the stranger was. Strange words usually come together with words you know. You can use the words you know to ask what the new words mean. What do you ask? You ask yourself, "What goes together with these words I know?"

☐ WAYS OF GOING TOGETHER: GROUPS

A word can go together with other words because it belongs to the same group.

 ### *Example*

Arnold took good care of his rake, hoe, pitchfork, and trowel.

rake
hoe
pitchfork
trowel ⟶ gardening tools

 ### *Explanation*

Rakes, hoes, and pitchforks are gardening tools. Trowels are in the same group. So, trowels must be a type of gardening tool, too. Circle the answer choice that defines trowel.

a. a small shovel   b. cactus   c. a tree   d. cabbage

If you circled *a*, you are right. A small shovel is the only answer choice that is a tool.

WORDS THAT GO TOGETHER

❑ Complete the sentence with any word that goes together with the other words.
 • Remember to *ask yourself:* What group is in this sentence? What belongs with this group? (hint: There are many words that could fit in each sentence.)

1. The children could not decide whether to play jump rope, _____ , or freeze tag.

2. Sharon went to the small animal house at the zoo to see the raccoons, _____ _____ , and foxes.

3. Italian food is good: I like spaghetti, ravioli, and _____ .

4. To grow, plants need good soil, the right temperature, light, and _____ _____ .

5. In the parade there was a band with trumpets, _____ , and _____ .

NAME THE GROUP

❑ Here are some sentences with groups of words in them. One of the words in each group is underlined.
 • *Ask Yourself,* "What group is in this sentence?"
 • Write the word that describes the group.

1. Sarah's mother asked her to buy some cream cheese, some American cheese, and some <u>gorgonzola</u> at the corner store.

   Think: Cream cheese and American cheese are foods but, more exactly, they are

   kinds of _____ .

   Inference: <u>Gorgonzola</u> is a kind of_____ .

2. Basil can play the harp, the organ, and the <u>concertina</u>.

   Inference: A <u>concertina</u> is a kind of _____ .

3. Imelda is good at basketball, <u>squash</u>, and swimming.

   Inference: <u>Squash</u> is a kind of _____ .

4. Would you rather live in a castle, a teepee, a <u>bungalow</u>, or an igloo?

   Inference: A <u>bungalow</u> is a kind of _____ .

5. On the shores of the lake, the noisy sea gulls, wild ducks, and <u>petrels</u> flapped their wings.

   Inference: <u>Petrels</u> are a kind of _____ .

☐ WAYS OF GOING TOGETHER: PICTURES

A word can go together with other words because it belongs in the picture the other words create.

Example

Just as Glenna was finishing the painting, her little brother came running in and spilled the <u>tempera</u> all over her picture.

Visualize this scene. Is <u>tempera</u> a liquid or is it hard and solid? _____

Which word tells you that <u>tempera</u> must be a liquid? _____

Is <u>tempera</u> something connected with gardening or with painting? _____

Which words tell you that <u>tempera</u> must be connected with painting?

_____

Explanation

The word <u>spilled</u> tells you that tempera must be a liquid. And, of course, the word <u>painting</u> tells you that tempera is connected with painting.

What is a liquid connected with painting? Paint! Circle the word below that defines <u>tempera</u>.

a. paint   b. paper   c. eraser   d. snow

☐ GO-TOGETHERS

☐ Complete the sentence with any word that goes together with the other words.
- Remember to visualize the picture. *Ask yourself:* What belongs in this picture?
- The first one has been done for you as an example.

1. Suddenly, two cars ___skidded___ into one another on the snowy road.

2. It was hard working on the farm; Emma's arms _____ from the constant hoeing and shoveling.

3. At night, in the pet shop, one of the _____ suddenly began to bark.

4. The mechanic called, "Hey, Chris, bring me the _____; I have to take this screw out."

5. Raoul was feeling worse; the nurse was very _____ and decided to call the doctor.

THE CONTEXT OF NEW WORDS

In the previous exercise you decided what word to put in the sentence, but you could not put in just any word. The other words in the sentence, the context, showed you what word to put in. You did not have too much choice. Imagine that sentence 1 had said:

Suddenly, two cars skidded and <u>collided</u> with one another on the snowy road.

You still would have known <u>collided</u> had to mean something like <u>crashed</u>, (or <u>slammed</u> or <u>ran</u>). It is what fits in the sentence and goes together with the other words. When you come across a new word with familiar words in a sentence, the familiar words give you a clue as to what the new word means. Remember to ask yourself, "What goes together with the other words in this sentence? What belongs in the picture the sentence creates?"

CONTEXT CLUES

❑ Read each sentence. Pay attention to the context of the underlined word.
  • *Ask yourself:* What kind of thing belongs in the picture this sentence creates? or What kind of group is the context for the underlined word?
  • Read the answer choices under the sentences.
  • Circle the answer choice that best explains or defines the underlined word.

1. On foggy days, the top of the skyscraper is not <u>visible</u> from the sidewalk.
   a. capable of being seen   b. reachable   c. lit   d. far away

2. The mole is an animal that <u>burrows</u> into the ground to make its home under the roots of plants.
   a. sails   b. digs   c. jumps   d. lifts

3. Carmela <u>confronted</u> the angry shopkeeper bravely; "I did not break anything in your store," she said.
   a. faced   b. ran away from   c. left   d. pleased

4. The police said, "There has been too much <u>negligence</u> on this corner; there have been three collisions, and a pedestrian was hit during the past week."
   a. love   b. carelessness   c. caution   d. tiredness

5. Mr. Sanchez has learned that one <u>breed</u> of cow gives more milk than any other.
   a. bread   b. tree   c. kind   d. trap

■ CHECK YOURSELF

❏ Check your answers. In the previous activity you read the sentences carefully to find the context clues for the underlined word. Then you found the words that defined or explained the underlined word. Now you can check your answers.

Sentence	Answer	The Context Clues
1.	a. capable of being seen	Think about the context: The top of a skyscraper is reachable (b) and it is lit (c) and far away (d) whether it is foggy or not.
2.	b. digs	Think about the context: A mole cannot sail (a) and does not jump (c) or lift (d) into the ground to make a home.
3.	a. faced	If you circled (b) "ran away from," you did not pay close attention to the word <u>bravely</u>; if you circled (d) "pleased," you did not pay close attention to the word <u>angry</u>.
4.	b. carelessness	Even if you did not know "negligence," you could eliminate all the other answer choices. None of them fits the context.
5.	c. kind	If you circled (a) "bread," you were fooled by a look-alike; *bread* is not *breed*.

READING BETWEEN THE LINES

❏ Read the passage. The information in all the sentences before and after the missing word will help you infer which of the choices in the margin belongs in the space.

• Circle the letter in front of the word that makes the most sense in the passage.

Many people take frozen foods for granted. We just don't spend much time thinking about __1__ . However, the process of freezing foods to preserve them (make them last longer) is responsible in part for much of our modern meals. Freezing lets us __2__ many foods all year. Many foods would be far too expensive in the winter if they hadn't been frozen during the summer and fall.

People have known since prehistoric times that food could be preserved by freezing. For centuries, people have put fresh caught fish on __3__ . The cold keeps the fish from going bad. The modern technique for freezing foods was first perfected by Clarence Birdseye in 1949. Since then, frozen foods have become very __4__ . Today practically everyone has tasted frozen foods.

Frozen foods can be so delicious that sometimes it is hard to tell the difference between fresh-picked and frozen flavor. Many people, though, prefer to cook __5__ foods whenever possible. They believe that just-picked fruits and vegetables are more nutritious.

Today, nearly every food imaginable can be found in the frozen food section of your supermarket. These foods can save you a lot of time in the kitchen. You can buy an entire __6__ in one box. You just microwave it and eat it. Most come in disposable containers. It's the __7__ way to do meal planning and clean-up.

1. a. you
   b. him
   c. them
   d. it
   e. her

2. a. smell
   b. eat
   c. grow
   d. ripen
   e. see

3. a. ice
   b. fires
   c. broilers
   d. plates
   e. oil

4. a. tasteless
   b. boring
   c. profitable
   d. watery
   e. common

5. a. frozen
   b. older
   c. other
   d. fresh
   e. foreign

6. a. dinner
   b. set
   c. watermelon
   d. table
   e. eggplant

7. a. best
   b. worst
   c. cheapest
   d. finest
   e. fastest

e-assessment

Blackline Master Pages 41-42

The Re-assessment uses the same format as the Assessment and asks the students to demonstrate the same understandings and strategies. Hand out copies of Blackline Master Pages 41-42. Tell students the Re-assessment has two parts. Ask them to read the directions carefully.

Answers for Blackline Master Page 41
1. a. trainee
2. c. set apart
3. c. rules of conduct
4. a. distinguish
5. d. become noticeable
6. d. ate
7. b. warm
8. c. moving heavily
9. a. dim
10. d. adequate

Answers for Blackline Master Page 42
1. c. unforgettable
2. e. share
3. b. curved
4. a. they
5. d. dangerous
6. c. painted
7. b. He

❏ Scoring

Score 1 point for each correct answer.

Mastery Level: 14 out of 17 points.

Re-assessment

❑ **Part 1 - Context Clues in Sentences**

- Read each sentence
- Circle the letter of the answer choice that best defines the underlined word.

1. Before you are allowed to join the union, you must spend two years working as an <u>apprentice</u>.

   a. trainee   b. bricklayer   c. messenger   d. carhop

2. The nurse explained that the hospital would <u>isolate</u> those patients who have the disease.

   a destroy   b. reserve   c. set apart   d. insult

3. It is necessary for all thoughtful people to live with a set of <u>principles</u>.

   a. heads of schools   b. straight lines   c. rules of conduct   d. bank statements

4. It is impossible for the human ear to <u>discern</u> certain sound-wave patterns.

   a. distinguish   b. see   c. reduce   d. produce

5. A pattern of consistent behavior will <u>emerge</u> if you take the time to study children's activities.

   a. change   b. cease   c. offend   d. become noticeable

6. The hungry young man <u>consumed</u> a huge amount of food.

   a. concealed   b. refused   c. sold   d. ate

7. Cora greeted the guests in a very <u>cordial</u> way that made them feel welcome.

   a. calm   b. warm   c. strained   d. angry

8. Maria and Fred came <u>lumbering</u> up the slope, breathing hard, carrying axes and firewood.

   a. skipping   b. marching   c. moving heavily   d. dealing with timber

9. The sky was <u>murky</u> and filled with heavy, rolling clouds.

   a. dim   b. unbalanced   c. metallic   d. liquid

10. I do not have a <u>sufficient</u> amount of cash. Will you take a check?

   a. mistaken   b. misjudged   c. paltry   d. adequate

- For each missing word, circle the letter in front of the word that makes the most sense in the passage.

If you are ever fortunate enough to visit Niagara Falls, you will certainly remember the spectacular sight for the rest of your life! The Falls are definitely __1__ . You can watch them crash down from a height of over 170 feet.

Niagara Falls are on the border between the United States and Canada. Canadians and Americans __2__ this natural wonder. That's because they belong in part to both countries. The falls are divided into two parts. The American Falls form a straight line. The Canadian Falls are __3__ . They are in the shape of a horseshoe. The narrow bit of rock between the two is known as Goat Island.

Niagara Falls are very powerful. Many believe that __4__ are the most wonderful natural feature on earth. The Falls have always been the object of great respect. Long ago, Native Americans named them "Thunderer of Water." Pioneer trappers exploring the area found the rapids very __5__ . They went many miles out of their way to go around them.

Writers and artists from all over the world have been drawn to Niagara Falls. Some have come to write about the area. Others have tried to capture the beautiful scene on canvas. One of the most famous of these was Frederick Edwin Church, who __6__ the falls in 1857. Copies of this artwork are hanging today in many homes around the world.

Tourists from far-off lands come to see Niagara Falls. Just recently, a tourist from a small town in China visited Niagara Falls. __7__ had heard about the Falls from a teacher, thirty years earlier. A visit to the Falls had been his fondest dream ever since.

1. a. dirty
   b. warm
   c. unforgettable
   d. dull
   e. artificial

2. a. destroyed
   b. dislike
   c. built
   d. like
   e. share

3. a. newer
   b. curved
   c. straighter
   d. colder
   e. older

4. a. they
   b. others
   c. oceans
   d. those
   e. canyons

5. a. tiring
   b. exciting
   c. beautiful
   d. dangerous
   e. meaningless

6. a. filmed
   b. discovered
   c. painted
   d. renamed
   e. photographed

7. a. They
   b. He
   c. She
   d. Tourists
   e. We

BLACKLINE MASTER

INSIGHTS: Reading as Thinking ©
Charlesbridge Publishing • (800) 225-3214

UNIT 2

Mood in Reading and Writing

Learning Objectives

The student will learn to infer the mood of character and setting in stories by
- inferring the mood implied by direct statements, actions, and dialogue
- locating connotative words suggesting emotions and attitudes
- inferring the character's mood from clues in the paragraph
- writing sentences that express given moods and feelings
- writing a character description to create a specific mood
- analyzing mood changes in a story
- noting complex mood changes in literature
- developing a story revealing characters' moods

Purpose of this Unit

In literature, and in life, students need to learn to use the subtle clues that make inferences possible. They will better appreciate the skills of authors of literature in which mood changes are basic.

Lesson 1: Defining literal and inferred mood of characters
Lesson 2: Inferring the mood of settings
Lesson 3: Using connotative words to infer mood
Lesson 4: Analyzing changes in mood
Assessment: Blackline Master Pages 79 through 81
    Extension: Observing details to describe mood
    Remediation: Additional Activities on Blackline Master Pages 87 through 94.
Re-Assessment: Blackline Master Pages 96 through 98.

Activating Prior Knowledge

Before beginning the unit, ask the students to define mood in their own words. Have volunteers suggest words to describe different moods they have felt. Write the connotative words on the chalkboard. Point out that in the passages they read in this unit, the students will be looking for words like these as clues to the mood of a character or setting.

❏ MOOD: LITERAL AND INFERRED

Have the students read the introductory paragraphs on page 29. Read aloud the Example. Have a volunteer read the Explanation. Ask students to explain the difference between literal and inferential comprehension. You may want to use examples of each type of comprehension from a book the students have read. Write the examples on the board and ask which require literal comprehension and which require inferential comprehension.

PREREQUISITES AND INTRODUCTION

In this unit, you will learn to identify the mood of both the characters and the setting in stories. You will also develop your ability to create mood when you write.

■ MOOD: LITERAL AND INFERRED

Mood refers to the overall emotional setting or atmosphere created by all of the elements of a written work. Two of the most powerful elements are the mood of the characters and the mood of the setting. Both of these elements have a big impact on the way you feel when you read. To recognize mood in a story, you use two important processes: literal and inferential comprehension.

Literal Comprehension: This means that the narrator, or one of the characters, tells you by direct statement what the mood is.

Inferential Comprehension: This means you use the clues in the text such as (a) the characters' dialogue and descriptions of the characters' actions, or (b) the details about where events take place. You combine these clues with the knowledge you have from your own experiences in order to figure out (infer) what the mood is.

 Example

	LITERAL	INFERRED
Narrator:	1. Sally was sad.	3. Hot tears trickled slowly down Sally's cheeks.
Character:	2. Sally said, "I am sad."	4. Sally said, "I have not been able to stop crying."

 Explanation

Sentences 1 and 2 require literal comprehension because the narrator and the character tell you directly what Sally's mood is.

Sentences 3 and 4 require inferential comprehension. You have to figure out Sally's mood from the clues. In each statement, Sally's mood is one of sadness.

Investigation A: DEFINITIONS

❑ Complete the statements using your own words.

1. Mood refers to _____ .

2. Two elements that work to create the overall mood of the passage or story are

_____ .

3. In a literal passage, the author tells you the mood of the characters and setting by

_____ .

4. Inferential comprehension _____

_____ .

5. A narrator may give you clues to the mood of the story in the form of _____

and _____ .

Investigation B: STATEMENTS OF MOOD

❑ Write **L** next to the statements that are literal.
  • Write **I** next to the statements for which you must make inferences.

1. _____ Max was really disappointed when he found out that he had not been chosen for the varsity basketball team.

   Think: The statement tells you how Max feels. It is, therefore, a

   _____ statement.

2. _____ Carla bit her lip and tiptoed quietly through the open door of the empty mansion.

3. _____ I am really sick and tired of cleaning this house every day.

4. _____ When Elmer learned he had to get his hair cut, he slammed his fist into his other hand.

5. _____ Len woke up, groped around in the dark, stood up slowly, and staggered back and forth as he tried to get his bearings.

INSIGHTS: Reading as Thinking ©
Charlesbridge Publishing • (800) 225-3214

Investigation A: DEFINITIONS

Have the students complete the definition statements on page 30. Have volunteers read their completed statements.

Answer Key

1. the emotional impact or atmosphere created by all the elements of a written work
2. the mood of the setting and the mood of the characters
3. direct statements
4. means you have to use the clues and your own knowledge to figure out the mood
5. dialogue, descriptions or details

Investigation B: STATEMENTS OF MOOD

Have students identify the type of comprehension required for each statement at the bottom of page 30. Discuss the clues that helped them decide whether the mood in each sentence is literal or inferred.

Answer Key

1. L, literal
2. I
3. L
4. I
5. I

❑ CONNOTATIVE WORDS

Have the students read the Example and the Explanation. Read aloud several sentences from a work of fiction. Ask the students which of the sentences have emotional impact. Write the word *blue* on the chalkboard. Ask the students to think of two sentences using the word: one which is neutral and one which has emotional impact. For example: 1. She wore a blue dress. 2. The blue wail of a saxophone filled the dim room. Point out that the context in which a word is used affects its emotional impact.

Investigation A: SENTENCES EXPRESSING MOOD

Have the students read the instructions at the bottom of page 31. Read the first statement aloud and have the class identify it as neutral or connotative. Then have the students identify the remaining sentences on their own.

Answer Key

1. C
2. N
3. N

☐ CONNOTATIVE WORDS

One key way in which authors create mood is by describing the setting and the appearance of the characters. Some descriptions are neutral (show no emotions). They do not tell you the emotion or attitude of the character. These descriptions do not create an emotional impact on you as the reader.

Other descriptions have emotional impact because they contain words that suggest emotions or attitudes. These are called connotative words. A connotation is the feeling or image that we associate with a word. For example, a smile connotes happiness, while a frown connotes sadness or displeasure. The reader infers the connotation of a word. The terms "connotative" and "descriptive" can sometimes be interchanged (exchanged). Connotative words are always descriptive, but descriptive words may not always be connotative.

Example

NEUTRAL	EMOTIONAL IMPACT
1. The girl blinked her blue eyes.	2. Her eyes were clouded with rage.

Explanation

In sentence 1, the word *blue* tells you nothing about how the character feels. It is neutral. In sentence 2, the words *clouded with rage* are connotative, words that have an emotional impact. From them, you know that the girl is angry.

Investigation **A**: SENTENCES EXPRESSING MOOD

❑ Write **N** for Neutral next to those sentences that do not tell you anything about the character's mood.
  • Write **C** for Connotative next to those sentences that do give clues to the character's mood.

1. _____ The conductor's face turned red as he stared at the violinist who kept hitting the wrong note.
Ask yourself: Are there clues to how the conductor feels?

2. _____ Louisa had a small birthmark just to the left of her mouth.

3. _____ After looking at the clock, James put his tools away, went into the kitchen, took the hamburger meat out, and started dinner.

INSIGHTS: Reading as Thinking ©
Charlesbridge Publishing • (800) 225-3214   **UNIT 2 – Mood in Reading and Writing** **31**

---

4. _____ As soon as Mary saw the new bike, she leaped up, let out a shriek, and gave her father a big hug.

5. _____ The shoemaker sat hunched over the workbench and pounded the leather as hard as he could; his breath came in short gasps, and he stared intently in front of him.

INFERRING A CHARACTER'S MOOD

A character's mood is the character's overall state of mind. It is not always the same as the mood of the story. In fact, one character's mood may be different from the mood of the story and different from the mood of the other characters. To infer a character's mood from his or her actions or appearance, you should—

1. Find the connotative words that the description includes. These are the words that give you clues about how a character feels.

2. Make inferences about mood. Using the descriptive words as clues, figure out what the character's mood might be. Use your own knowledge of similar situations. Remember, not all descriptive words are connotative, but all connotative words are descriptive.

⭐ Example

DESCRIPTION	INFERENCE
1. Hugo often sat on the bed and <u>pounded</u> his <u>fists</u> <u>into</u> the <u>pillow</u>.	He was angry or frustrated.
2. Her <u>eyes</u> <u>opened</u> <u>wide</u> when she saw the new car.	She was surprised or overjoyed.

☆ Explanation

The underlined words in the left column have emotional impact. From these clues you can make an inference about the character's mood as shown in the right-hand column.

Investigation **A: IDENTIFYING MOOD CLUES**

❏ Underline the connotative words that are clues to the mood of the character.
  • Circle the letter in front of the word that best describes the mood you infer from the clues.

UNIT 2 – Mood in Reading and Writing   *INSIGHTS: Reading as Thinking* ©
        Charlesbridge Publishing • (800) 225-3214

Investigation A: SENTENCES EXPRESSING MOOD *continued*

Have students identify the last two sentences as neutral or connotative. Discuss their choices.

Answer Key
4. C
5. C

❏ INFERRING A CHARACTER'S MOOD

Discuss the process of inferring a character's mood from his or her actions or appearance. Elicit from the students examples of descriptive phrases which may be connotative in some contexts but not in others. For example, in the sentence, "The girl's eyes were squinted," the connotation is uncertain. It is a neutral description if the sentence reads "The girl's eyes were squinted as she looked towards the sun." But if the sentence is changed to "The girl's eyes were squinted and she was scowling," you may infer that she is very angry.

Have students read the introductory paragraph on page 32. Ask volunteers to read the Example and Explanation.

Investigation A: IDENTIFYING MOOD CLUES

Have the class read the instructions at the bottom of page 32 for identifying mood clues.

Investigation A: IDENTIFYING MOOD CLUES *continued*

Help students identify the connotative words in the first sentence and infer the mood implied by them. Elicit other words that express the same idea. For instance, the words *happy*, *joyful*, and *enthusiastic* could all be used to describe the mood in the first sentence. Have students underline the mood clues and identify the mood in the remaining sentences. When you discuss their answers, elicit synonyms for each mood.

Answer Key
1. b. happy; underlined words: smiling, skipped
2. b. angry; underlined words: frowned, sternly, handed him a parking ticket
3. a. eager; underlined words: smiled broadly, welcomed
4. b. dutiful; underlined words: busy, hurried
5. c. happy; underlined words: gentle goodnight kiss, smiling
6. a. enthusiastic; underlined words: cheered loudly, wildly
7. c. proud; underlined words: leaned back, exclaimed, early
8. a. concerned; underlined words: clutching, rushed
9. b. joyful; underlined word: laughing
10. c. persuasive; underlined words: moving her hands forcefully, emphasize, appealed

---

1. The smiling girl skipped down the street.
   - a. nervous
   - b. happy
   - c. shocked

   Think: *Smiling* is the best clue that the girl is happy, but *skipped* also indicates happiness.

2. The police officer frowned at the driver and sternly handed him a parking ticket.
   - a. timid
   - b. angry
   - c. lonely

   Ask yourself: What emotion would the police officer probably be feeling if he or she is frowning and stern?

3. The librarian, who smiled broadly, welcomed the visitors.
   - a. eager
   - b. tired
   - c. jealous

4. The busy nurse hurried down the corridor.
   - a. indifferent
   - b. dutiful
   - c. confused

5. The baby received a gentle goodnight kiss from his smiling father.
   - a. disgusted
   - b. unsure
   - c. happy

6. The girl in the audience cheered loudly and wildly at the end of the concert.
   - a. enthusiastic
   - b. indifferent
   - c. sarcastic

7. The clerk leaned back in his chair and exclaimed to his boss, "I've finished it a day early!"
   - a. envious
   - b. sad
   - c. proud

8. Clutching her bag, the doctor rushed towards the hospital.
   - a. concerned
   - b. happy
   - c. excited

9. The boy with the laughing eyes joined the other children.
   - a. mysterious
   - b. joyful
   - c. dishonest

10. Moving her hands forcefully to emphasize her words, the candidate appealed to the crowd.
    - a. friendly
    - b. unbelieving
    - c. persuasive

INSIGHTS: Reading as Thinking ©
Charlesbridge Publishing • (800) 225-3214 **UNIT 2 – Mood in Reading and Writing** **33**

MOOD IN PARAGRAPHS

Now that you see how mood clues may be expressed in a sentence, you are ready to identify the mood clues in a paragraph. The mood clues in a paragraph describe how the character acts and feels.

Investigation **A: IDENTIFYING MOOD IN A PARAGRAPH**

❏ Underline the descriptive words in the following paragraph.

Mrs. Meacham walked slowly into the classroom and the students quieted down immediately. She started talking, and her voice sounded like the sea rising and falling in gentle waves. When students had something to say, she looked directly at them with eyes that twinkled. Lightly, she folded her hands. When she heard something that amused her, her mouth widened slowly into a broad smile.

What mood is expressed by the details? (Circle your answer.)

1. her voice:	2. her eyes:	3. her hands:	4. her mouth:
a. wild	a. confused	a. nervous	a. friendly
b. suspicious	b. cheerful	b. relaxed	b. evil
c. calm	c. bored	c. angry	c. afraid

5. What overall mood does this paragraph express?
   a. shy and retiring
   b. evil and threatening
   c. friendly and relaxed

INFERRING A CHARACTER'S MOOD FROM ACTIONS

Another way in which writers create images with words is by choosing their verbs (action words) carefully so that they have connotative value. Read the examples given below to see how an idea can be expressed differently with the use of different words. The way a character walks can express different moods.

 Example

character rushes	. . . . .	feels hurried
character shuffles	. . . .	feels tired and defeated
character swaggers	. . .	fees proud and conceited
character saunters	. . .	feels relaxed

UNIT 2 – Mood in Reading and Writing   *INSIGHTS: Reading as Thinking* ©
                                         Charlesbridge Publishing • (800) 225-3214

❏ MOOD IN PARAGRAPHS

Have students read the introductory paragraph. Suggest that it is sometimes easier to identify the mood in paragraphs because there are more clues to work from.

Investigation A: IDENTIFYING MOOD IN A PARAGRAPH

Have the students underline the connotative words in the paragraph, then decide what mood is expressed by the paragraph details. Have students explain the connotative words that helped them to identify the mood of the complete paragraph.

Answer Key

Underlined words: slowly, quieted, sea rising and falling in gentle waves, looked directly, eyes that twinkled, lightly, folded her hands, mouth widened slowly, broad smile.

1. c. calm
2. b. cheerful
3. b. relaxed
4. a. friendly
5. c. friendly and relaxed

❏ INFERRING A CHARACTER'S MOOD FROM ACTIONS

Have students read the introductory paragraph and the Example. Provide another verb such as *look*. Ask students to think of alternate words for it, such as *glance* and *stare*. Write these on the board, and discuss the connotations.

❏ INFERRING A CHARACTER'S MOOD FROM ACTIONS
continued

Read the first Explanation with the students. Then have volunteers read the following Example and Explanation. Have students begin a list of actions as mood clues in a short story or novel they are reading for class.

Investigation A: IDENTIFYING MOOD CLUES

Have the students underline the mood clues in each sentence, and then circle the letter of the mood that the clues suggest.

Answer Key
1. b. proud; underlined words: smiled, eyes lit up
2. a. happy; underlined words: raced, hugged
3. a. suspenseful; underlined words: crept silently

Explanation
This example shows how one type of movement may be described with a variety of verbs. Each verb may be a clue to the mood.

Example

VERBS	MOOD EXPRESSED
strut	to be self-confident
sulk	to be in an unhappy or disgusted mood
bawl	to be overcome with grief
sprawl	to be totally relaxed
stare	to be very interested in something

Explanation

Verbs can be vivid mood clues. When you read, pay attention to the verbs the author is using and use those verbs as clues to the character's mood.

Investigation **A**: IDENTIFYING MOOD CLUES

❏ Underline the words in each sentence that are clues to the mood of the character who is the subject of that sentence.
   • Circle the answer choice that best describes the mood you infer from the clues.

1. The mother smiled, and her eyes lit up as she watched her daughter cross the stage and take her diploma.

   a. shy   b. proud   c. conceited

2. As her sister walked through the door, Amy raced up to her and hugged her as hard as she could.

   a. happy   b. brave   c. nervous

3. The yellow cat crept silently up the tree toward the bird.

   a. suspenseful   b. gallant   c. relaxed

INSIGHTS: Reading as Thinking ©
Charlesbridge Publishing • (800) 225-3214

UNIT 2 – Mood in Reading and Writing   **35**

---

4. As Herman felt himself falling off the branch, he stared wild-eyed at the ground far below.

   a. kind   b. doubting   c. terrified

5. His skin pale and his eyes half-closed, the old clown sagged back in his seat while letting out a long sigh.

   a. impatient   b. tired   c. bold

6. The woman entered the room, glared down at those seated before her, and snapped, "Why can't you be on time?"

   a. bad-tempered   b. light-hearted   c. adventurous

7. The boy bounced out the door, leaped down the front steps, yanked the car door open, and plopped down into the driver's seat.

   a. mysterious   b. fearful   c. excited

8. The little girl sobbed on and on, her tiny shoulders shaking.

   a. deeply upset   b. tired   c. surprised

9. Dudley frantically flipped through all his books and papers; then he searched the room for his keys.

   a. uncaring   b. depressed   c. anxious

10. Their hands grasping the arms of their seats, Dorine and John watched the screen with eyes that were as big as saucers.

    a. honest   b. amazed   c. forgiving

❑ MOOD IN LONGER PASSAGES

In many stories and novels, the author will describe a whole series of actions that reveal the character's mood. These actions may be described in one paragraph or throughout an entire passage. In order to identify the mood of an action-packed story, use the following steps.

> Step 1: Identify the verbs in the passage that are clues to the mood.
>
> Step 2: Using the verbs as clues, figure out the mood by using your own knowledge of similar types of actions.

INSIGHTS: Reading as Thinking ©
Charlesbridge Publishing • (800) 225-3214

Answer Key

4. c. terrified; underlined words: stared wild-eyed

5. b. tired; underlined words: pale, eyes half-closed, sagged, long sigh

6. a. bad-tempered; underlined words: glared, snapped

7. c. excited; underlined words: bounced, leaped, yanked, plopped

8. a. deeply upset; underlined words: sobbed, shoulders shaking

9. c. anxious; underlined words: frantically flipped

10. b. amazed; underlined words: grasping the arms of their seats, big as saucers

❑ MOOD IN LONGER PASSAGES

Discuss the steps for identifying the mood in a passage. Explain that sometimes a series of actions all express the same mood. Point out that a clear sense of mood in a story makes the reader feel involved in the events the author is describing. A series of actions or descriptions that all express the same mood usually make the mood easier to identify.

Investigation A: IDENTIFYING MOOD IN A PASSAGE

The paragraph's overall mood is pressure or urgency. Have the students read through the passage twice, the first time to get a sense of the mood, and the second time to underline the words that reflect the mood. As a class, discuss students' answers to the three questions following the passage.

Answer Key

Accept all reasonable answers.
Underlined words: in a bind, phone kept ringing, salespeople kept lining up, few minutes before 5:00 PM, grabbed his coat and hat, rushed, just minutes to spare, raced, pulled on the handle, door was locked, turned and looked, it had to be!, picked up his briefcase and ran.

1. They define a problem that must be solved. The father needs to buy a present for his son, but has not had time to do so.
2. All the action words describe how rushed (concerned, panicked, anxious) Chuck is to find a gift
3. They describe Chuck's frantic search for a gift.

Investigation A: IDENTIFYING MOOD IN A PASSAGE

❑ Read the passage that follows.
   • Underline the words or phrases that help to create an overall mood of pressure.
   • Complete the sentences that follow the passage.

No Time for the Present

(1) Chuck was really in a bind. (2) It was his son's birthday, and he wanted to go home that night with a present. (3) But the day had slipped by, the phone kept ringing, the salespeople kept lining up to talk to him, and when he finally looked at his watch, it was a few minutes before 5:00 PM. (4) He grabbed his coat and hat, told his secretary he would not take another phone call, and rushed into the street to find a department store that was still open. (5) Most of the stores on the street closed at 5:30 PM on Wednesday, so he knew he had just minutes to spare. (6) He raced down to Gordon's Department Store, a block away from his office. (7) He pulled on the handle; the door was locked. (8) He peered in and saw the salespeople putting cloths over the counters. (9) He turned and looked. (10) What was still open? (11) About a block down the street was a large drugstore. (12) It would be open; it had to be! (13) People stopped in there to pick up their evening newspapers. (14) He picked up his briefcase and ran, thinking about what the drugstore might have that would please his ten-year-old son.

1. Sentences 2 and 3 create a mood of being under pressure because _____
_____
_____ .

2. Sentence 4 creates a mood of pressure because _____
_____
_____ .

3. Sentences 8, 9, and 14 continue to create a mood of pressure because _____
_____
_____ .

INSIGHTS: Reading as Thinking ©
Charlesbridge Publishing • (800) 225-3214

WRITING DESCRIPTIONS OF CHARACTERS

At this point in the unit, you have read descriptions of a character's appearance and actions and inferred the character's mood. Now you are ready to write descriptive sentences of your own. The key to writing good descriptive sentences is to select details that give clues to the character's overall mood, not just the character's feelings at that moment.

1. *Physical details:* details about the character's facial features, physical build, or anything else. These details should be chosen to be clues to the character's mood.
2. *Actions:* actions by the character that reveal his or her overall mood, such as a certain habitual way of doing something.

Investigation A: WRITING DESCRIPTIVE SENTENCES

❑ Read the phrases below and the description with the first phrase.
  • Write a description that expresses the mood in phrases 2-10. Use complete sentences in your descriptions; try not to include the underlined words.

1. a <u>slow</u>, <u>lazy</u> turtle — The turtle cautiously inched its way across the rocks in its

bowl as if it were wandering across a great desert, stopping repeatedly for rest

and careful examination of the things around it.

2. a comedian who is <u>nervous</u> on stage — _____

_____

_____

3. a <u>confused</u> child — _____

_____

_____

_____

4. a salesperson who is extremely <u>friendly</u> and <u>outgoing</u> — _____

_____

_____

❑ WRITING DESCRIPTIONS OF CHARACTERS

Have two volunteers read aloud the definitions of physical details and actions. Discuss the differences between the two, and the effect they have on the reader. Explain that good writers try to use both in their writing.

Investigation A: WRITING DESCRIPTIVE SENTENCES

Have students read the instructions and the example sentence. Have students suggest alternate sentences whose mood corresponds with a turtle that is *slow* and *lazy*.

Encourage the students to use both physical details and actions in each description. The descriptions need not be more than a sentence long, although some students may prefer longer descriptions.

Investigation A: WRITING DESCRIPTIVE SENTENCES
continued

Call on volunteers to read their descriptions aloud. Discuss the words that different students have used to convey the same mood. Elicit the idea that there are many different ways to describe a situation.

Curriculum Connection

Music: Play two or more pieces of music that reflect distinctly different moods. Ask students to try to infer the mood from each piece. Provide at least one example of instrumental music. Explain that mood can be inferred from the sound of the music, not just the words. Encourage students to choose a favorite song and to describe the mood the music inspires.

Art: Show the students art prints or slides of various works of art. Discuss with the students how artists visually express mood in paintings, photographs, and sculpture. Ask students to share their impressions of the mood each picture evokes.

5. an athlete who is <u>totally dedicated</u> to winning — _____

_____

_____

_____

6. a <u>lost</u> tourist — _____

_____

_____

_____

7. a grandmother who <u>longs for the "good old days"</u> — _____

_____

_____

_____

_____

8. a firefighter <u>exhausted</u> after fighting a fierce fire all night — _____

_____

_____

_____

_____

9. a dancer who is completely <u>lost in concentration</u> — _____

_____

_____

_____

10. a person who is <u>astonished</u> at seeing an unexpected face in the crowd — _____

_____

_____

_____

INSIGHTS: Reading as Thinking ©
Charlesbridge Publishing • (800) 225-3214

Mood of a Setting

Strategy
Lesson

MOOD OF A SETTING

In Strategy Lesson 1, you learned that connotative descriptions of people may include more than just their physical features. From a clear and vivid description, using connotative words, you get a sense of the character's feelings. This lesson will focus on descriptions of the setting of stories.

 INFERRING THE MOOD OF THE SETTING

Strictly speaking, setting refers to the time and place of a story, for example, *during World War II, at night, in Memphis, on a farm.*

More broadly defined, setting refers to all the details about time (when) and place (where). Writers often give the setting a particular mood or atmosphere so readers will have strong feelings about the action taking place in the story.

The mood of the setting may be different from the mood of the story or the mood of the characters. Read the following Example carefully. Try to see, feel, and hear for yourself what Lila sees, feels, and hears.

 Example

Lila walked along the beach.

Explanation

There are no setting details about the beach. We, therefore, do not know what the mood of the setting is. Nor do we know how Lila feels about the beach she is walking on.

 Example

Lila walked along the warm, sandy beach and felt the radiant heat from the sun and the soft spray of the waves as they slapped gently against the shoreline.

Examine the descriptive details closely. On the line below write two or three words that describe the mood of the setting.

Mood: _____

INSIGHTS: Reading as Thinking ©
Charlesbridge Publishing • (800) 225-3214

Discuss why authors need to convey not only the moods of characters, but also the moods of a story's settings.

❏ **INFERRING THE MOOD OF THE SETTING**

Have students read the opening paragraphs.

Read the Example and the Explanation aloud. Discuss the absence of connotative details in the sentence. Elicit the idea that without descriptive details, the reader is left in the dark.

Ask a volunteer to read the second Example aloud. At the bottom of the page, have the students write words that describe the mood of the setting.

❏ INFERRING THE MOOD OF THE SETTING *continued*

Ask volunteers to read aloud the Explanation and the next Example. Ask students to underline the descriptive details in the Example. Discuss how the underlined words make the Examples sound very different from each other. Ask the students which connotative verb in the last Example contributes to the overall mood. (struggled)

Answer Key

Example 3
Underlined words: cold, howling wind; crashing, swirling waves; pounded the beach.
Mood: stormy and angry

Investigation A: IDENTIFYING MOOD IN SETTING

Have the students read the instructions on the bottom of page 41. Discuss the first sentence and the *Think* statement.

Explanation

Did you describe the scene as warm, relaxed, comfortable, calm, or inviting? To make the inference about mood, you should have gone through this two-step process:

Step 1: Examine the details of the sentence for clues to mood.

Step 2: Infer the mood from these clues and your own prior knowledge.

Now read the next Example, in which the opposite mood is created.

Example

Lila struggled to walk against the cold, howling wind and the crashing, swirling waves as they pounded the beach.

Underline the descriptive details. Then write what you think the mood of the setting is.

Mood: _____

Explanation

Did you underline *cold, howling wind*, *crashing, swirling*, and *pounded the beach*? For the mood, you might have written *threatening*, *dangerous*, or some other word that expresses the wild, destructive nature of the waves.

As you have seen from the examples, authors can create a strong emotional impact with the setting just as they can with a character's behavior.

Investigation : IDENTIFYING MOOD IN SETTING

❏ Underline the descriptive words that help create the mood in each sentence.
   • Circle the choice that best describes the mood created in each sentence.

1. In the animal shelter, the cages were spotlessly clean, the windows sparkled, and there was a clean, fresh smell coming from the cages.

   a. nervous and tense   b. dirty and unpleasant   c. cheerful and tidy

   Think: The descriptive details in the sentence are *spotlessly clean*, *sparkled*, and *clean, fresh smell*. These details create a mood of cheerfulness and tidiness.

INSIGHTS: Reading as Thinking ©
Charlesbridge Publishing • (800) 225-3214

---

2. In another animal shelter, the cages were filthy and foul-smelling, and there were mounds of old food piled in the corners.

   a. exhilarated and joyous   b. disgusting and dirty   c. indifferent and unconcerned

   Ask yourself: What are the descriptive details in the sentence? Underline them. What atmosphere do these details create?

3. The air was cool and refreshing as Kevin parachuted toward the earth, which looked like a green, brown, and golden-patched pillow as he lazily approached it.

   a. concerned   b. panicky   c. comfortable

4. The house on top of the hill was always dark, and all the windows were blocked by thick iron bars.

   a. mysterious   b. fresh   c. lively

5. The dimly lit store could barely hold the crowds of pushing, shoving people who scattered tangled garments all over the shelves.

   a. attractive and pleasant   b. unpleasant and chaotic   c. lonely and beautiful

6. As far as the eye could see were hills of rich, dark soil, green pasturelands, cottages, and farmhouses.

   a. appealing   b. dirty   c. depressing

7. Outside Jennifer's window, which reflected the grayness of the shadows within, weeping willows trembled in the wind.

   a. cruel   b. hopeful   c. sad

8. As Ralph walked along the street, the long, dark shadows of ancient elm trees seemed to follow him, and he heard the sounds of hungry dogs howling in the distance.

   a. warm   b. hopeful   c. scary

9. Snow rested like a mantle on the mountain peak, and the sun blazed overhead like a huge, yellow crown.

   a. destructive   b. magnificent   c. dull

Investigation A: IDENTIFYING MOOD IN SETTING *continued*

Have students identify the mood implied by the settings in sentences 2-9. Discuss their answers and ask them to suggest other details that would fit in each setting.

Answer Key

1. c. cheerful and tidy; underlined words: spotlessly clean, sparkled, clean, fresh smell
2. b. disgusting and dirty; underlined words: filthy, foul-smelling, mounds of old food, piled
3. c. comfortable; underlined words: cool, refreshing, pillow, lazily
4. a. mysterious; underlined words: dark, blocked, thick iron bars
5. b. unpleasant and chaotic; underlined words: dimly lit, crowds, pushing, shoving, scattered, tangled
6. a. appealing; underlined words: rich, dark, green
7. c. sad; underlined words: greyness, shadows, trembled
8. c. scary; underlined words: dark shadows, ancient, seemed to follow, howling
9. b. magnificent; underlined words: mantle, blazed, huge, yellow crown

❏ MOOD OF SETTING IN A PARAGRAPH

Have students read the introduction and the steps for identifying the mood of a setting. Ask volunteers to paraphrase the two steps. Discuss the use of setting in stories and novels that you have assigned. Provide, or ask volunteers to provide, descriptions of two very different settings from a book the class is currently reading. Have the students identify the mood of each setting.

Investigation A: IDENTIFYING MOOD OF SETTING IN A PARAGRAPH

Have the students read the paragraph, underline the descriptive details, and identify the mood of the setting. Then have them write the details that express the mood of each aspect of the setting listed. Ask volunteers to read the details they wrote.

Answer Key
Underlined words: frozen, hard crust, cracked into jagged holes, stung my skin, pushed through them, had to keep moving, keep from freezing, icy wasteland, dropped from exposure, worry about enemy troops
1. b. cold and dangerous
2. cracked into jagged holes (Accept all reasonable answers)
3. stung my skin as I pushed through them
4. snow; frozen, hard crust; had to keep moving to keep from freezing; icy wasteland; dropped from exposure
5. until I dropped from exposure; worry about enemy troops

❏ MOOD OF SETTING IN A PARAGRAPH

In short stories and novels, the author will often take at least one complete paragraph to create the mood of a setting. To tell what the mood of the paragraph is, go through the same steps:

Step 1: Identify the details in the description. These are the features of the setting that you can see, hear, or feel.

Step 2: Infer the mood that these details create. You can infer the overall feeling about the setting from how it is described.

 Investigation : IDENTIFYING MOOD OF SETTING IN A PARAGRAPH

❏ Underline the details in the paragraph that help create the mood of the setting.
• Circle the choice that best completes statement 1.
• Write the details that express the mood in 2-5.

As the moon rose in the sky, each minute seemed an hour. I tried to figure out my position as I trudged on through the snowdrifts. The frozen, hard crust on the top of each snowdrift cracked into jagged holes as the weight of my boots broke through it. The twigs of the frozen scrub oak stung my skin as I pushed through them. I had to keep moving, though, to keep from freezing. The brightness of the stars was my one advantage. I would follow the North Star across this icy wasteland until I dropped from exposure or daylight came. Either way, I promised myself not to worry about enemy troops.

1. The mood of the entire paragraph is
   a. mysterious and spooky   b. cold and dangerous   c. suspenseful and terrifying

2. the snow: _____

_____

3. the scrub oak: _____

_____

4. the temperature: _____

_____

5. the danger: _____

_____

INSIGHTS: Reading as Thinking ©
Charlesbridge Publishing • (800) 225-3214

☐ WRITING DESCRIPTIONS OF SETTINGS

At this point in the unit, you have inferred the mood of a setting from a series of details. Now you will write descriptions of settings that create different moods.

An excellent way for you to start writing a description is by brainstorming, which means to think of everything you can without worrying whether the ideas are good or not. When you brainstorm you let your mind think randomly or freely. Later, you organize your thoughts logically.

Investigation A: WRITING A SETTING DESCRIPTION

☐ Select one of the settings below and brainstorm vivid details about that setting.
- On a piece of paper, jot down all the details you think of.
- From this list, choose details to create a paragraph with a strong atmosphere or mood. Each description should be at least a few sentences long. The first one has been written as an example.

1. A blizzard: What is it like to be caught in a blizzard? Describe what it is like so that the reader will understand what you heard, saw, and felt at the time.

   As I stood on Western Avenue waiting for the bus, the cyclone of snow

   raced toward me. It reached me, and the vicious winds cut my skin and drove

   the sharp flakes into my eyes. Soon I could see no farther than six inches in

   front of me because of the thick, swirling sheet of snow.

2. Your bedroom: What is your room at home like? Is it a cozy, inviting place? messy? tidy? Describe what the room is like.

   _____

   _____

   _____

   _____

   _____

☐ WRITING DESCRIPTIONS OF SETTINGS

Ask students to read the introductory paragraphs. Discuss the use of brainstorming to generate ideas. Ask the students to brainstorm a list of details for one of the topics provided in the following writing assignment.

Investigation A: WRITING A SETTING DESCRIPTION

Have each student choose one of the topics on pages 44 and 45, and brainstorm a list of details. Ask them to brainstorm a special list of verbs and connotative phrases. After they have written their descriptions, have them exchange papers, read each other's paragraphs, and identify the mood that the author has created.

Accept all descriptions that effectively convey mood.

Investigation A: WRITING A SETTING DESCRIPTION
continued

These are three of the five settings students may choose as the basis of a written description with a strong atmosphere or mood.

 Literature Connection

Choose two or three poems for the class to read. Either read them aloud or provide copies of them for the students. Have the students identify the mood in each poem. Discuss the words in the poem that helped them to infer the mood.

3. A cozy kitchen: Create a picture of a warm, cozy kitchen that is the center of the household activity.

_____

_____

_____

_____

_____

4. A gloomy forest: Have you ever been alone in a gloomy and heavily wooded forest? Or can you imagine what it would be like? Describe such a forest, and make the reader feel what it is like.

_____

_____

_____

_____

_____

5. Crowded city sidewalk: Have you ever been downtown on the day after Thanksgiving, when the sidewalks are mobbed with rushing, determined shoppers? Describe the scene on one of the downtown streets.

_____

_____

_____

_____

_____

_____

Mood in Longer Passages

MOOD IN LONGER PASSAGES

You have been inferring mood from connotative words. The key to inferring the mood of a passage is the ability to spot the connotative words the author uses to create the mood.

Inferring mood from longer passages involves the same process as inferring mood from short passages. Authors use connotative words when they describe the setting (the time and place of the story) and when they describe the characters in the story.

Connotative words add color to stories because they cause an emotional reaction in the reader. For instance, someone who writes the phrase *the baby* will not cause much emotional reaction in the reader. But, by writing *the cooing, chubby infant*, an author not only presents the image of a child, but also suggests a mood of contentment and well-being.

The word *mud* creates no emotional response in itself, but if the author uses the phrase *oozing, slimy, smelly mud*, the reader is likely to react with disgust.

◼ DESCRIBING THE SETTING OF A STORY

The setting of a story is very important in creating the mood. That is why most horror stories take place at night in eerie, mysterious surroundings.

It is important to realize that a particular setting does not always create the same mood. The same setting can create two completely different moods. The connotative words used to describe the setting at a given time and place make the difference. For example, in both of the following paragraphs, the setting is the same city block at 10 o'clock on a summer night.

In this lesson, students analyze longer passages to find clues to the mood of characters and settings. Have them read the introductory paragraphs on page 46.

❑ DESCRIBING THE SETTING OF A STORY

Ask the students to name books they have read in which the setting affects the story. Discuss the importance of setting for the mood of any story. Ask if a vivid description of setting has ever affected a student's own mood – if the bats and haunted houses in a scary story have made them feel scared, or the description of waves pounding the shore has made them feel peaceful, and so on. The mood of the setting often affects the mood of a character in a similar way.

INSIGHTS: Reading as Thinking ©
Charlesbridge Publishing • (800) 225-3214

❑ DESCRIBING THE SETTING OF A STORY *continued*

Ask students to read the two paragraphs in the Example. Ask the students to imagine the events in both paragraphs as occurring on the same street to illustrate the importance of mood in the setting. Have students read and complete the Explanation. Discuss the connotative words that help the reader to identify the mood in each paragraph.

Answer Key

"The Walk" – holding hands; enjoying; quiet, summer night; whispered in the gentle, warm breeze; neighbors sat on their front porches; talking quietly; laughing at each other's jokes.

"The Fire" – piercing shriek; shattered; roared; red lights flashing; yelled; jumped; trapped; chopped; confronted by tongues of flame.

Investigation A: MOOD OF SETTING IN A STORY

Have the students read the instructions on the bottom of page 47.

 Example

The Walk

Jim and his girlfriend, Rosa, walked down the street holding hands, enjoying the quiet, summer night. The leaves of the trees whispered in the gentle, warm breeze. A few neighbors sat on their front porches, talking quietly and laughing at each other's jokes.

The Fire

The piercing shriek of the siren shattered the silence as the fire truck roared down the street, its red lights flashing in the darkness. "Hurry up," a man yelled to the firefighters as they jumped off the truck. "There's a lady with a baby trapped on the second floor!" Two firefighters ran to the front door and chopped it down with their axes, only to be confronted by tongues of flame.

☆ *Explanation*

The mood of "The Walk" is peaceful. The mood of "The Fire" is very different. Which of the three words listed below do you think best describes the mood of the second paragraph?

a. relaxed   b. dangerous   c. happy

If you chose *dangerous*, you correctly inferred the mood. Now go back to each paragraph and <u>underline</u> at least five connotative phrases that the author uses to create a mood.

Investigation : MOOD OF SETTING IN A STORY

❑ Read the passage on the following page.
  • Reread it and find four details about the setting.
  • Write them on the lines below the passage.
  • Then, write what you infer from each detail.

INSIGHTS: Reading as Thinking ©
Charlesbridge Publishing • (800) 225-3214

Pitfall

When Deneen and Michelle stepped into the elevator, it seemed very large and comfortable. Deneen pushed a button, and they started down. Suddenly, the lights blinked, and the elevator jerked to a stop. Michelle's heart started to beat quickly. They knew what had happened, but neither could speak. Deneen laughed nervously, but Michelle could see fear in her eyes.

The blank, white walls seemed to be closing in on them, and the ceiling looked as though it were going to collapse. The seconds ticked on like hours, and they wondered how long it would be before one of them admitted to being afraid. A shrill, panic-stricken voice broke the silence. It was Deneen screaming, "What if the elevator falls to the bottom of the shaft?"

Michelle broke out in a cold sweat. The air seemed to be getting thinner. Then, as if the elevator had heard Deneen's scream, it dropped a foot. Nothing else happened. Everything was silent again. Deneen crawled into a corner. Michelle just sat in the middle of the floor, stunned, not believing what was happening. Her mouth was dry, and she felt as if she were suffocating. She took a deep breath and prayed quietly.

Abruptly, there was a whine in the gears, and the elevator jerked upward. There was no time to think. Two hearts were beating rapidly. The elevator door opened with a groan. Deneen jumped to her feet and snatched Michelle out with lightning speed.

They stood outside the elevator, relieved and totally awed by what had happened. Deneen looked at Michelle and gave a slight smile. She said, "From now on, let's take the stairs."

Detail 1: _____

_____

This detail shows that _____ .

Detail 2: _____

_____

This detail shows that _____ .

Detail 3: _____

_____

This detail shows that _____

_____ .

Detail 4: _____

_____

This detail shows that _____ .

INSIGHTS: Reading as Thinking ©
Charlesbridge Publishing • (800) 225-3214

Investigation A: MOOD OF SETTING IN A STORY *continued*

Have the students read "Pitfall," identify four details about the setting and write their inferences about each detail. There are more than four details in the story, so answers may vary. Ask students to explain how they arrived at their inferences.

Answer Key

Accept any appropriate inferences. Here are four possible answers:

1. The lights blinked, and the elevator jerked to a stop.
   Something is wrong with the elevator.
2. The blank white walls seemed to be closing in on them, and the ceiling looked as though it were going to collapse.
   The girls feel cramped in a small place because they are panicking.
3. The air seemed to be getting thinner.
   The girls feel that they cannot breathe in their panic, or that they are using up the oxygen.
4. Abruptly, there was a whine in the gears.
   The elevator is not in good working condition.

❏ DESCRIBING CHARACTERS IN A STORY

Have students read the introductory paragraphs and the Example paragraphs aloud. Discuss the differences between the two paragraphs in the Example. Have the students complete the two statements in the Explanation.

Answer Key
Accept reasonable alternatives.
1. satisfaction
2. worry

 Curriculum Connection

Cut out a newspaper or magazine article and photocopy it for the students. Ask them to infer the mood of the person who wrote the article. If the article contains quotations, ask them to infer the speakers' moods as well.

 DESCRIBING CHARACTERS IN A STORY

The characters in a story also contribute to its mood. If their actions are calm and unhurried, the mood will probably be peaceful. But if their actions are frantic or nervous, then a different mood will be created.

The two paragraphs below have the same character, a man named Wally. In both paragraphs, Wally is rowing a boat. However, the mood is different in each paragraph.

⭐ *Example*

Gone Fishing

Wally lifted the oars out of the water and let the boat glide through the silvery water of the lake. The hot sun felt good on his bare back, and he was pleased with all the fish he had caught. He dipped the oars back into the water and rowed with smooth, even strokes that barely disturbed the water as he thought about how good the fish would taste at lunch. He smiled, glad that he and his wife had decided to buy a summer home on the lake.

The Emergency

Wally's forehead creased with a worried frown. He pulled hard on the oars of the boat. The craft pushed through the hostile water as Wally clenched his teeth and rowed hard, the oars slapping at the water and splashing it across the back of the boat. Beads of sweat dotted his forehead and he rowed on and on for what seemed like hours. His youngest daughter was very sick with a high fever, and he had to get the doctor from the town on the far side of the lake.

 Explanation

The use of connotative words has created very different moods in two paragraphs with the same setting and the same character. Complete the sentences below.

1. The mood in "Gone Fishing" is one of _____ .

2. The mood in "The Emergency" is one of _____ .

INSIGHTS: *Reading as Thinking* ©
Charlesbridge Publishing • (800) 225-3214

Investigation A: MOOD OF CHARACTERS IN A STORY

❏ Read the passage and complete the sentences following the passage.

(1) The spaceship landed on the cold, desolate planet. (2) Jephtha stepped out onto the jagged rocky surface and tripped on a twisted knife-edged boulder. (3) Thunder, which sounded like angry men fighting, echoed in the distance. (4) Jephtha picked his way forward as his eyes warily scanned the horizon. (5) Suddenly, he saw a great, dark shape lift itself and advance steadily forward like a shark plowing through the ocean.

(6) An icy hand gripped Jephtha's stomach; his eyeballs froze in his head. (7) Afraid to look away from the dark shape coming toward him, he screamed. (8) He backed slowly toward his spaceship. (9) "Oh, no," Jephtha whispered to himself. (10) "What is that huge hulk?" (11) Frantically, he fumbled for his radio and called. (12) "Alien life form sighted. (13) Help needed. (14) Hurry." (15) His voice trembled. (16) No response came from the radio. (17) It seemed to be as dead as the silence around him. (18) "Help," he pleaded. (19) "Do you copy? (20) Over." (21) There was no answer.

(22) Jephtha continued to inch cautiously toward his spaceship, which seemed to be a million light-years away. (23) Now the menacing form was closer. (24) His legs were like two iron rods that had been welded to the ground. (25) Beads of sweat burned his forehead like little chunks of red-hot coals. (26) He had never experienced such raw fear before. (27) Was the creature advancing faster? (28) Jephtha could not really tell. (29) He only knew that the distance between them was becoming shorter and shorter. (30) What was to be his fate?

1. Sentences 1 through 10 produce a mood of fear because _____

_____

_____

_____ .

2. Sentences 11 through 21 produce a mood of anxiety because _____

_____

_____

_____ .

3. Sentences 23 through 30 produce a mood of lost hope and doom because _____

_____

_____ .

INSIGHTS: *Reading as Thinking* ©
Charlesbridge Publishing • (800) 225-3214

Investigation A: MOOD OF CHARACTERS IN A STORY

Have the students read the story and complete the sentences. Discuss the clues students found to the mood.

Answer Key

1. Jephtha is isolated on a strange, unfamiliar planet where he suddenly comes in contact with an unknown and frightful looking creature.
2. Jephtha is trying to reach his spaceship but does not seem to be getting any response.
3. The distance between Jephtha and the menacing shape is becoming shorter and shorter.

 Curriculum Connection

Obtain a recording of a speech by a famous political figure. Explain that a speaker expresses mood through 1) the quality and tone of his or her voice, and 2) the choice of words. After listening to the speech, discuss the moods or feelings evoked by the tone of voice and by the choice of words.

Investigation B: CREATING A MOOD COLLAGE

Have the students read the directions for creating a mood collage. Answer any questions they may have. Allow the students at least a few days to work on their collages. Display the completed collages, letting students infer the mood in each.

 Literature Connection

Choose, or have each student select, a short story. Elicit from the students the kinds of clues that will help them infer mood (connotative expressions, and descriptions of characters, actions, events, and settings).

After reading the story, have the students write a paragraph describing its mood.

 Investigation **B**: CREATING A MOOD COLLAGE

In this activity, you will make a poster in which you create a mood.

1. Select a particular mood. On the lines at the bottom of this page, list the words that convey your chosen mood.

2. Go through magazines and newspapers at home and look for pictures of settings that create your chosen mood. The pictures could be of house interiors and exteriors, forests, farms, meadows — any place, anywhere, any period of time.

3. All the pictures should create or express a similar mood or feeling. They might all be gloomy, cheery, or any other mood.

4. Cut out the pictures and mount them together on poster board to make a collage (a collection of pictures or photos) that creates a mood.

5. When you have finished pasting down the photos, write your name and a short description of the mood on the back of the poster board.

6. When all the posters are done, share your poster with the class. See whether the rest of the students can infer the mood expressed by the photos.

_____

_____

_____

_____

_____

_____

_____

_____

INSIGHTS: Reading as Thinking ©
Charlesbridge Publishing • (800) 225-3214

Strategy
Lesson
4 MOOD CHANGES IN A STORY

Very often, the mood of a story changes as the author tells the story. Usually, this happens when the character faces a problem and tries to solve it, or when the setting changes. Sometimes the author deliberately starts the story in one mood so that when the mood changes, you, the reader, are taken by surprise.

As you read the story below, notice the way the mood changes from contentment to danger. Also, notice that the mood changes when the problem appears, that is, when Juan's son is in danger. Finally, pay attention to the connotative words. At the beginning of the story, the author is using words that connote peacefulness. When the problem occurs, the writer uses words that connote panic and terror.

★ *Example*

The Accident

Juan and his wife, Inez, were sunning themselves at the end of the dock as they watched their son, Gabriel, drive their new motorboat back and forth on the sparkling water of the quiet lake. A flock of birds flew lazily overhead as Inez and Juan smiled at their son, who waved happily to them from the middle of the lake. As they talked about Gabriel, who would be starting high school in the fall, Juan suddenly noticed a wildly lurching speedboat on the far side of the lake. Flying along at top speed, the driver was obviously joy-riding. The speedboat roared to the middle of the lake, turned sharply to avoid hitting Gabriel, and sent a huge, foaming wave into the small boat, which pitched and turned over, throwing Gabriel into the water.

Inez screamed as Juan dove into the water and swam frantically to the middle of the lake. Juan tried to spot Gabriel, but all he could see was the overturned boat bobbing in the cold, dark water. His stomach ached with worry. As he neared the boat, he spotted Gabriel's yellow life jacket, but the boy was not moving. He must have hit his head when the boat overturned. Juan swam to the boy, pulled him to the surface, and began to swim to the capsized boat.

 Explanation

In order to recognize mood changes, you must do the following:

Step 1: Assess the mood at the beginning of the story by establishing the mood of the setting and the characters.

Step 2: As you continue to read, examine the descriptions of the characters and the setting for each of the events to see if they suggest a different mood.

INSIGHTS: Reading as Thinking ©
Charlesbridge Publishing • (800) 225-3214

Explain that the mood often changes within a story, particularly in a longer one. Have students read the introductory paragraphs. Ask two volunteers to each read a paragraph of the story in the Example. Discuss the two steps used to identify the mood changes in a story. Have the students complete the sentences on the following page.

❏ MOOD CHANGES IN A STORY *continued*

Have the students read the *Think, Inference,* and *Ask yourself* prompts. Ask them to complete each statement.

Answer Key

Below are the concepts to complete the statements. Accept all reasonable answers.

Think – In the first part of the story the lake is described as sparkling and quiet, with a flock of birds that flew lazily overhead.

Inference – The connotative words are sunning, smiling, and happily.

Ask yourself – The descriptive words are cold and dark.

Inference – Inez screams, and Juan dives.

The strategy involves thinking a long series of thoughts. This thinking process is described below. Complete the sentences with connotative words from the story.

Think: about the setting

In the first part of the story, the lake is described as _____

and _____ , with a flock of birds that flew _____ .

Inference: The words *sparkling, quiet,* and *lazily* express a calm mood. The author uses words with pleasant connotations such as _____ and

_____ to tell us what Juan and Inez are doing at the

beginning of the story. Their son waves _____ .

Think: about the characters

Inference: *Sunning, smiling,* and *happily* suggest that the characters are in a pleasant and relaxed mood.

Ask yourself: When does the mood change?

Water is an important part of the story in both parts. The words used to

describe the water in the second part of the story are _____ and

_____ .

Think: about the setting

Inference: *Cold and dark* suggest that the water is threatening and dangerous. This contrasts with the sparkling, quiet lake described earlier.

Juan and Inez were sunning themselves and smiling in the first part. In the

second part, Inez _____ and Juan _____ into the water

and swims frantically.

Think: about the characters

Inference: Something is wrong. The scream helps to build a sense of danger and fear and lets you know that Juan dives into the water because something unpleasant is happening. His frantic swim confirms that the mood is one of danger.

INSIGHTS: Reading as Thinking ©
Charlesbridge Publishing • (800) 225-3214

Investigation : MOOD CHANGE

❑ Read the passage and answer the questions after it.

Anticipation

Mai Chung was not the only student whose eyes were locked on the principal, Mr. Brown. He stood at the front of the room looking through the report cards of Ms. Aaron's class. The room was filled with a tense, strained silence.

As Mr. Brown passed out the report cards, the students would know whether or not they had been promoted. Mai sat up straight in her chair and nibbled on her fingernails. She crossed her legs and tried to ignore the butterflies in her stomach, but her left foot swung nervously back and forth under her desk.

"I have good news for all of you," Mr. Brown said. "Everyone has been promoted. You will all graduate." The room echoed with a sigh of relief. Mai leaned back in her chair and smiled. Her smile grew even bigger when she thought of how proud her parents would be that she had succeeded. When Mr. Brown finished passing out the report cards, Ms. Aaron dismissed the class. Mai breezed down the hall to the front door. Once outside, she jumped up and down and screamed happily. Her friends screamed, too, and they hugged one another in celebration.

1. In the first part of the story, what two words describe the silence in the room?

   _____

2. In the first paragraph of the story, what connotative words show us that Mai is worried about her report card? _____

3. In the second paragraph of the story, what did Mai do that showed she was worried?

   _____

   _____

4. What is the mood in the first part of the story? _____

5. When does the mood of the story change? _____

   _____

   _____

INSIGHTS: Reading as Thinking ©
Charlesbridge Publishing • (800) 225-3214

Investigation A: MOOD CHANGE

Have the students read the story. The questions that follow it relate to the character's change from one mood to another. Have the students answer the questions, then discuss their answers.

Answer Key

1. tense, strained
2. eyes were locked on the principal, Mr. Brown
3. She sat straight in her chair, nibbling on her fingernails, her left foot swaying back and forth under her desk.
4. nervous (Accept reasonable alternatives)
5. when the principal says everyone has been promoted

Investigation A: MOOD CHANGE *continued*

Have the students answer the rest of the questions. Discuss their answers when they are finished.

Answer Key

6. the room echoed with a sigh of relief
7. Accept any three: leaned back, smiled, smile grew even bigger, breezed down the hall, jumped up and down, screamed happily
8. screamed, hugged one another in celebration
9. joyful

❑ COMPLEX MOOD CHANGES IN STORIES AND CHARACTERS

Have students read the introductory paragraphs. Discuss how much more interesting or suspenseful a story can become when the mood of the setting changes and affects the characters or vice versa.

Investigation A: COMPLEX MOOD CHANGES

Have the students read the instructions on page 55. They will read two long passages, and then answer questions about the mood of the characters and the overall mood.

---

6. In the second part of the story, what connotative phrase tells us that the students are relieved? _____

   _____

7. In the second part of the story, what are three connotative words or phrases that tell us Mai is happy?

   a. _____

   b. _____

   c. _____

8. In the second part of the story, what do Mai's friends do that shows they are happy?

   _____

   _____

9. The mood in the second part of the story is_____.

▦ COMPLEX MOOD CHANGES IN STORIES AND CHARACTERS

Sometimes, in stories like "Anticipation," the mood of the passage and the mood of the characters are similar. However, this is not always the case. Some happy stories have sad characters in them, and a horror story can have a kind, pleasant character who never scares anyone and who is always in a good mood.

Each passage that follows is divided into two parts. The mood of the story and the mood of the characters are the same in the first part. In the second part, the mood of the characters changes, but not all of the characters are in the same mood.

Investigation **A**: COMPLEX MOOD CHANGES

❑ Read each passage, keeping in mind the difference between the mood of the passage and the mood of the characters.
   • Underline the mood clues.
   • Answer the questions following the passage.

INSIGHTS: Reading as Thinking ©
Charlesbridge Publishing • (800) 225-3214

Winter Night

(1) When the bus pulled up to the corner, Bill and Tom Murphy stepped into the howling wind of the winter night. The bone-chilling gusts tore through the boys' jackets as they pulled their hats over their ears, stuffed their hands deep into their pockets, and started on the two-block walk to their home.

(2) They walked quickly, eager to escape the icy wind. Their breath froze in the air and trailed behind them like streams of exhaust as they hurried down the dark street.

(3) "You think Mom and Dad are home yet?" Tom asked through chattering teeth.

(4) "I suppose so. It's after 7:00 now," Bill shivered.

(5) "Good. I hope one of them made some soup tonight. I'm really cold," Tom said with a shiver, as the boys turned into the courtyard of their building. The gusting wind pushed them along the sidewalk toward the back door. The boys went in and climbed the stairs to their apartment on the second floor, their cheeks still numb from the cold.

(6) The boys hung their jackets in the front hall closet and went to the kitchen, which was bright and warm and rich with the aromas of food. A pot of thick soup bubbled contentedly on the stove. Pork chops sizzled merrily under the broiler, while a pot of potatoes and another pot of green beans steamed quietly on the back burners.

(7) "Hi, Dad, hi, Mom, we're home," Tom said, crossing the kitchen and kissing his mother on the cheek as she buttered the rolls she had just taken out of the oven.

(8) "That really smells good, Mom," Bill said, taking the plate of rolls from her and kissing her forehead.

(9) "Well, if it tastes as good as it smells," laughed Mr. Murphy, "then we are going to have a mighty fine meal." The boys laughed along with their father, helped their parents serve the food, and all four of them sat down at the table.

(10) "You know, I'm very proud of you boys, working after school selling those newspapers," Mr. Murphy told the boys. "The money you make sure helps out."

(11) The two boys smiled shyly, pleased by their father's compliment. As they ate their dinner, Tom told his parents all about his day at school and at the newsstand. Mrs. Murphy laughed at all the funny things he told her, but noticed that Bill did not have a word to say.

(12) When Tom went to his room to do his homework, Mrs. Murphy said, "What's the matter, Bill? You are so quiet tonight."

(13) "Oh, Mom, I feel so badly. I lost my watch today while we were selling newspapers." Bill's eyes were clouded with pain and hurt.

(14) "I know how badly you feel, Bill, because that's the way I felt when I lost my graduation ring. It just makes you sick to think about it, but in time it passes, and you get back to feeling normal." She wrapped her arms around him, and he felt a little better, knowing she understood how he felt and was not angry with him for losing the watch.

INSIGHTS: Reading as Thinking ©
Charlesbridge Publishing • (800) 225-3214

Investigation A: COMPLEX MOOD CHANGES *continued*

Have the students read the story. As they read the passage, they should be underlining connotative words and mood clues.

Investigation A: COMPLEX MOOD CHANGES *continued*

Have the students answer the questions about the setting and the characters in the story on page 56. Encourage them to reread parts of the story when answering the questions. This is often helpful, and absolutely essential here to find specific details.

Answer Key
<u>Winter Night</u>

1. bone-chilling gusts
2. their breath froze; it trailed behind them like streams of exhaust
3. wintry, painfully cold (Accept reasonable alternatives)
4. bright, warm, rich with the aromas of food
5. sizzled
6. warm
7. chattering teeth
8. shivered
9. cold and uncomfortable
10. laughed
11. smiled
12. warm

Questions About Setting

1. What connotative phrase in paragraph 1 tells us the wind is cold?
   _____

2. What connotative phrase in paragraph 2 tells us what happened to the boys' breath? _____

3. What mood is created by these connotative words? _____

4. What connotative words or phrases in paragraph 6 describe the kitchen?
   _____

5. What connotative word in paragraph 6 describes the pork chops?
   _____

6. The mood created by the connotative words in paragraph 6 is _____ .

Questions About Characters

7. What connotative words in paragraph 3 show us that Tom is cold?
   _____

8. What connotative word in paragraph 4 shows us that Bill is cold?
   _____

9. The mood created by the connotative words in paragraphs 2 and 3 is _____
   _____ .

10. What connotative word in paragraph 9 shows us that Mr. Murphy is a pleasant father? _____

11. What connotative words in paragraph 11 show us that the boys are pleased by their father's compliment? _____

12. The mood created by the connotative words in paragraphs 10 and 11 is _____ .

INSIGHTS: Reading as Thinking ©
Charlesbridge Publishing • (800) 225-3214

Questions About the Mood of the Story

13. The mood of the first part of the story is _____ .

14. When does the mood change? _____

15. The mood of the second part of the story is _____ .

16. Bill's mood in paragraph 13 is _____ .

Passage from *A Separate Peace* by John Knowles

(1) "You work too hard," Finny said, sitting opposite me at the table where we read. The study lamp cast a yellow pool of light between us. "You know all about history and English and French and everything else. What good will trigonometry do you?"

(2) "I'll have to pass it to graduate, for one thing."

(3) "Don't give me that line, Gene. Nobody at Devon has ever been surer of graduating than you are. You aren't working for that. You want to be head of the class, valedictorian,* so you can make a speech on Graduation Day—in Latin or something boring like that probably—and be the boy wonder of the school. I know you."

(4) "Don't be silly, Finny, I wouldn't waste my time on anything like that."

(5) "You never waste your time. That's why I have to do it for you."

(6) "Anyway," I grudgingly added, "somebody's got to be the head of the class."

(7) "You see. I knew that's what you were aiming at," Finny concluded quietly.

(8) "Fooey," I said to him.

(9) What if I were, I thought a moment later. It was a pretty good goal to have, it seemed to me. After all, he should talk. He had won and been proud to win the Galbraith Football Trophy and the Contact Sport Award, and there were two or three other athletic prizes he was sure to get this year or next. If I were head of the class on Graduation Day and made a speech and won the Ne Plus Ultra Scholastic Achievement Citation,** then we would both have come out on top, we would be even, that was all. We would be even . . .

(10) Was that it? My eyes snapped from the textbook toward him. Did he notice this sudden glance shot across the pool of light? He didn't seem to; he went on writing down his strange curlicue notes about Thomas Hardy in Phineas Shorthand. Was that it?

* valedictorian—a person graduating at the head of a class
** Ne Plus Ultra Scholastic Achievement Citation—an award for excellent academic performance at the boys' school
From *A Separate Peace* by John Knowles (New York: Macmillan Co., 1959), pp. 41 – 43. Copyright© by John Knowles, 1959. Reprinted by permission of Curtis Brown, Ltd.

INSIGHTS: Reading as Thinking ©
Charlesbridge Publishing • (800) 225-3214

Investigation A: COMPLEX MOOD CHANGES *continued*

Have the students answer the questions relating to the mood of the story on page 56. Discuss and accept all reasonable answers.

Answer Key
13. anticipation, suffering
14. before dinner, when the boys enter the kitchen
15. cheerful, loving
16. sorrowful, sad, or depressed

Have the students read the passage from *A Separate Peace* by John Knowles on pages 58 and 59 . You may wish to give the students some information about the book, to encourage them to read the rest of it.

A Separate Peace, is about two friends; one is an introverted intellectual and the other is a handsome, daredevil athlete. The story takes place in England at the beginning of World War II and involves jealousy, anger, and treachery that begins with a tiny incident. The mood changes are distinct and powerful.

Investigation A: COMPLEX MOOD CHANGES *continued*

When students finish reading, have them answer the questions and complete the statements about connotative words.

Answer Key
Passage from *A Separate Peace*
1. My eyes snapped from the textbook toward him.
2. surprise (Accept reasonable alternatives.)
3. he went on writing down his strange curlicue notes
4. preoccupation or concentration (Accept reasonable alternatives.)

With his head bent over in the lamplight I could discern a slight mound in his brow above the eyebrows, the faint bulge which is usually believed to indicate mental power. Phineas would be the first to disclaim* any great mental power in himself. But what did go on in his mind? If I were the head of the class and won that prize, then we would be even. . .

(11) His head started to come up, and mine snapped down. I glared at the textbook. "Relax," he said. "Your brain'll explode if you keep this up."

(12) "You don't need to worry about me, Finny."

(13) "I'm not worried."

(14) "You wouldn't —" I wasn't sure I had the control to put this question — "mind if I wound up head of the class, would you?"

(15) "Mind?" Two clear, green-blue eyes looked at me. "Fat chance you've got, anyway, with Chet Douglass around."

(16) "But you wouldn't mind, would you?" I repeated in a lower and more distinct voice.

(17) He gave me that half-smile of his, which had won him a thousand conflicts. "I'd kill myself out of envy."

(18) I believed him. The joking manner was a screen; I believed him. In front of my eyes the trigonometry textbook blurred into a jumble. I couldn't see. My brain exploded. He minded, despised the possibility that I might be the head of the school. There was a swift chain of explosions in my brain, one certainty after another, — up like a detonation** went the idea of any best friend, up went affection and partnership and sticking by someone and relying on someone absolutely in the jungle of a boys' school, up went the hope that there was anyone in this school — in this world — whom I could trust. "Chet Douglass," I said uncertainly, "is a sure thing for it."

*disclaim — to deny
**detonation — a loud explosion

Connotative Words

1. What phrase in paragraph 10 conveys sudden movement?

   _____

2. The mood created by this phrase is one of_____

3. What phrase in the same paragraph tells you about Finny's state of mind?

   _____

4. The mood created by this phrase is one of_____ .

5. What phrase in paragraph 17 gives you a description of Finny's manner?

   _____

6. The mood created by this phrase is one of_____.

7. In paragraph 18, what does the phrase "The trigonometry textbook blurred into a jumble" mean? _____

Mood Inferences

8. At the start of the passage, how does Finny behave toward the narrator?

   _____

9. When Gene, the narrator, says, "Was that it?" in paragraph 10, he realizes that Finny is _____.

10. The relationship between Gene and Finny can best be described as _____

    _____.

11. In paragraph 11, Gene snaps his head down and stares at the textbook. At this point, how does he feel about Finny? _____

12. In paragraph 18, Gene says that Finny's "joking manner was a screen." What mood or feeling is Finny hiding? _____

13. In Paragraph 18, what mood is indicated by phrases like "the trigonometry textbook blurred into a jumble" and "My brain exploded"? _____

14. What is Gene's mood when he says at the end of the passage. "Chet Douglass is a sure thing for it"?_____

INSIGHTS: Reading as Thinking ©
Charlesbridge Publishing • (800) 225-3214

Investigation A: COMPLEX MOOD CHANGES *continued*

Have the students answer the remaining questions about connotative words and mood inferences from the excerpt of *A Separate Peace*. When they have completed the questions, discuss their answers. Point out that mood changes in many novels are as complex as these.

Answer Key

5. which had won him a thousand conflicts
6. charm, confidence, etc.
7. the boy could not see clearly
8. friendly and accepting
9. jealous or envious
10. troubled, uncertain, competitive, etc.
11. angry
12. jealousy
13. anger or resentment
14. depressed, not confident

 ## Curriculum Connection

Ask the students to write a poem about a setting that they know very well. The students should use descriptive language and images in their poems to recreate their own feelings about that setting.

Investigation B: WRITING A STORY

Have the students read the four situations and select one to develop as a story. Some students may wish to use their own topics. Explain that a mood change must be included in the story. Have the students work on their stories outside of class, perhaps as a weekend assignment.

 Curriculum Connection

Language Arts: After the students have read a work of fiction, discuss mood by listing the mood of each major character and the mood of the setting on the chalkboard and having the students find details in the story that help express those moods. Write the details on the board as the students volunteer them.

Investigation **B**: WRITING A STORY

Below are brief descriptions of four situations that could all be developed into stories. Choose any one situation and develop it into a story that has a beginning, a middle, and an end. In the story, try to reveal the characters' moods.

☐ STORY SITUATIONS

1. Two friends go into a cave because one talks the other into exploring it. Once they enter, they find that it is very dark and gloomy, but one friend persuades the other to explore deeper and deeper into the cave. One of them is brave, while the other is very frightened.

   My characters are _____.

2. A large ocean liner has sunk, and three people manage to climb onto a lifeboat. The sea is extremely hazardous — high waves, heavy winds, a hard rain. To make matters worse, the people on the lifeboat are cold and hungry and are beginning to irritate each other.

   My characters are _____.

3. Two friends are talking. One friend is angry with the other because he or she has been pulling away and spending more time with a group whom the first friend does not like. They argue about this situation as they wait for their first class to start in the morning.

   My characters are _____.

4. A student transfers to a new school in September. The other students seem to be unfriendly, and for the first few days, make him or her feel unwelcome. The new student feels miserable, lonely, and isolated. Finally, an incident occurs that helps the new student to make friends.

   My characters are _____.

INSIGHTS: Reading as Thinking ©
Charlesbridge Publishing • (800) 225-3214   UNIT 2 – Mood in Reading and Writing **61**

Self-evaluation

Self-evaluation

1. What strategies did you learn?

_____

_____

2. What part of the unit was easiest?

_____

_____

3. What part of the unit was the most difficult? Why?

_____

_____

4. When can you use the unit strategy?

_____

_____

_____

5. Write one question you think should be on a test of this unit.

_____

_____

_____

6. Circle the number that shows how much you learned in this unit.

1	2	3	4	5	6	7	8	9	10

DIDN'T LEARN   LEARNED A LITTLE   LEARNED SOME   LEARNED MOST   LEARNED ALL

❑ STUDENT SELF-EVALUATION

Have the students complete the Self-evaluation. Encourage them to use the Self-evaluation to identify areas in which they need further preparation. Discuss any areas of concern with students before conducting the unit assessment.

Assessment

A student's performance on the Assessment is rated against a predetermined level of mastery. The Assessment is used as a diagnostic tool to provide feedback on the learner's progress.

Blackline Master Pages 79-81

Hand out copies of Blackline Master Pages 79-81 to each student. Ask the students to read the story through once before answering any of the questions.

Collect and score the Assessments before returning them and discussing them with the students.

Answers for Blackline Master Pages 80-81
1. Accept any three: exploded, roaring cheers, clapped her hands in time with the other Spanaker students, students went wild, screaming with delight, joined the other students in cheering
2. Accept any reasonable answer such as delighted, excited, enthusiastic, or worked-up.
3. glanced nervously at the clock
4. Accept any reasonable answer such as happy, excited, glad, anxious, or nervous.
5. Accept either: screamed with delight, or jumped up and down.
6. Accept any reasonable answer such as excited, delighted, thrilled, glad, or tense.
7. Accept any reasonable answer such as excitement, happiness, enthusiasm, or tension.
8. Accept any two: cool, gentle afternoon breeze; a few cars slowly passed; the grey light of the afternoon was slowly fading.
9. Accept any reasonable answer such as calmer, quieter, pleasant, relaxed, peaceful, or serene.
10. Accept any of the following: a sour frown on his face; stuffed his hands in his pockets; stared at the traffic light; angry glare in Fernando's eyes.
11. Acceptable answers include tense, jealous, angry, or envious.
12. Accept any of the following: surprised, smiled back, excitedly talking about the basketball game.
13. Accept any reasonable answer such as caring, concerned, interested, or attentive.
14. Accept any reasonable answer such as pleasant, happy, friendly, cheerful, or enjoyable.
15. Accept any of the following: after the game, as Fernando and Lawanda walk home, or when they talk about Fernando's brother.

❏ SCORING

Score 1 point for each correct answer.

Mastery Level: 12 out of 15 points.

Assessment

❏ Read the story and answer the questions on the following pages.

 Winning the Game

(1) The ball went through the hoop, and the Spanaker School gym exploded with the roaring cheers of the delighted students. With just a minute left in the basketball game, the Spanaker Pythons had taken the lead over the Brownville Bombers.

(2) Fernando Gonzales leaned over to Lawanda Reed and yelled in her ear, "If we hold on to this lead, we will win the junior high championship."

(3) Lawanda nodded her head to show she understood as she watched the Brownville guard dribble the ball up the floor. Her face was flushed and perspiring with heat and excitement as she clapped her hands in time with the other Spanaker students.

(4) Fernando glanced nervously at the clock – only 30 seconds left in the game. The guard dribbled the ball into the corner of the court. He tried to pass it over to the center. Fernando's younger brother, Manuel, reached in front of the center and grabbed the ball. As the Spanaker students went wild, screaming with delight, Manuel dribbled to the other end of the floor and scored with an easy lay-up shot.

(5) The buzzer sounded, and the game was over. The Spanaker Pythons were the champs. Lawanda screamed with delight and jumped up and down. Fernando raised his arms in victory and joined the other students in cheering, "We're number one!"

(6) When the team members ran into the locker room, the students began to file out of the gym. Fernando was glad to be out in the cool, gentle afternoon breeze after the heat of the gym. A few cars slowly passed by as Fernando and Lawanda walked down the street. The grey light of the afternoon was slowly fading as Lawanda talked about the game and excitedly relived every basket the Pythons had scored.

(7) They had walked two blocks before Lawanda noticed that Fernando was not listening to her. "What is the matter?" she asked. "You don't seem excited at all that we are the champs."

(8) "Oh, I'm excited all right," Fernando answered, a sour frown on his face as he stuffed his hands in his pockets and stared at the traffic light across the street.

(9) "You sure have a funny way of showing it," Lawanda said. "Aren't you glad your brother played so well?"

(10) Fernando took a deep breath before he answered. "No, not really. I mean, it's easy for you to be excited about his playing well, but you don't have to live in the same house with him. He's so stuck up about being a basketball star that he's a big pain in the neck."

(11) Lawanda was really surprised by the angry glare in Fernando's eyes. "Don't be jealous, Fernando. You get better grades than he does, and you are the captain of the baseball team. He doesn't say you're stuck up because of that."

(12) Fernando tried to stay angry, but he knew Lawanda was telling the truth and that he was being childish. Slowly, a small smile creased his lips. Lawanda smiled back. The light turned green, and they crossed the street, excitedly talking about the basketball game.

1. What are three connotative words or phrases that the author uses to describe the noise in the gym in the first half of the story?

   a. _____

   b. _____

   c. _____

2. What is the mood of the setting in this part of the story?

   _____

   _____

3. In Paragraph 4, what connotative word or phrase describes Fernando's feelings?

   _____

   _____

4. What word describes Fernando's mood in the first part of the story?

   _____

   _____

5. How does the author describe Lawanda's mood at the end of the game? (Write one connotative phrase.)

   _____

   _____

6. What word describes Lawanda's mood in the first part of the story?

   _____

   _____

7. What is the overall mood in the first part of the story?

   _____

   _____

8. How does the author describe the setting after the game? (List two connotative words or phrases.)

   a. _____

   b. _____

BLACKLINE MASTER
INSIGHTS: *Reading as Thinking* ©
Charlesbridge Publishing • (800) 225-3214

9. What is the mood of the setting in paragraph 6 of the story?

_____

_____

10. What connotative words or phrases describe Fernando's mood when he is talking about his brother? (List two.)

    a. _____

    b. _____

11. What is Fernando's mood in this part of the story?

_____

_____

12. What connotative word or phrase describes Lawanda's mood during her conversation with Fernando about his brother? (Give one.)

_____

_____

13. What is Lawanda's mood in this part of the story?

_____

_____

14. What is the mood in the last part of the story?

_____

_____

15. When does the mood change?

_____

_____

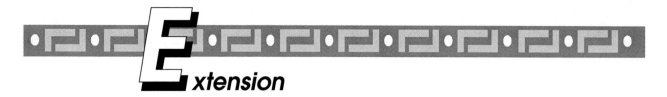

Extension

Students who work on the Extension may choose one or both of the activities listed below. Since the activities are time-consuming, they may be completed outside of class. Both of these activities emphasize writing skills.

❏ DESCRIBING A PERSON

You may wish to have the students work on steps 1 and 2 in class, and assign the writing segment as homework. Collect their notes as well as their finished story. Have the writers read their stories to the class. Discuss the mood each story evoked, and ask the writer if that was the mood he or she intended to convey.

❏ WRITING A SHORT STORY

Encourage the students to look back at any mood words that they have written or read in this unit. Encourage them to use these words and similar ones to describe physical details and actions. They may want to write a story in which two characters have different moods, the mood of the setting is different from the characters' mood, or the mood changes.

Extension

Choose one of the following activities and use your powers of observation to write mood descriptions. By being a careful observer you can become a better writer, too.

◻ DESCRIBING A PERSON

Describe how another person feels. Remember, good writers are careful observers who pay close attention to how people look, how they dress, how they act, and what they say. Use the following three steps:

Step 1: Observation   Step 2: Taking Notes   Step 3: Writing

Step 1: Observation
Pick a person you want to write about, for instance your friend, a neighbor, someone at a supermarket, or someone from your family. There are many situations in which you can observe people without letting them know that you are doing so.

Step 2: Taking Notes
Make a list of twenty-five details about the person you observed. The notes should include everything you observed: hair color, facial features, physical build, expressions.

Step 3: Writing
When you have finished taking notes, write a complete description of the person you just observed. Remember, you must describe the person in such a way that the reader can recognize the feelings or the mood of the person. For example: was the person happy, sad, excited, or afraid?

◻ WRITING A SHORT STORY

Write a short story relating to your own experiences. First, look at the mood words you have written and read as you went through this unit. Then, select a category of words you wish to use in the story. Think of a personal experience that best fits the category of words you have selected. Finally, write a short story about your experience using as many words as possible from your selected category. Give your story a clear beginning, middle, and an ending.

As you are writing the story, remember the ways in which an author uses the words to connote a mood. Use the same techniques of writing dialogue and description for creating both literal and inferred mood.

INSIGHTS: Reading as Thinking ©
Charlesbridge Publishing • (800) 225-3214

Additional Activities

The Additional Activities are designed as the remediation for those students who did not achieve mastery on the Assessment. They are included as Blackline Master Pages 87 through 94.

❏ FIVE TERMS TO REMEMBER

Blackline Master Page 87

Hand out copies of Blackline Master Page 87. Have the students read and discuss the five definitions, encouraging them to try to remember them. Explain that understanding these terms is key to understanding the unit.

❏ MATCHING DEFINITIONS

Have the students match the definitions to the terms on Blackline Master Page 87.

Answers for Blackline Master Page 87
1. B. where and when a story takes place
2. E. what is directly stated in a story
3. D. how the characters in a story feel
4. A. conclusion that is not directly stated
5. C. specific fact or example

❏ INFERRING MOOD FROM DETAILS

Blackline Master Page 88

Hand out copies of Blackline Master Page 88. This section of the Additional Activities calls for students to observe skits performed by their classmates and to make a chart for each skit listing details and mood.

1. Ask volunteers to work in pairs to act out a very short story based on one of the following situations:
   a. a comedian who is nervous on stage
   b. a confused child
   c. a salesperson who is extremely friendly and outgoing
   d. an athlete who is totally dedicated to winning
   e. a lost tourist
   f. a grandmother who longs for the "good old days"
   g. a fire fighter exhausted after fighting a fierce fire all night
   h. a person who is astonished to see an unexpected face in the crowd.
2. The players should take 10 minutes to prepare their skits. The skits themselves should last for no more than three minutes each. In the skits, the players should try to reveal the moods or feelings of the characters they are portraying.
3. While these players are preparing their skits, direct the other students doing the Additional Activities to read Blackline Master Page 88 and to prepare their charts.

4. As the skits are presented, the audience tries to infer each character's mood.

5. After each skit, give the observers a few minutes to fill in their charts with details and moods. Afterwards, you might discuss the observations they made and the conclusions drawn from these observations.

6. Collect the observers' charts and evaluate them to see how well the students observed detail and how accurately they described the mood of each of the actors in the skit.

❏ IDENTIFYING DETAILS THAT CREATE MOOD

Blackline
Master Pages
89-90

Ask students to read the descriptions and explanations on Blackline Master Page 89. Explain to the students that they will use the same thinking process to infer mood from stories that they used when inferring mood from the skits.

❏ INFERRING MOOD FROM DETAILS

Have the students read the two passages on Blackline Master Pages 89 and 90. For the first passage, help the students select a detail that expresses mood and write it on the chart.

Have the students complete the chart. Help them to find two details in the second passage and to identify the mood each detail creates. Discuss their charts as a class, explaining that there are several correct answers.

Answers for Blackline Master Pages 89-90
Accept any answer in which the detail corresponds with the mood the student has identified. Here are some possible answers.
Passage I
  1. deserted gas station – isolated
  2. only one or two cars passed by – lonely
  3. an abandoned car which looked as if it had been left there for days – scary
  4. there were no signs of people – isolated

Passage II
  5. crunch of horses slamming to the ground – threatening
  6. thick cloud of dust made it harder and harder to tell just what in the world was going on – confusing
  7. shouts and screams of soldiers – dangerous
  8. vague red and blue forms wrestling with one another – destructive

❏ UNDERSTANDING THE MOOD OF THE CHARACTERS AND THE SETTING

Blackline Master Pages 91-92

Hand out copies of Blackline Master Pages 91 and 92. Explain that changes in the setting often work as signals to changes in the mood of the character. Tell students that the story on Blackline Master Page 91 is an example of this technique.

❏ IDENTIFYING MOOD WORDS

Have the students read through the story silently before they begin responding to the questions. As they read the passage, have them underline words according to the directions.

Answers for Blackline Master Page 91

Accept all reasonable answers. Words and phrases to be underlined are indicated below.

Part 1 – It was so nice just lying there; felt at peace; usually at peace with himself; it was just so pleasant right now.

Part 2 – could not breathe; no air moving, not the smallest whiff; curtains hung limply.

Part 3 – "Goodness, it's hot"; "I wake up in an oven"; headed for a cold shower; "not only could you fry an egg on the sidewalk today, you could fry the whole chicken"; he had seen hot days before, but nothing quite like this; the heat felt different, or maybe it was just him.

Part 4 – Suddenly, the sky opened and the rain came; it came down like a gigantic waterfall; watched steam rise; the rain bombarded the sidewalk in front of him.

Part 5 – watched as the rain washed away the specks of dirt and paper; something about watching falling rain that was soothing and refreshing; as he watched the rain fall, he could also feel some of his tensions wash away; he was beginning to feel like himself again – cool, calm, and collected.

❏ INFERRING MOOD IN A STORY

Discuss the three steps the students have been using to infer the mood of a passage. Explain that as they read more stories, observing details and inferring the mood will become an automatic process.

❏ MOOD IN A STORY

Blackline
Master Pages
93-94

Hand out copies of Blackline Master Pages 93-94. Have the students read the instructions on the bottom of Blackline Master Page 92, before they proceed to read "The Bean" and to answer the questions that accompany it. As they read, they should look for connotative words that will help them infer the mood, and for changes in mood within the story. Discuss the variety of words and phrases the author uses to convey each mood.

Answer Key for Blackline Master Pages 93 and 94
1. Accept any three: sun danced, quiet, silent, except for the sound of pages turning, occasional cough.
2. Accept any reasonable answer such as the following: busy, occupied, studious, or quiet.
3. Accept any three: eyes were wide with amazement, excited, smiled, "That's really great."
4. Accept any reasonable answer such as delighted, amazed, pleased, interested, or curious.
5. Accept any one: was frowning, read about the Incas hurriedly, waited for the lunch bell to ring.
6. Accept any reasonable answer, such as bored, impatient, fed-up, or uninterested.
7. Accept any reasonable answer, such as quiet, studious, or busy.
8. buzzing with the happy chatter of students
9. Accept any reasonable answer, such as cheerful, happy, pleasant, talkative, or fun.
10. Accept any one: eyes bright, laughed, or giggled.
11. Accept any reasonable answer, such as laughing, imaginative, creative, or funny.
12. Accept any one: laughed, giggled, smiled.
13. Accept any reasonable answer, such as amused, interested, or involved.
14. Accept any reasonable answer, such as humorous, fun, or enjoyable.
15. Accept any one: when the girls enter the lunchroom, when they talk, after class.

Additional Activities

■ FIVE TERMS TO REMEMBER

From time to time, you might say, "I'm in a good mood" or "I'm in a bad mood" — meaning that you feel a certain way. Unfortunately, the characters in a story do not always show their feelings so clearly. Therefore, you have to know what clues to look for in order to tell how characters feel. This activity is about finding those clues and deciding what feelings they indicate.

First, read the following definitions. You should memorize what these words mean because they are used in the rest of the unit.

1. An **inference** is a conclusion you make with the help of clues. When you infer, you decide that something is true even though it is not stated by the author.

2. **Literal meaning** refers to the actual facts that are stated by the author.

3. **Details** are specific facts or examples of an item.

4. **Setting** is the time and place of the story.

5. **Mood** is the feelings that the author creates about the characters or setting in a story.

■ MATCHING DEFINITIONS

❏ Match the definitions on the right with the terms on the left by writing the letter of the definition next to the correct term.

1. _____ setting

    A. conclusion that is not directly stated

2. _____ literal meaning

    B. where and when a story takes place

3. _____ mood

    C. specific fact or example

4. _____ inference

    D. how the characters in a story feel

5. _____ detail

    E. what is directly stated in a story

◻ INFERRING MOOD FROM DETAILS

You will watch several skits acted out by other students in your class.

1. Observe closely for details.

   Take note of as many details as you can about each actor in the skit. What are their facial expressions? How do they walk? What gestures do they make with their arms? What emotions do their eyes express?

2. Infer each character's mood from the details that you observe.

   Each gesture and expression is a clue telling you about the character's mood or emotional state. In order to infer mood, use your knowledge of people. In your daily life, you automatically infer what a person's mood is from the way he or she behaves because you know from your own experience what the behavior means or represents.

   In the skits you are watching, decide what feelings each of the characters is expressing. Is he or she happy? sad? nervous? relaxed?

3. Make a chart of details and mood.

   Using a separate sheet of paper, make the following chart for each skit:

   a. Make a chart with three columns: one for the names of the actors, one for details, and one for inferences about moods.

NAMES	DETAILS	MOODS

   b. In the Details column, write facial expressions, gestures, and other things you observed during the skit.

   c. In the Moods column, write the moods expressed by each of the actors in the skit. Make sure your inference about mood follows from the details you observed.

IDENTIFYING DETAILS THAT CREATE MOOD

You just saw some skits and observed details that told you about the characters' feelings. Now try observing similar details as you read a story.

1. Characters — facial expressions; appearance; gestures; manner of walking; clothing

2. Setting — things about the environment that can be seen, heard, or touched, for example, the inside of a house, a forest, a meadow.

After you have noted the details, you should make inferences about the mood — just as you did when you watched the skit.

You can use the details as clues to the mood. To do so, remember to draw on your personal experience.

INFERRING MOOD FROM DETAILS

❏ Read the two short passages, each expressing a different mood.
  • In the left-hand column of the chart that follows, write four details from each passage. The details should express mood.
  • In the right-hand column, write a word or phrase that identifies the mood.

I — No One To Be Seen

What a time to get a flat tire — at 2:30 in the morning! Grace did not like it at all, especially because she was by herself. She stepped out of the car, opened the trunk, and hauled out the jack. Stopping to rest for a moment, she could hear the buzz of the street lights overhead. An occasional car sped by, but too fast for her to see the driver. At the top of the hill was a deserted gas station with the neon sign turned off; there were no signs of people.

Fifteen minutes passed as she worked on taking the wheel with the flat tire off her car, and only one or two cars passed by. She looked over to the other side of the expressway. Beyond the feeble (weak) reach of the streetlights, there was only darkness. Almost directly across from her was an abandoned car which looked as if it had been left there for days. The buzz of those street lights seemed louder than ever, compared to the silence of everything else. She worked harder at the wheel, finally put the spare one on, and threw the flat one into the trunk. She glanced one more time at the abandoned car across the way, shivered, climbed into her own car, and drove out onto the road—more anxious than ever to go home.

II — What's Going On?

The roar of the battle was almost too much for Peterson. He lay on the ground, his leg hurting too much for him to move, waiting and hoping that one of the other soldiers in blue would take pity and help him. Red and blue forms rushed by him, not looking out for him or for each other. He could hear the crunch of horses slamming to the ground and the shouts and screams of soldiers.

Confusing blasts of guns and cannons combined to create an almost unbelievable racket near him. A thick cloud of dust made it harder and harder to tell just what in the world was going on. But he could see enough to know that the ground was completely torn up and to see vague red and blue forms wrestling with one another. The longer he looked, the more everything just seemed to melt together, until he could no longer even keep his eyes open. He rested on the ground, praying that it would all end. It was all so . . . senseless.

PASSAGE		SETTING DETAILS	MOOD/ATMOSPHERE
I.	1.		
	2.		
	3.		
	4.		
II.	5.		
	6.		
	7.		
	8.		

BLACKLINE MASTER   INSIGHTS: Reading as Thinking ©
Charlesbridge Publishing • (800) 225-3214

UNDERSTANDING THE MOOD OF THE CHARACTERS AND THE SETTING

Most authors provide many statements and clues about the setting and the characters. Usually, the mood of the setting and the character are related to the overall mood. A change in one may cause a change in the other. Thus, if you can see clearly that the mood of the setting has changed, you can expect the character's mood to change. In the story that follows, the mood of the setting and characters has been shown by dividing the story into parts. As you work through the story, be alert to how changes in the weather (the setting) bring on or seem to cause changes in the mood of the character.

IDENTIFYING MOOD WORDS

❑ Read the following story.
  • Underline the words in Part 1 that show the peacefulness that Quincy feels.
  • Underline the words in Part 2 that describe the heat (the mood of the setting).
  • Underline the words that show how Quincy responds to the heat in Part 3. Be careful: Do not underline the words which describe the setting in this part.
  • Underline the words that describe the storm (a change of setting) in Part 4.
  • Underline the words that describe how Quincy responds to the storm in Part 5 – only the key connotative words and phrases, not whole sentences.

The Heat and the Cool

(Part 1)

Quincy really hated to get up. It was so nice just lying there, watching the curtains move gently in the cool morning breeze. Somewhere a dog was barking. He felt at peace with himself and with everything around him. But there was nothing unusual in that; he was usually at peace with himself. The refreshing breeze forced its way past the curtains and enveloped him. He could not believe the temperature would go as high as the weather report said it would. He knew how changeable the weather was in New Orleans, but it was just so pleasant right now. He hoped it would stay that way.

He had two houses to paint today. On a cool day like this, he could finish them quickly with no problems. He could afford to sleep just a few more minutes.

(Part 2)

He woke up and could not breathe. There was no air moving, not the smallest whiff. He looked at the window. The curtains hung limply. He felt as though someone had drenched (soaked) him in water.

(Part 3)

"Goodness, it's hot," he thought. "What a difference a couple of hours can make. I doze off, feeling as if I'm on a cool ocean, and I wake up in an oven."

(Continued on following page)

(Continued from previous page)

He headed for a cold shower. The bathroom was so hot that it became a steambath instead. He tried to dress in a hurry, but it was difficult because everything seemed to stick to him.

He walked outdoors. "Boy," he thought to himself, "not only could you fry an egg on the sidewalk today, you could fry the whole chicken." He looked at the Spanish moss that usually swished in the breeze. Today it just hung there, like soggy dish rags. The magnolia trees, which were usually stately-looking, seemed to droop from the heat. He looked at the sky, he could almost smell the rain and, for some strange reason, he could almost feel it, too. He had seen hot days before, but nothing quite like this; this heat felt different, or maybe it was just him. He pondered (thought about) this as he walked to the shop.

(Part 4)

Suddenly, the sky opened and the rain came; it came down like a gigantic waterfall. Quincy ran to a doorway for cover. He stopped there watching the sheets of rain fall. A few minutes elapsed (passed). Quincy watched steam rise as the rain bombarded the sidewalk in front of him.

(Part 5)

He watched as the rain washed away the specks of dirt and paper. There was something about watching falling rain that was soothing and — ah, yes— refreshing. That is how he was beginning to feel. As he watched the rain fall, he could also feel some of his tensions wash away. He was beginning to feel like himself again — cool, calm, and collected.

▆ INFERRING MOOD IN A STORY

So far you have been using these steps:
1. observing details in character and setting,
2. inferring characters' moods from details,
3. making inferences about the mood of the setting from details.

Now you are ready to put these steps together while reading a complete story.

☐ MOOD IN A STORY

☐ Read the following story and answer the questions that follow the story.

The Bean

(1) As the late morning sun danced into the quiet of Mr. Singh's classroom, the students were reading in their social studies book about the Incas, the people who built a huge empire in South America centuries ago. The room was silent except for the sound of pages turning and an occasional cough as the students answered the questions at the end of the reading selection.

(2) As Pam Lee read, her eyes were wide with amazement. She was excited about the accomplishments of the Incas, who built huge palaces and forts, had a system of highways that reached all parts of their empire, and used a system of knotted strings to keep records. When she read that they also wrote messages on lima beans, she smiled. "That's really great," she thought.

(3) Kate Willard, who sat across the aisle from Pam Lee, was frowning. She did not like social studies a bit. She thought it was boring. She read about the Incas hurriedly, answered the questions, and waited for the lunch bell to ring.

(4) When the class ended, Pam wheeled her chair into the lunchroom, which was buzzing with the happy chatter of students. She sat at the same table where Kate was already eating a peanut butter sandwich. "Aren't those Incas wonderful?" she asked Kate.

(5) "What are you talking about? I thought they were boring," Kate answered.

(6) "Not really. Just use your imagination. If we wrote on lima beans instead of on paper, there would not be any mail. There would be limagrams, and the lima man would carry them in bean bags and deliver them to bean boxes. If someone told you to spill the beans, they would want you to send them a letter," said Pam, her eyes bright.

(7) Kate smiled as her imagination led her into a sunlit, fantasy world. "I think I know what you mean," Kate said. "We would not be reading newspapers; we would read newsbeans, sold at bean stands."

(8) "Right, and you would not be writing with a pen. You'd write with a lima liner." Both girls giggled.

(9) "And when you went to school," Kate said, "the teacher would say, 'Put your name at the top of the bean and get ready for a test'." The girls laughed. "This is fun, Pam," said Kate. "Do you always make up jokes about the things you learn?"

(10) "Whenever I can," Pam answered. "It makes it fun to learn, and it helps me to remember things, too."

(11) "You're unbelievable, Pam Lee," Kate laughed. She paused and then said, "Maybe I should try it."

(12) "Well, if you decide to, I have a great assignment for you. The Incas also read knots."

"What?" asked Kate unbelievingly.

"The Incas had a very advanced system of accounting. They used color-coded strings with knots in them to keep a record of their food supplies, for example. Learning about the knots will be as much fun as the lima beans," smiled Pam.

1. What are the three connotative words or phrases the author uses to describe Mr. Singh's classroom?

   _____

2. What is the mood of the setting in the first part of the story?

   _____

3. What are three connotative words or phrases used in paragraph 2 to describe Pam Lee's mood?

   _____

4. What is Pam's mood in paragraph 2? _____

5. What connotative word or phrase in paragraph 3 describes Kate Willard's mood?

   _____

6. What is Kate's mood in this part of the story? _____

7. What is the overall mood in the first part of the story? _____

8. What connotative word or phrase does the author use to describe the lunchroom?

   _____

9. What is the mood of the setting in this part of the story? _____

10. What connotative word or phrase describes Pam's mood in the lunchroom?

    _____

11. What is Pam's mood in this part of the story? _____

12. What connotative word or phrase describes Kate's mood in this part of the story?

    _____

13. What is Kate's mood in this part of the story? _____

14. What is the mood in the last part of the story? _____

15. When does the mood change? _____

Re-assessment

Blackline
Master Pages
96-98

The Re-Assessment uses the same format as the Assessment and asks the students to demonstrate the same concepts and strategies. Hand out copies of Blackline Master Pages 96-98. Have the students read the story through at least once before answering the questions that follow it.

Answers for Blackline Master Page 96-98
1. murky darkness
2. Accept any reasonable answer such as threatening, scary, frightening, tense, or intimidating.
3. Accept any three: hands were clammy and cold, her stomach was knotted with tension, cold beads of sweat dotted the back of her neck and trickled down her spine, it loomed in front of her like a vast canyon, she licked her lips and wished her mouth were not so dry, she wiped her hands and shivered.
4. Accept any reasonable answer such as nervous, worried, scared, insecure, frightened, or anxious.
5. grinning at her
6. Accept any reasonable answer such as confident, secure, happy, or assured.
7. Accept any reasonable answer such as suspenseful, tense, anxious, or apprehensive.
8. Accept either one: the stage exploded into a sea of light, the audience roared with delight.
9. Accept any reasonable answer such as frenzied, excited, or chaotic.
10. Accept any three: rich, sweet, strong, pleasing them and herself, her voice rolled across the audience.
11. Accept any reasonable answer such as confident, calm, comfortable, assured, or enthusiastic.
12. He was still smiling, pushed her onto the stage, guitar pounding out the beat for her, smiled his approval.
13. Accept any reasonable answer such as confident, enthusiastic, approving, or happy.
14. Accept any reasonable answer such as exciting, enthusiastic, approving, cheerful, or happy.
15. Accept any reasonable answer such as the following: when the announcer announced the group, when The Tams went on stage, when Sarita began singing, when the audience roared with delight.

❏ SCORING

Score 1 point for each question.

Mastery Level: 12 out of 15 points.

Re-assessment

❏ Read the story and answer the questions on the following pages.

Hot Lights

(1) The palms of Sarita's hands were clammy and cold as she stood in the wing of the theater and looked out at the murky darkness of the stage. She would be performing on it in a few minutes, and her stomach was knotted with tension. This would be her first appearance as the lead singer with the rock band The Tams, and she was worried that the waiting fans would not like her performance.

(2) Cold beads of sweat dotted the back of her neck and trickled down her spine as her eyes scanned the stage. It loomed in front of her like a vast canyon, threatening to swallow her up.

(3) She licked her lips and wished her mouth were not so dry. The Tams were the hottest band in town, and she knew she would be a star if she sang well. She wiped her hands on her jeans and shivered in the chilly air that blew down on her from the air conditioner.

(4) "Have those butterflies under control?" asked a voice from behind her.

(5) Sarita turned to find The Tams' guitarist, Roger, grinning at her. "Not really, Roger. I guess you could say I am scared to death."

(6) "Don't worry, Sarita. We're a good band, and we'll make sure that you just knock them off their feet," he said reassuringly.

(7) Before she could answer, the announcer yelled into the microphone, "Here they are — The Tams." The stage exploded into a sea of light, and the audience roared with delight. Roger, still smiling, pushed her out onto the stage. She ran to the microphone as the band members hurried to their instruments and played the opening chords of the first song.

(8) With shaking hands, she took the microphone from the stand and waited for her cue. As she began to sing, her voice rolled across the audience, rich and strong and sweet, pleasing them and herself. The fans swayed and clapped along with the song, and Sarita could see that they were enjoying her singing.

(9) As she went into the chorus of the song, Roger's guitar pounding out the beat for her, her knees stopped shaking, and she began to revolve around the stage as if she owned it. The sparkling spotlights washed away her nervousness and covered her with their comforting warmth.

(10) She strutted as she sang, and the audience stood up and applauded, screaming for more. When she finished the song, Sarita looked at Roger, who smiled his approval. She smiled back, glad that she was on her way to becoming a rock star.

BLACKLINE MASTER

INSIGHTS: Reading as Thinking ©
Charlesbridge Publishing • (800) 225-3214

1. What connotative word or phrase does the author use to describe the stage?

   _____

2. What is the mood of the setting in this part of the story?

   _____

3. What are three connotative words or phrases that describe Sarita's mood?

   a. _____

   b. _____

   c. _____

4. What is Sarita's mood in this part of the story?

   _____

5. What connotative word or phrase suggests Roger's mood?

   _____

6. What is Roger's mood in this part of the story?

   _____

7. What is the overall mood in the first part of the story?

   _____

8. What connotative word or phrase does the author use to describe the stage after The Tams are announced? (Give one.)

   _____

9. What is the mood of the setting in paragraph 7?

   _____

10. What are three connotative words or phrases in paragraph 8 that describe how Sarita sang?

    a. _____

    b. _____

    c. _____

11. What is Sarita's mood in paragraph 9?

    _____

12. What connotative words or phrases describe Roger's relationship to Sarita in the second half of the story?

    a. _____

    b. _____

    c. _____

13. What is Roger's mood in this part of the story?

    _____

14. What is the overall mood of the second part of the story?

    _____

15. When does the mood change?

    _____

BLACKLINE MASTER

INSIGHTS: *Reading as Thinking* ©
Charlesbridge Publishing • (800) 225-3214

UNIT 3
Comprehending Comparisons

Learning Objectives

In this unit, the student will analyze and explain various types of comparisons and contrasts by

- differentiating between explained and implied comparisons
- identifying signal words suggesting similarities and differences
- inferring similarities in similes and metaphors
- deconstructing unexplained negative comparisons
- deriving underlying similarities from apparent differences
- differentiating comparisons from non-comparisons
- analyzing similarities and differences of characters in literature

Lesson 1: Analyzing comparisons
Lesson 2: Analyzing contrasts
Lesson 3: Interpreting similes and metaphors as comparisons
Lesson 4: Making charts to compare characters
Assessment: Blackline Master Pages 129-130
    Extension: Writing comparisons of people, places, and things
    Remediation: Additional Activities on Blackline Master Pages 135-140
Re-assessment: Blackline Master Pages 142-143

Purpose of the Unit

This unit provides students with strategies for analyzing both explained and unexplained comparisons. Comparisons are the basis of much thinking involving such constructs as analogies, figurative language, literary analysis, and the structure of meaning itself. Many abstractions can only be defined through comparison: we can define truth most easily by comparing it to false-hood.

Activating Prior Knowledge

Ask the students to define *compare* and *contrast* in their own words. Explain that *com* means together; *par* means equal or on equal footing with someone or something. So to compare means to examine how things are equal or similar.

Explain that *contrast* comes from the root *contra*, meaning the opposite or against. So to contrast means to examine the differences between things.

❏ WHAT COMPARISON IS

Have the students read page 65. Provide examples of comparisons from novels and short stories the students have read. Discuss examples showing similarities and differences.

Examples:

Both Anne of *Anne of Green Gables* and Jo of *Little Women* loved to write.

Aslan, the lion in *The Lion, the Witch, and the Wardrobe,* has power that everyone in the kingdom is aware of, but Charlotte in *Charlotte's Web* has power that no one recognizes.

PREREQUISITES AND INTRODUCTION

In this unit you will learn to identify two types of comparisons: those showing similarities and those showing differences. You will also learn that some comparisons are fully explained while others are not. You will find examples of both in this lesson when you learn about similes and metaphors that authors use in a passage.

▣ WHAT COMPARISON IS

Frequently in everyday language we use the word *comparison* when we want to show how things are similar. Any number of things may be compared: people, places, objects, events, and ideas. In formal English, however, the word *comparison* is used to show how things are similar and how they are different. This unit will focus on both types of comparisons.

Two Types of Comparisons

    a. **Comparisons showing similarities.** These comparisons show how two or more things are alike. For example: The ocean lay still, like a sleeping child. In this example, the two things being compared are an *ocean* and *a sleeping child.* They are alike because both are still and quiet.

    b. **Comparisons showing differences.** These comparisons show how two or more things are different. For example: Oceans are always larger than lakes or seas. In this example, the things being compared are *oceans, lakes,* and *seas*; oceans are different from lakes and seas because oceans are larger. Another word for differences is *contrast.*

Fully Explained and Unexplained Comparisons

    a. **Fully explained comparisons.** In making comparisons, it is useful to keep in mind that some comparisons are fully explained. This means that the author tells you exactly how the things being compared are alike or different.

    b. **Unexplained comparisons.** Frequently, however, the author decides to let you infer (work out) the meaning of the comparison yourself.

Example

1. A fully explained comparison: Sasha's face was as round and shining as the moon.

2. An unexplained comparison: Sasha's face was like the moon.

Explanation

In comparison 1, the two things being compared are Sasha's face and the moon. The author tells you how they are alike: both are round and shining. You do not have to infer how her face is like the moon.

In comparison 2, the two things being compared are also Sasha's face and the moon. Here, however, the author does not explain how the two things are alike. You, the reader, have to infer the ways in which they are similar. This is done by asking yourself about the main characteristics of the objects being compared.

Ask yourself: What are the characteristics of the moon that might relate to a face? The moon is round and shining. You can infer that Sasha's face is round and shining.

Investigation **A: DEFINITIONS**

❑ Complete the sentences in your own words.

1. A comparison showing similarities explains how _____

_____ .

2. A comparison showing contrasts explains how _____

_____ .

3. Any of the following things may be compared: a) people, b) _____ ,

c) _____ , d) _____ , and e) _____ .

4. A fully explained comparison is _____

_____ .

5. An unexplained comparison is _____

_____ .

Have the students read each Example. Suggest that they visualize the comparison. Some students may have mental pictures that suggest another comparison. Other reasonable inferences would be that Sasha's face is softly glowing or partially hidden. Point out that each reader can make a different inference that is correct as long as it is based on the clues the author gives and connects those clues in a logical manner.

Investigation A: DEFINITIONS

Have the students complete the definitions.

Answer Key

1. A comparison showing similarities explains how two or more things are alike.

2. A comparison showing contrasts explains how two or more things are different.

3. Any of the following things may be compared: people, places, objects, events, and ideas.

4. A fully explained comparison is one in which the author tells you exactly how the things being compared are alike or different.

5. An unexplained comparison is one in which the author does not explain the meaning of the comparison. The reader must infer it.

❏ SIMILARITY SIGNAL WORDS

Have students read the signal words.

Elicit comparisons using any of the signal words listed.

Choose one of the comparisons and use it to show students how to apply each of the steps for identifying the kind of comparison being made.

Investigation A: IDENTIFYING COMPARISONS

Read aloud the first two sentences and ask students whether or not they contain comparisons. In the second sentence there is a comparison. Ask students to identify the similarity signal word and the meaning of the comparison.

Answer Key

1. NC
2. S
3. S
4. S

SIMILARITY SIGNAL WORDS

Similarities may be expressed by any of the following signal words.

1. like/alike
2. as/as if, similarly
3. both/and
4. also
5. similar
6. same/identical
7. share
8. have in common
9. resemble

Most of these signal words have more than one use. Seeing one in a sentence may or may not signal a comparison. When you read, be alert to signal words. A comparison using the words *like* or *as* is called a **simile**. Use the following strategy to decide what kind of comparison is implied.

Step 1: *Think:* This sentence contains a similarity signal word.

Step 2: Decide what things are being compared.

Step 3: Decide how they are alike.

Step 4: *Think:* If it is an unexplained comparison, I need to infer the meaning by thinking of how the things being compared are similar.

Investigation **A**: IDENTIFYING COMPARISONS

❏ Read each of the following sentences.
- Write **S** if the sentence contains a comparison showing similarities.
- Write **NC** if the sentence does not contain a comparison showing similarities.

_____ 1. Some people did not understand why Harry asked so many questions all the time.

_____ 2. Both water and certain mirrors can distort (change) your reflection because their surfaces are curved.

_____ 3. Some early models of airplanes had wings shaped like saucers.

_____ 4. Crocodiles and alligators are almost identical in the way they look and in the way they live.

Investigation B: ANALYZING COMPARISONS

Investigation B: ANALYZING COMPARISONS

❑ Read each of the following sentences.
  • Circle the words that signal a comparison of similar things.
  • Underline the things being compared.
  • Write the meaning by describing the similarity. Be sure to include the two things being compared in the sentence.

1. One reason both the Roman and British empires declined (lost their power) was that the lands they controlled were too widespread to be governed effectively.

   Think: This is a fully explained comparison using a signal word. The author tells you exactly how the empires are alike.

   Meaning: The lands of the _____ and the _____ _____ were too _____ to be governed effectively.

2. Professional football players are like professional basketball players because both must think only about the game while they play.

   Think: This is a fully explained comparison using signal words.

   Meaning: _____ _____

3. Apes and humans share many characteristics; both are mammals, walk upright, and have strong family ties.

   Think: This is a fully explained comparison using signal words.

   Meaning: _____ _____

4. The red ants poured out of the anthill like molten lava.

   Think: This is an unexplained comparison with a signal word. I need to infer how the movement of ants could be like molten lava.

   Meaning: _____ _____

5. Did you know that sea horses and kangaroos have something in common? They carry their young in pouches.

   Meaning: _____ _____

INSIGHTS: Reading as Thinking ©
Charlesbridge Publishing • (800) 225-3214

Investigation B: ANALYZING COMPARISONS

Read the instructions. Ask students to write the meaning so that it is a sentence naming the two things being compared. Use the first sentence as a model, identifying the signal words and the items being compared, and providing the meaning of the comparison. Have the students complete sentences 2-5 independently.

Answer Key

1. Signal words: both
   Compare: the Roman to the British Empire
   Meaning: The lands of the Roman Empire and the British were too widespread to be governed effectively.

2. Signal words: like, both
   Compare: professional football players to basketball players
   Meaning: Professional football and basketball players must think only about winning while they play.

3. Signal word: both
   Compare: apes to humans
   Meaning: Apes and humans are mammals, walk upright, and have strong family ties.

4. Signal word: like
   Compare: red ants to molten lava
   Meaning: Both burning lava and ants are red. Both move as a solid mass.

5. Signal words: in common
   Compare: sea horses to kangaroos
   Meaning: Both sea horses and kangaroos carry their young in pouches.

Investigation B: ANALYZING COMPARISONS *continued*

Have students continue finding the signal words, comparisons, and their meaning for sentences 6-12.

In discussing their answers, point out that things being compared may be alike in more than one way, which means that inferred comparisons may be different as long as they are logical.

Answer Key

6. Signal word: like
   Compare: rusty old car to a workhorse
   Meaning: A workhorse looks tired and worn out at the end of the day, in the same way an old car looks worn out.
7. Signal word: similar
   Compare: grasshoppers to frogs
   Meaning: Both grasshoppers and frogs undergo a change in form.
8. Signal word: share
   Compare: the Nootka to other Native Americans in the Pacific Northwest
   Meaning: Both the Nootka and other Native Americans live in large log houses.
9. Signal word: as
   Compare: flies to mosquitoes
   Meaning: Flies and mosquitoes both buzz during flight, crawl on people and/or food, carry germs, and bite.
10. Signal words: same, as
    Compare: hang gliding to airplane flying
    Meaning: Both hang gliding and airplane flying are based on the same principles of flight.

---

6. The rusty old car moved down the street like a workhorse at the end of a hard day.

   Think: This is an unexplained comparison using a signal word. How would a workhorse feel at the end of a hard day?

   Meaning: _____

   _____

7. Grasshoppers and frogs are similar because they undergo a metamorphosis, changing from one form in infancy to another form as they grow older.

   Meaning: _____

   _____

8. The Nootka and other Native Americans in the Pacific Northwest share a tradition of living in large log houses.

   Meaning: _____

   _____

9. Flies can be just as irritating as mosquitoes in the summertime.

   Meaning: _____

   Hint — This comparison is only partly explained. Think of all the different ways that flies and mosquitoes can be irritating.

10. Hang gliding, a sport involving human flight, is based on the same principles as airplane flying.

    Meaning: _____

    _____

11. The news spread like wildfire.

    Meaning: _____

    _____

12. That rock is like a piece of glass.

    Meaning: _____

    _____

11. Signal word: like
    Compare: news to wildfire
    Meaning: The news spread from person to person just as quickly as wildfire does.
12. Signal word: like
    Compare: a rock to a piece of glass
    Meaning: The rock has a smooth surface like glass, or it has sharp edges like glass.

13. My vivid poster will be as effective as her clever speech.

Meaning: _____

_____

14. Dean flew down the street, flapping his arms like a bird.

Meaning: _____

_____

15. Marlene suddenly looked as if she were an icicle.

Meaning: _____

_____

16. It was like a furnace in the basement.

Meaning: _____

_____

Investigation **C**: WRITING SIGNAL WORDS

❏ Write as many signal words as possible without referring back to page 67.

1. _____   6. _____

2. _____   7. _____

3. _____   8. _____

4. _____   9. _____

5. _____   _____

Investigation B: ANALYZING COMPARISONS *continued*

After students complete items 13-16, discuss these sentences. Elicit alternate ways of interpreting the meaning of each comparison.

Answer Key

13. Signal word: as
    Compare: a vivid poster to a clever speech
    Meaning: A vivid poster can have as powerful an effect on people as a clever speech.
14. Signal word: like
    Compare: Dean to a bird
    Meaning: Dean ran, moving his arms up and down like a bird in flight.
15. Signal words: as if
    Compare: Marlene to an icicle
    Meaning: Marlene did not move, as if she were frozen stiff.
16. Signal word: like
    Compare: a furnace to a basement
    Meaning: The basement was very hot.

Investigation C: WRITING SIGNAL WORDS

Have students write the signal words from memory.

Answer Key

1. like/alike
2. as/as if, similarly
3. both/and
4. also
5. similar
6. same/identical
7. share
8. have in common
9. resemble

❑ COMPARISONS WITHOUT SIGNAL WORDS

Have a student read the Example and the accompanying Explanation. For the second sentence, ask students what the car really did. (It probably made a grinding noise or backfired.) Discuss why writers use personification. Two reasons for using personification are to create new and interesting comparisons and to help the reader identify with non-living things.

Have students complete the sentences. Then discuss their metaphors.

▣ COMPARISONS WITHOUT SIGNAL WORDS

So far, the comparisons in this unit have contained signal words. However, comparisons can be made without using the words *like* or *as* or other signal words. These unexplained comparisons are called **metaphors**. You must infer their meaning. There are two types of metaphors: metaphors with personification, and metaphors without personification.

Example

Two Types of Metaphor:

1. The fog blanketed the city. (metaphor without personification)

2. The rusty old car coughed and stopped. (personification metaphor)

Explanation

In each of the Example sentences, there is a comparison showing a similarity without the use of signal words.

In sentence 1, you know there is a metaphor because a fog is not a blanket in reality. The fog (a thing) is being compared to a blanket (a thing). This comparison is an unexplained metaphor. You must infer that the fog is like a blanket because it covers the city.

In sentence 2, you know that the comparison is an unexplained metaphor because cars do not cough in reality. Humans cough. Thus, the car is being compared to a human being who is coughing; that is, the car sounds like a person coughing. This is called *personification*.

Now create two of your own metaphors by completing the following sentences.

a. The falling rock_____

   _____.

b. The pair of old sneakers _____

   _____.

Investigation A: ANALYZING METAPHORS

❑ Read each of the following sentences and circle the metaphors.
- Write the meaning of each sentence.

1. The cart groaned under its heavy load as it made its way up the hill.

   Think: A cart does not groan. A person might groan when tired or in pain.

   Things compared: The cart is compared to a human.

   Meaning: _____

   _____

2. The newsroom hummed with the noise of computers.

   Think: A room cannot hum. When many people talk softly, it makes a humming sound.

   Things compared: The sound of the computers is compared to the sound of humans humming.

   Meaning: _____

   _____

3. Catherine ruled with an iron hand.

   Think: This is a metaphor. People do not have iron hands.

   Things compared: Catherine's style of leadership is compared to the hardness and coldness of iron.

   Meaning: _____

   _____

4. A good book is a treasure chest of knowledge.

   Think: This is a metaphor. A book is not a treasure chest.

   Things compared: The book is compared to a treasure chest.

   Meaning: _____

   _____

INSIGHTS: Reading as Thinking ©
Charlesbridge Publishing • (800) 225-3214

Investigation A: ANALYZING METAPHORS

Have the students read the instructions on page 72. Use the first sentence to model the strategy. Have the students circle the metaphor and write the meaning for the second sentence. Point out that the *Think* statement is omitted after sentence 5. Ask student volunteers to describe how they know each sentence is a metaphor.

Answer Key

1. Metaphor: cart groaned
   Meaning: The cart is loaded with so much weight that it makes noises like a person groaning in pain.
2. Metaphor: computer hummed
   Meaning: The computer made a pleasant sound like people humming.
3. Metaphor: iron hand
   Meaning: Catherine's leadership is like iron because both are hard and unfeeling.
4. Metaphor: treasure chest of knowledge
   Meaning: A good book contains as many wonderful and precious pieces of information as a chest full of jewels and gold.

Investigation A: ANALYZING METAPHORS *continued*

Answer Key *continued*

5. Metaphor: icing on the cake
   Meaning: The money is an additional bonus that will be as enjoyable as a sweet food.
6. Metaphor: legs turned to jelly
   Meaning: Julio was so scared that he could not move his legs to run away.
7. Metaphor: Mr. Matthews erupted
   Meaning: Mr. Matthews was so angry because of the delay in the mail that his anger exploded or poured out like lava from a volcano.
8. Metaphor: chained him to the house
   Meaning: Tom was confined to his house just as if he were in chains and unable to escape.
9. Metaphor: invaded my thoughts
   Meaning: The metaphor suggests that Leslie's voice is an unwelcome intrusion, just as an invasion is unwelcome.
10. Metaphor: garden's thirst
   Meaning: The metaphor suggests that the garden needed water just as a thirsty person does.

---

5. The extra money you receive will be icing on the cake for a job well done.

   Think: This is a metaphor. Money is not icing on a cake.

   Things compared: The extra money is compared to icing on a cake.

   Meaning: _____

   _____

6. Julio was so scared that his legs turned to jelly.

   Things compared: Julio's legs are compared to jelly.

   Meaning: _____

   _____

7. Mr. Matthews erupted when the mail finally arrived — two hours late.

   Things compared: Mr. Matthews's behavior is compared to an eruption.

   Meaning: _____

   _____

8. Tom's inability to drive chained him to the house.

   Things compared: The inability to drive is compared to being chained.

   Meaning: _____

   _____

9. Leslie's voice invaded my thoughts.

   Things compared: Leslie's voice is compared to an invasion.

   Meaning: _____

   _____

10. The summer shower quenched the garden's thirst.

   Things compared: The garden is being compared to a thirsty person.

   Meaning: _____

   _____

 Literature Connection

Have students find examples of similes and metaphors in books they are reading and share them with the class. Discuss the meaning of each example they find.

Comparisons Showing Differences

COMPARISONS SHOWING DIFFERENCES

In the previous lesson you compared two or more things or ideas that are similar. In this lesson you will compare two or more things or ideas that are different. When you compare differences, you are making a contrast. Listed below are some contrast signal words that indicate differences between things.

1. than	5. in contrast (to)	9. however
2. while	6. in comparison (to)	10. on one hand
3. but	7. difference/different	11. on the other hand
4. although	8. unlike	12. whereas

Example

1. Silk is smoother *than* wool.
2. *Although* silk is smooth, wool is rough.
3. Silk is smooth, *but* wool is not as smooth.
4. *In contrast to* wool, silk is smooth.
5. Silk is smooth in *comparison to* wool.
6. Silk is smooth, *compared to* wool.
7. *Whereas* silk is smooth, wool is rough.
8. *Unlike* wool, silk is smooth.
9. Silk is smooth; *however,* wool is rough.
10. *While* silk is smooth, wool is rough.

Explanation

In each of the Example sentences, the same two items are being compared: wool and silk. The comparison contrasts silk and wool; it tells how they are different.

 Investigation : IDENTIFYING CONTRASTS

❑ Read each of the following sentences.
  • Write **D** if the sentence contains a comparison showing differences.
  • Write **NC** if the sentence contains no comparison.
  • Underline the contrast signal word in the sentences that you mark with a **D**.

INSIGHTS: Reading as Thinking ©
Charlesbridge Publishing • (800) 225-3214

As a review, call on students to list the similarity signal words and suggest appropriate comparisons.

Have students read the opening paragraphs and the list of contrast signal words.

Call on a volunteer to read each sentence in the Example and to suggest another sentence that uses the same contrast signal word.

Investigation A: IDENTIFYING CONTRASTS

Ask a student to read the instructions aloud. This activity is parallel to the one on page 67 for comparisons showing similarities.

Investigation A:
IDENTIFYING CONTRASTS
continued

Read aloud the first two sentences and ask students whether or not they contain contrasts. In the first sentence there is a contrast. Ask students to identify the contrast signal word and the meaning of the contrast.

Answer Key
1. D; signal word: Although
2. NC
3. NC
4. D; signal word: compared
5. D; signal word: but

❏ FULLY EXPLAINED AND UNEXPLAINED CONTRASTS

Ask volunteers to read the Examples and Explanations aloud.

Discuss how students can use the context to help them make inferences.

If your school is a magnet, charter, or private school or requires an entrance exam, the topic of this Example may require further discussion.

_____ 1. Although the city has industry and construction jobs, rural areas have ranching and farming jobs.

_____ 2. There are a number of high-rise apartments and office buildings in the city.

_____ 3. The city also has lots of street lights, neon lights from signs, and traffic lights.

_____ 4. There are many cars, buses, and motorcycles in the city, compared to rural areas.

_____ 5. Fruits and vegetables are often sold in outdoor markets in many rural areas, but in the city fruits and vegetables are usually sold in supermarkets.

◻ FULLY EXPLAINED AND UNEXPLAINED CONTRASTS

Recall that comparisons may be fully explained by the author, or they may be unexplained so that you have to infer the meaning of the contrast.

 Example

A fully explained contrast: While Alexandra had been accepted at the school of her choice, Anne had received no notices from the schools to which she had applied.

 Explanation
The two people being compared are Alexandra and Anne. The author has told you exactly how the two girls are different: In this example the signal word is *While*. One has received notice of an acceptance, but the other has received no notices.

 Example

An unexplained contrast: Unlike Anne, Alexandra had been accepted at the school of her choice.

 Explanation
In this example, the contrast is not fully explained. You must infer or figure out how the two girls are different. Generally speaking, when you have an unexplained negative comparison, you may infer that the things compared are opposites. Thus, you could infer from the example that Anne had *not* been accepted at the school of her choice.

INSIGHTS: Reading as Thinking ©
Charlesbridge Publishing • (800) 225-3214

To understand a comparison showing differences, you use almost the same strategy that you used for comparisons showing similarities.

> **Step 1:** *Ask yourself:* Are there signal words or is it an unexplained comparison?
>
> **Step 2:** Decide what things are being compared.
>
> **Step 3:** Decide how the things are different.
>
> **Step 4:** *Think:* If it is an unexplained comparison, I need to infer the meaning.

Investigation **A**: ANALYZING CONTRASTS

❑ Read each of the following sentences and circle the contrast signal words.
  • Explain the meaning of each contrast.

1. In contrast to the monkey, the chimpanzee uses tools to catch and eat food.

   Meaning: The monkey does not use tools to catch and eat food,

   but the chimpanzee does.

2. Unlike the chimpanzee, the monkey has a tail.
   Meaning: _____

   _____

3. There are four chief kinds of chimpanzees compared to three kinds of monkeys.
   Meaning: _____

   _____

4. While chimpanzees seldom fight among themselves, monkeys will threaten members of their own group.
   Meaning: _____

   _____

5. Usually, people say that both monkeys and chimpanzees are intelligent animals, but the chimpanzee is really more intelligent than the monkey.
   Meaning: _____

   _____

INSIGHTS: Reading as Thinking ©
Charlesbridge Publishing • (800) 225-3214

Ask student volunteers to read the strategy for understanding a comparison showing differences.

Investigation A: ANALYZING CONTRASTS

Have students read the instructions. Apply the four-step strategy to the first sentence for your students. Have them use the strategy independently to analyze the remaining sentences.

Answer Key

1. Signal words: In contrast
   Meaning: The monkey does not use tools to catch and eat food, but the chimpanzee does.
2. Signal word: Unlike
   Meaning: The monkey has a tail but the chimpanzee does not.
3. Signal word: compared
   Meaning: There are more kinds of chimpanzees than kinds of monkeys.
4. Signal word: While
   Meaning: Monkeys fight with members of their own group; chimpanzees do not.
5. Signal word: but
   Meaning: The chimpanzee is more intelligent than the monkey.

❏ UNEXPLAINED NEGATIVE COMPARISONS

After students have read the introductory paragraph, have volunteers read the Example and Explanation. Suggest that students apply the four-step strategy to the sentences in the Example. Point out that although the first sentence has the signal word *like*, it also has the negative signal word *not*, which indicates it is a negative comparison.

Investigation A: ANALYZING NEGATIVE COMPARISONS

Ask a volunteer to read aloud the instructions. Demonstrate the steps of the strategy using the first sentence.

Answer Key

1. Signal word: Unlike
   Compare: two cats
   Meaning: Fluffy and Patches are different, because Patches likes to go outdoors, whereas Fluffy does not.

❏ UNEXPLAINED NEGATIVE COMPARISONS

Negative comparisons are comparisons which show differences using negative signal words such as *not, but,* and *unlike*. Unexplained negative comparisons are difficult to understand because they are sometimes mistaken for statements containing similarities and differences. They are also difficult to understand because they are unexplained. You have to infer their meaning. Consider this example.

Example

1. The caddis worm does not look like a worm; to protect its body from water, it builds a unique covering of pebbles and twigs.

2. Unlike his brother, Milo was allowed to stay out late because he had good grades.

Explanation

In both sentences, there is a negative comparison showing differences between two or more things. In sentence 1, the purpose of the comparison is to show how the caddis worm is *different* from other worms.

In sentence 2, the purpose of the comparison is to contrast the behavior of Milo and his brother. The use of the word *unlike* means that they are different. The sentence does not directly state that Milo's brother had lower grades and, therefore, could not stay out late, but both of these facts are clearly implied by the negative comparison words.

Investigation **A**: ANALYZING NEGATIVE COMPARISONS

❏ Read each of the following sentences and circle the contrast signal words.
   • Complete the statements that follow each sentence.

1. Unlike Fluffy, our cat Patches loves to go outdoors.

The things compared are _____ : Patches and Fluffy.

This comparison suggests that _____

_____ .

---

2. In contrast to other mammals, whales live in the sea.

   The things compared are _____ .

   This comparison suggests that _____

   _____ .

3. Unlike other twentieth-century Presidents, President Eisenhower was a general in the U.S. Army.

   The things compared are _____ .

   This comparison suggests that _____

   _____ .

4. In Britain, the Prime Minister is the head of state; whereas in the United States, the President is the head of state.

   The things compared are _____ .

   This comparison suggests that _____

   _____ .

5. In contrast to long days of travel in the early part of this century, people today can reach any part of the United States within a few hours.

   The things compared are _____ .

   This comparison suggests that _____

   _____ .

6. Australia is not as large a continent as South America or North America.

   The things compared are _____ .

   This comparison suggests that _____

   _____ .

INSIGHTS: *Reading as Thinking* ©
Charlesbridge Publishing • (800) 225-3214

Investigation A: ANALYZING NEGATIVE COMPARISONS
continued

After students complete the analysis of the sentences, discuss how they used the strategy to explain the comparisons.

Answer Key

2. Signal words: In contrast to
   Compare: other mammals to whales
   Meaning: The whale is different from other mammals. Other mammals live on land but the whale lives in the sea.

3. Signal word: Unlike
   Compare: President Eisenhower to other twentieth-century Presidents
   Meaning: President Eisenhower was different from other twentieth-century Presidents because he had a military background that the other Presidents did not have.

4. Signal word: whereas
   Compare: Britain to the United States
   Meaning: This comparison suggest that while both countries have heads of states, their leaders have different official titles.

5. Signal words: In contrast to
   Compare: past to present travel
   Meaning: In the past it took people a long time to travel in the United States, but today people are able to travel quickly.

6. Signal word: not
   Compare: Australia to South and North America
   Meaning: Australia is not as big in size as South or North America.

Have students read aloud the introductory paragraph and the Example. Discuss what is being compared and the kind of comparison being made. Then call the students' attention to the Explanation. Ask volunteers to tell what they visualize for each statement.

Investigation A: ANALYZING SIMILARITIES

Have students read the instructions. Use the first group of words to demonstrate how you visualize the following: Marlene excited about running in her first race; William was angry with himself for failing to save his story on the computer, etc.

After you have shared your visualization for each item, discuss what all the words in the group have in common. (All are human emotions.) Have students identify the similarities among the items in the second group.

Answer Key

1. excited, angry, resentful, eager: All are human emotions.
2. a telephone book, a bulletin board, a newspaper, an invitation: All are used to communicate information, may be made of paper, or contain print.

 SIMILARITIES UNDERLYING APPARENT DIFFERENCES

Sometimes you will come across information that seems to present differences. If you look at the information again closely, you may discover that there are actually some features in common after all.

★ *Example*

Heidi lived in the only chalet high up the side of the mountain.
Sam lived in a cottage in the middle of the forest.
Tony lived in a lighthouse.

☆ *Explanation*

On the surface, it appears that all three people lived in different types of housing. While this is true, it is also true that all of their houses have something in common. Can you guess what it is? Reread each of the Example sentences and try to visualize each housing site. *Ask yourself* (as you read and visualize): What do these housing sites have in common? *Answer:* All of the housing sites are isolated.

Investigation : ANALYZING SIMILARITIES

□ Read each of the following groups of items. You may need to look up some of the words in a dictionary.
- *Ask yourself:* What do these items have in common?
- In the column on the right, state how they are similar. There may be more than one similarity.

ITEMS	SIMILARITIES
1. excited, angry, resentful, eager	
2. a telephone book, a bulletin board, a newspaper, an invitation	

ITEMS	SIMILARITIES
3. cave, nest, tent, apartment	
4. a kite, a hang glider	
5. flock, school, gaggle, herd	
6. teammate, deputy, sidekick, conspirator	
7. baby chickens, dandelions, the sun, egg yolk	
8. halo, wreath, crown, collar	
9. telephone, megaphone, microphone	
10. cattle, bumblebees, cats	

INSIGHTS: Reading as Thinking ©
Charlesbridge Publishing • (800) 225-3214

Investigation A: ANALYZING SIMILARITIES *continued*

Encourage students to use the dictionary if they are not sure of a word's meaning. Have them identify the similarities among the words in each group.

Answer Key

3. cave, nest, tent, apartment: All are places to live, or structures that give shelter.
4. a kite, a hang glider: Both are unmotorized objects that fly, or both are guided by people.
5. flock, school, gaggle, herd: Each word represents a group of animals; each word is a collective noun.
6. teammate, deputy, sidekick, conspirator: Each word represents a person who helps another person, or persons, do something.
7. baby chickens, dandelions, the sun, egg yolk: Each word represents something that is yellow.
8. halo, wreath, crown, collar: All have a circular or ringlike shape.
9. telephone, megaphone, microphone: All three are used to communicate human speech.
10. cattle, bumblebees, cats: All three are living creatures.

Analyzing Similes and Metaphors

This lesson continues the work begun with similes and metaphors. In this lesson they are used to make more abstract comparisons. As a review, have the students complete the definitions of simile and metaphor.

Investigation A: INTERPRETING THE MEANING OF SIMILES

Have the students visualize each simile and use their mental pictures to interpret them.

Answer Key

1. a. Compare: redwood trees to skyscrapers
   b. The simile suggests that redwoods are very tall.
2. a. Compare: Latisha to a rag
   b. The simile suggests that at the end of the day, Latisha felt tired and wrung out.
3. a. Compare: baby brother to a kitten
   b. The simile suggests that Aneze's baby brother was very frisky and playful.
4. a. Compare: Hubert's heart to a drum
   b. The simile suggests that Hubert's heart beat very loudly.
5. a. Compare: people to elephants
   b. The simile suggests that some people are very good at remembering events.

Strategy
Lesson **3**

ANALYZING SIMILES AND METAPHORS

Similes and metaphors compare two or more things or ideas. Complete the sentences below.

1. A simile is _____

_____.

2. A metaphor is_____

_____.

Investigation **A**: INTERPRETING THE MEANING OF SIMILES

❑ Read each of the following similes and complete the statements.

1. The giant redwood trees stood like skyscrapers.

   a. The two things compared are _____.

   b. The simile suggests that _____.

2. Latisha felt as limp as a rag by the end of the day.

   a. The two things compared are_____.

   b. The simile suggests that_____.

3. Aneze's baby brother was as playful as a kitten most of the time.

   a. The two things compared are_____.

   b. The simile suggests that _____.

4. Hubert's heart beat like a drum.

   a. The two things compared are_____.

   b. The simile suggests that _____.

5. Some people act like elephants when they have events to remember.

   a. The two things compared are_____.

   b. The simile suggests that _____.

---

6. Jeff turned as red as a beet when he tripped over his own feet.

   a. The two things compared are _____ .

   b. The simile suggests that _____ .

7. The darkness enveloped us like a cloak (cape).

   a. The two things compared are _____ .

   b. The simile suggests that _____ .

8. The puppies were as alike as two leaves on a tree.

   a. The two things compared are _____ .

   b. The simile suggests that _____ .

Investigation **B**: INTERPRETING METAPHORS

❏ Read each of the following metaphors.
   • Complete the statements that follow each metaphor.

1. Rob's daydreams came crashing down when he heard the bell ring.

   a. The metaphor is _____ .

   b. The metaphor suggests that _____

   _____ .

2. Lucian's voice thundered down the street as he called after his son.

   a. The metaphor is _____ .

   b. The metaphor suggests that _____

   _____ .

INSIGHTS: Reading as Thinking ©
Charlesbridge Publishing • (800) 225-3214

Investigation A: INTERPRETING THE MEANING OF SIMILES
continued

Remind students to visualize what is described in each simile. Discuss the prior knowledge it takes to interpret these similes.

Answer Key

6. a. Compare: Jeff's face to a beet
   b. The simile suggests that Jeff blushed because he was embarrassed.
7. a. Compare: darkness to a cloak
   b. The simile suggests that the darkness was all around them.
8. a. Compare: puppies to leaves on a tree
   b. The simile suggests that the two puppies were nearly identical.

Investigation B: INTERPRETING METAPHORS

Interpret the first metaphor as an example. Have students interpret the rest independently. Discuss their interpretations.

Answer Key

1. a. Metaphor: dreams came crashing
   b. Suggests that Rob's imaginary world collapsed when he heard the bell ring.
2. a. Metaphor: voice thundered
   b. Suggests that Lucian's voice was as loud and as harsh as thunder and could be heard far down the street.

Investigation B: INTERPRETING METAPHORS *continued*

Have students work independently to interpret the meaning of each metaphor. Suggest that visualizing can be useful in identifying metaphorical comparisons.

Answer Key

3. a. Metaphor: memories were sunshine
   b. Suggests that the memories were a bright spot in her life.
4. a. Metaphor: mind was flooded
   b. Suggests that many thoughts came rushing into Cassandra's mind.
5. a. Metaphor: Loren and friends stampeded
   b. Suggests that the boys charged through the house like a herd of animals.
6. a. Metaphor: showered with affection
   b. Suggests that Sally gave her daughter lots of affection.
7. a. Metaphor: graduates were harvested
   b. Suggests that the top graduates were chosen for the best jobs.
8. a. Metaphor: Lester's arguments muddied
   b. Suggests that Lester's arguments made the issue unclear, as muddy water is unclear.

3. Sylvia's memories were the sunshine in her life.

   a. The metaphor is_____ .

   b. The metaphor suggests that _____

   _____ .

4. Cassandra's mind was flooded with thoughts.

   a. The metaphor is_____ .

   b. The metaphor suggests that _____

   _____ .

5. Every day after school, Loren and his friends stampeded through the house to the refrigerator.

   a. The metaphor is_____ .

   b. The metaphor suggests that _____

   _____ .

6. Sally showered her daughter with affection.

   a. The metaphor is_____ .

   b. The metaphor suggests that _____

   _____ .

7. The top graduates were harvested for the best jobs.

   a. The metaphor is_____ .

   b. The metaphor suggests that _____

   _____ .

8. Lester's arguments muddied the issue.

   a. The metaphor is_____ .

   b. The metaphor suggests that _____

   _____ .

INSIGHTS: Reading as Thinking ©
Charlesbridge Publishing • (800) 225-3214

UNIT 3 – Comprehending Comparisons   **83**

Investigation : WRITING COMPARISONS

❑ Think of a novel or story you have read.
  • Write the title and the name of the author on lines 1 and 2.
  • Select two characters in the story who have something in common (for example, physical appearance, interests, activities, or character traits).
  • Describe one or more of these similarities in sentence form.
  • Write the same information about another book and describe character differences.

Similarities

1. Title of the book or story: _____

   _____

2. Author: _____

3. Characters: A. _____

   B. _____

4. _____ and _____ are alike because

   _____

   _____ .

Differences

1. Title of the book or story: _____

   _____

2. Author. _____

3. Characters: A. _____

   B. _____

4. _____ and _____ are different because

   _____

   _____ .

INSIGHTS: *Reading as Thinking* ©
Charlesbridge Publishing • (800) 225-3214

Investigation C: WRITING COMPARISONS

Have the students as a group make comparison and contrast statements about characters in a book they have all read in class. Write these on the board. Have each student choose one statement to use as the basis of a paragraph. The writing may be done as homework.

Literature Connection

Have students analyze the similarities and differences in the plots of two books they have read, two recent programs on television, or two movies of the same or different genres.

Putting It All Together

As a review, ask students to write the comparison signal words and the contrast signal words. The lists of signal words are shown on student pages 67 and 74.

❏ RECOGNIZING COMPARISONS AND NONCOMPARISONS

Ask a volunteer to read the introductory paragraph. The signal words do not always signal a comparison so the strategy on the following page is important.

PUTTING IT ALL TOGETHER

It is important to recognize signal words in sentences. Comparison signal words are very common. Just for fun, see how many similarity signal words you can remember without looking back.

1._____	8._____
2._____	9._____
3._____	10._____
4._____	11._____
5._____	12._____
6._____	13._____
7._____	14._____

Now try to write as many contrast signal words as you can without looking back.

1._____	7._____
2._____	8._____
3._____	9._____
4._____	10._____
5._____	11._____
6._____	12._____

▢ RECOGNIZING COMPARISONS AND NONCOMPARISONS

In the previous lessons, you worked with similarity comparisons or difference comparisons, or comparisons with both similarities and differences. This lesson provides you with a thinking strategy to use when comparisons are mixed with sentences containing no comparisons. In this situation you need to be alert to comparisons with and without signal words.

INSIGHTS: Reading as Thinking ©
Charlesbridge Publishing • (800) 225-3214

STRATEGY FOR READING COMPARISONS

While you are reading, if you think the sentence contains a comparison, think through these steps.

> 1. *Ask yourself:* Are there signal words? Is it an unexplained comparison (metaphor)?
>
> 2. *Ask yourself:* What things are being compared?
>
> 3. *Ask yourself:* How are the things alike or different?
>
> 4. *Think:* If the comparison is unexplained, I need to infer the meaning.

Remember, common words such as *and*, *but*, *as*, and *than* have many different uses. Just because a sentence contains one of these words does not necessarily mean that the text contains a comparison. You can use the strategy above to establish whether or not the sentence contains a comparison and to interpret the comparison. At each step of the strategy, you might decide that the answer is *No* and that there is no need to continue because there is no comparison.

Investigation **A**: ANALYZING DESCRIPTIONS OF LITERATURE

❑ Read each description of a book.
  • Write **S** if the sentences contain a comparison showing similarity.
  • Write **D** if the sentences contain a comparison showing difference.
  • Write **S/D** if the sentences show a similarity and a difference.
  • Write **NC** if the sentences contain no comparisons.

_____ 1. In *Charlie and the Chocolate Factory* by Roald Dahl, Charlie is a nice, well-behaved boy, but all of the other children are very mischievous. You would probably enjoy reading the book.

_____ 2. In *Plain Girl* by Virginia Sorensen, Esther more or less accepts the stern ways of the Amish people. In contrast, her older brother, Daniel, questions the Amish ideas about not singing happy songs, not wearing buttons, and not using any appliances such as toasters.

86 UNIT 3 – Comprehending Comparisons

INSIGHTS: Reading as Thinking ©
Charlesbridge Publishing • (800) 225-3214

❑ ## STRATEGY FOR READING COMPARISONS

Ask a student to read the strategy for reading comparisons and the paragraph that follows it. Discuss the other uses for the signal words.

Investigation A: ANALYZING DESCRIPTIONS OF LITERATURE

Have the students read the instructions. Demonstrate how to use the strategy with the first two descriptions.

Description 1.
Step 1: There is one signal word – *but*. It is a contrast signal word. There is no metaphor.
Step 2: Charlie is compared to other children.
Step 3: Charlie's behavior is good, while the other children are mischievous.
Step 4: I don't need to infer the meaning, because the comparison is explained.
Answer is D.

Description 2.
Step 1: The signal words are *In contrast*. There is no metaphor.
Step 2: Esther is compared to Daniel.
Step 3: Esther accepts Amish ways; her brother Daniel does not.
Step 4: The comparison is partly explained. The term *more or less* leaves the reader to infer that Esther does not accept everything without question.
Answer is D.

Investigation A: ANALYZING DESCRIPTIONS OF LITERATURE
continued

Have the students use the strategy to analyze the descriptions to find whether they contain similarities, differences, both, or neither. Call on volunteers to explain the answers. For homework, have students write a description of a favorite book. Ask them to include at least one simile, one metaphor, and one comparison showing a difference.

Answer Key

3. S
4. S
5. D
6. NC
7. S/D
8. D
9. D

_____ 3. In the book *Treasure Island* by Robert Louis Stevenson, a boy named Jim Hawkins has several exciting adventures. He is kidnapped by the famous pirate, Long John Silver. He meets a strange sailor named Ben Gunn, who has been left behind on Treasure Island. Finally, he takes part in an exciting search to find the buried treasure of pirates. The book *Peter Pan* by Sir James Barrie has a similar plot and other similar features.

_____ 4. The book *Where the Red Fern Grows* by Wilson Rawls is about a boy's love for two dogs. The dogs' love for each other is as deep as the love that humans feel for each other.

_____ 5. Autobiographies and biographies both present details of a person's life. However, an autobiography can tell a person's thoughts and feelings because it is written by the person about herself or himself. An example of an autobiography is *Story of My Childhood* by Clara Barton. A biography is written about someone other than the author. An example of a biography is *Abraham Lincoln — the Prairie Years* by Carl Sandburg.

_____ 6. *Sounder* by William H. Armstrong is a beautiful story of an African-American family, their love for each other, and their love for their dog, Sounder.

_____ 7. In *Lisa, Bright and Dark* by John Neufeld, Lisa can no longer control her behavior. On some days she does what most other people do (her bright days), but on other days she does things that others would not do (her dark days). Her parents refuse to believe that she needs help. Fortunately, however, her friends realize that she is mentally ill and are able to help her.

_____ 8. Unlike youths who live in the city and in suburbs, Mr. Boyer's children live in the backwoods of Florida. *Strawberry Girl* by Lois Lenski is a very interesting novel that describes the Boyers' way of life. You will really appreciate all the things that happen to Birdie, their daughter.

_____ 9. In *The Outsiders* by S. E. Hinton, Darry, Sodapop, and Ponyboy are brothers who love each other very much, but feel very differently about school and work.

Investigation B: ANALYZING MEANING

☐ Read each of the following sentences.
   • Explain the meaning of each sentence.
   • Be specific about the similarities and differences. Some sentences have more than one similarity or contrast.
   • For unexplained comparisons, first identify what the simile or metaphor is comparing, then explain how the two things are alike or different.

1. Both basketball and swimming test the skills and stamina of the individual.

   Meaning: _____

   _____

   _____

2. Some people have to put in many hours of practice before they are able to swim like a fish.

   Meaning: _____

   _____

   _____

3. However, while basketball is a team sport, swimming is essentially an individual sport.

   Meaning: _____

   _____

   _____

4. The basketball team must practice hard in order to have all the members of the team move on the court like the parts of a well-oiled machine.

   Meaning: _____

   _____

   _____

INSIGHTS: Reading as Thinking ©
Charlesbridge Publishing • (800) 225-3214

Investigation B: ANALYZING MEANING

Have students read the instructions. Use the first two sentences to demonstrate the strategy.

Sentence 1.
Step 1: There is one signal word – *Both*. There is no metaphor.
Step 2: Basketball is compared to swimming.
Step 3: The two sports are alike because they both test a person's skill and stamina.
Step 4: The comparison is explained so it is not necessary to infer it.

Sentence 2.
Step 1: There are no signal words. There is a simile – *swim like a fish*.
Step 2: People are compared to fish.
Step 3: This simile compares people who are good swimmers to fish that swim easily and naturally.
Step 4: The comparison needs to be inferred. A person does not grow gills and fins. The attributes of a fish that a person can acquire are limited to ease in the water.

Discuss students' answers for items 3 and 4 before they go on to analyze the remaining sentences.

Answer Key

3. Meaning: The two sports are different because basketball is played with a team, while swimming requires only a single person.

4. Meaning: This simile compares a basketball team to a machine. Just as a well-oiled machine works smoothly, with every part doing its job well, the players on the basketball team must learn how to do their respective tasks well so that the team plays smoothly.

Investigation B: ANALYZING MEANING *continued*

Have the students continue to analyze the meaning of each of the comparisons.

Answer Key

5. Meaning: The metaphor – *teams explode* – suggests that the two teams start playing with a sudden burst of speed and noise.

6. Meaning: The rules for swimming are different from the rules for basketball – a swimmer is disqualified for breaking one rule, while a basketball player is allowed to make five fouls.

7. Meaning: Basketball and swimming are similar in that they rely on good coaching. But the two sports are different in that a basketball coach guides the players at all times, whereas a swimming coach provides detailed guidance mostly before a meet.

8. Meaning: The metaphor – *beats the clock* – means that the swimmer races against time. The sentence contrasts this type of goal with the goal of basketball, which is to outscore the opposing team.

5. The basketball referee can be identified by his striped shirt. At the sound of his whistle, the two opposing teams explode into action.

   Meaning: _____
   _____
   _____

6. Unlike the rules for a swim meet, where a single infraction can disqualify the swimmer, a player on a basketball team can commit five fouls before a disqualification.

   Meaning: _____
   _____
   _____

7. Good coaching is very important for both basketball and swimming. In basketball, the coach advises the players before, during, and after practice or a game. In contrast, a swimming coach provides the swimmer with most of the coaching before the meet, with a detailed workout plan to sharpen a particular skill before a swim meet.

   Think: This passage has both similarities and differences.

   Meaning: _____
   _____
   _____
   _____

8. In a sense, the swimmer beats the clock while the basketball players beat the opposite team.

   Meaning: _____
   _____
   _____
   _____

INSIGHTS: Reading as Thinking ©
Charlesbridge Publishing • (800) 225-3214

❏ COMPARISONS IN PROSE

You will find comparisons to interpret whenever you read. In this section, you can use the strategy to comprehend comparisons in a prose selection with several paragraphs.

Investigation **A**: CHARTING COMPARISONS

❏ Read the story. It describes the similarities and differences between two characters.

Baumgarten and Costello

No one could ever mistake Coach Costello for Coach Baumgarten — least of all the members of the Dover High School Basketball team. To them, Baumgarten was the head coach, the drill sergeant, the one the school could count on to mold raw students into disciplined players. A short, stocky man, Baumgarten could be spotted from a great distance by his stark, white hair and his loud voice.

Woe to the player whom Baumgarten found missing from practice. Not a day passed without the players gathering under the beady eyes of the coach for a two-hour practice, shooting baskets, repeating special plays, or just running laps around the court because one of their team had failed to show spirited footwork. At these sessions, Baumgarten would be found flailing his arms, yelling at his players for a broken play or a missed ball, or just barking at them to hustle more. Coach Baumgarten's voice was known to all — it was like a booming cannon.

In contrast, no one was afraid of Coach Costello's voice at Penscott High — at least at first. Tall, lean, and dignified, Coach Costello's polite voice could talk the spots off a leopard. Costello could convince a missing player that his contribution was important for the team, even while telling him that his next absence would mean a loss of playing time. Coach Costello had fewer practices; he let the team devise many of their own plays, and it was rare to find any Penscott player running laps at practice.

Yet, no player could be caught napping under Costello's alert gaze. He watched every one of their moves on the court; his eyes demanded every ounce of effort each player could squeeze out. All of his players were constantly aware of his presence, even without hearing him.

When the players of the two teams met, they sometimes talked among themselves. They knew that the differences between their coaches did not matter. The two coaches were like the flip sides of the same coin. Coach Baumgarten might shout, "If you don't start passing, you'll be on the bench," while Coach Costello might say gently, "Let's play as a team, fellas." But the result was the same. Each team played its best and each coach was admired and respected. Maybe that is why Dover and Penscott High Schools were known to have the best two teams in the high school basketball league.

INSIGHTS: Reading as Thinking ©
Charlesbridge Publishing • (800) 225-3214

❏ COMPARISONS IN PROSE

As students read books and stories, they interpret the similes and metaphors and make comparisons between characters. The following passage and chart will help them apply the strategy to take notes about comparative text.

Investigation A: CHARTING COMPARISONS

Have students read the instructions. Ask them to read the passage once straight through. Then, have them reread it as needed to complete the chart and answer the questions.

Investigation A: CHARTING COMPARISONS *continued*

Have students work independently to complete the chart and the questions following it. After the students have finished, discuss their answers.

Answer Key

Coach Baumgarten
1. short stocky
2. yelled in a loud, booming voice
3. a. had frequent practice
   b. provided a detailed plan
   c. penalized the players for unspirited footwork
4. authoritative and concerned
5. through authority

Coach Costello
1. tall, lean
2. spoke gently, politely
3. a. less frequent practices
   b. allowed players to devise their own plays
4. lenient but firm
5. encouragement or persuasion
6. Their similarities were more important because both inspired admiration and respect, which led the players to play their best game.
7. voice like a booming cannon, or like the flip sides of the same coin
8. mold raw students into disciplined players; was the drill sergeant; talk the spots off a leopard; just barking at them; etc.

❑ List the ways in which Coach Baumgarten and Coach Costello were similar and different. The first item has been completed for you as an example.

	Coach Baumgarten	Coach Costello
1. physical build	short, stocky	tall, lean
2. manner of talking		
3. manner of coaching		
4. attitude toward players		
5. manner of inspiring loyalty		

6. In your own words, were Coach Baumgarten and Coach Costello's similarities or differences more important? Why? _____
_____
_____

7. List one simile from the story. _____
_____
_____

8. List one metaphor from the story. _____
_____
_____

INSIGHTS: Reading as Thinking ©
Charlesbridge Publishing • (800) 225-3214

UNIT 3 – Comprehending Comparisons   **91**

Self-evaluation

elf-evaluation

1. What strategies did you learn?

_____

_____

2. What part of the unit was easiest?

_____

_____

3. What part of the unit was the most difficult? Why?

_____

_____

4. When can you use the unit strategy?

_____

_____

_____

5. Write one question you think should be on a test of this unit.

_____

_____

_____

6. Circle the number that shows how much you learned in this unit.

1	2	3	4	5	6	7	8	9	10
DIDN'T LEARN		LEARNED A LITTLE		LEARNED SOME		LEARNED MOST		LEARNED ALL	

INSIGHTS: Reading as Thinking ©
Charlesbridge Publishing • (800) 225-3214

❑ STUDENT SELF-EVALUATION

Have the students complete the Self-evaluation. Encourage them to use the Self-evaluation to identify areas in which they need further preparation. Discuss any areas of concern with students before conducting the unit Assessment.

Assessment

A student's performance on the Assessment is rated against a predetermined level of mastery. The Assessment is used as a diagnostic tool to provide feedback in the learner's progress.

Blackline Master Pages 129-130 Hand out copies of Blackline Master Pages 129 and 130. Tell students to read the instructions carefully and ask any questions about what is to be done before they start.

Answers for Blackline Master Pages 129-130

Part 1
  1. S
  2. S
  3. D
  4. NC
  5. S/D

Part 2
  1. Accept any three of the following: They were both chimpanzees. They could both use sign language. They could both talk (communicate). They both had trainers. They were both females.
  2. Accept any two of the following: They lived in different places. They had different owners. One of them (Washoe) was studied, the other was not. One lived in a farmhouse; the other lived in a special home.
  3. The two things compared are Lucy's movement and lightning. The simile suggests that Lucy moved very quickly, like lightening.
  4. The metaphor is *light up*. The metaphor suggests that Washoe's eyes appeared as bright as a light bulb whenever she saw her favorite foods.
  5. Accept any two of the following: Lucy was naughty, but Washoe was not. Lucy smothered the mailman with kisses; Washoe did not. Lucy emptied the vacuum cleaner, but Washoe did not.
  6. The metaphor is *Lucy is a clown*. The metaphor suggests that Lucy's behavior was like that of a clown, or she was funny, unpredictable, and made people laugh.

❏ SCORING:

Part 1: Score 1 point for each answer.

Part 2: Score 2 points for each answer.

Mastery Level: 14 out of 17 points.

Assessment

❏ **PART 1**

- Read each sentence.
  - Write **S** if the sentence contains a comparison showing a *similarity*.
  - Write **D** if the sentence contains a comparison showing a *difference*.
  - Write **S/D** if the sentence contains a similarity and a difference.
  - Write **NC** if the sentence contains no comparisons.

_____ 1. Sea turtles, like land turtles, lay about a hundred eggs, which take about two months to hatch.

_____ 2. The rhino beetle and the goliath beetle are two of the largest beetles in the world; both measure about five to six inches long.

_____ 3. The rhino beetle is from South America, whereas the goliath beetle is from Africa.

_____ 4. An eleven-year-old boy, who has a large collection of insects, has a goliath beetle that is six inches long.

_____ 5. Although robins and stickleback fish both build nests, unlike robins, it is only the male stickleback fish that builds the nest.

❏ **PART 2**

- Read each comparison and answer the questions in complete sentences.

1. Lucy and Washoe are female chimpanzees who can use sign language to talk to their trainers.

   In what ways are Lucy and Washoe similar? Give at least three similarities.

   _____

   _____

2. Lucy lived with a couple in a farmhouse in New England, whereas Washoe spent most of her life in a special home that had equipment to study animals.

   In what ways were Lucy and Washoe different? Give at least two differences.

   _____

   _____

INSIGHTS: Reading as Thinking ©
Charlesbridge Publishing • (800) 225-3214

BLACKLINE MASTER

UNIT 3 – Comparisons
Assessment

129

3. Lucy moved as fast as lightning when she heard the doorbell ring.

   What is the simile? What does the comparison mean?

   _____

   _____

   _____

4. Washoe's eyes would light up whenever she saw her favorite foods.

   What is the metaphor? What does the comparison mean?

   _____

   _____

   _____

5. Unlike Washoe, Lucy was quite naughty from time to time: she smothered the mailman with kisses whenever she could, and she emptied the vacuum cleaner on the floor.

   In what ways are Lucy and Washoe different? Give at least two differences.

   _____

   _____

   _____

6. Lucy was quite a clown and proved to be a challenge to live with.

   What is the metaphor? What does the comparison mean?

   _____

   _____

   _____

BLACKLINE MASTER

INSIGHTS: Reading as Thinking ©
Charlesbridge Publishing • (800) 225-3214

Extension

Extension

At this point in the unit, you may read a book of your choice, or do the writing activity described below.

■ WRITING COMPARISONS

1. Choose a familiar person — someone that you see often and know well. Write five sentences to describe the person.

2. Choose an object or place, and write five ways that it is like the person. Use your imagination!

3. Choose another person. Write five ways the two people are alike.

4. Write five ways the two people are different.

5. Go back to your sentences and underline any metaphors. If there are none, make at least one.

❏ WRITING COMPARISONS

The Extension is an independent activity for students who have demonstrated mastery on the Assessment.

The Extension provides an opportunity for students to create their own comparisons and contrasts using people, places, or things with which they are familiar.

Additional Activities

The Additional Activities are designed as remediation for those students who did not achieve mastery on the Assessment.

Draw on the board two pairs of faces: a happy pair and a sad pair. Ask students how each pair is alike and how the pairs differ from one another. Ask students what signal words they used to make their comparisons. Have students find the pages in the unit that list the similarity signal words (page 67) and the contrast signal words (page 74). Have the students write each list on a sheet of paper. Suggest they use the following memory technique, called overlearning, to help them remember the signal words – first, study each list forward, starting with number one. Then study them backward. As homework, have the students find the definitions given in the unit for the following words: *comparison*, *similarity*, and *contrast*, and write the definitions on a sheet of paper. Encourage students to think of other examples of comparisons showing a similarity or a contrast.

❏ RECOGNIZING COMPARISONS

Blackline
Master Pages
135-136

Hand out copies of Blackline Master Pages 135-136. Read aloud the steps for recognizing comparisons.

❏ RECOGNIZING COMPARISONS IN CONTEXT

Help the students follow the steps to identify the signal words in the first two sentences Ask the students to identify the similarities and contrasts in the items 2-5, helping them as necessary.

Answers for Blackline Master Pages 135-136

1a. S	2a. S	3a. C	4a. C	5a. S
1b. C	2b. C	3b. S	4b. S	5b. C

❏ EXPLAINED AND UNEXPLAINED COMPARISONS

Read and discuss the introductory paragraphs with the students. Have the students read the Example and Explanation. Ask students what else the antlers look like. (wings of a bird) Point out that if you had never seen moose antlers, you could not make that inference. When an author writes, he or she makes many requirements on the reader's prior knowledge and experience.

❏ TWO TYPES OF COMPARISONS

Blackline
Master Pages
137-138

Hand out copies of Blackline Master Pages 137-138. Have students read the directions. Discuss the first pair of descriptions. Point out that the first sentence is an explained comparison because it compares the cereal to wet tissues by saying they are both tasteless and soggy, whereas the second sentence lets the reader infer those qualities. Discuss each pair with the students until they see the distinction between explained and unexplained comparisons.

Answers for Blackline Master Page 137

| 1a. E | 2a. U | 3a. U | 4a. E | 5a. U |
| 1b. U | 2b. E | 3b. E | 4b. U | 5b. E |

❏ COMPARISONS WITHOUT SIGNALS OR EXPLANATIONS — METAPHORS

Have students read the paragraph about unexplained comparisons. Discuss the steps for inferring the meaning of metaphors and have students use them to interpret the metaphors in each Example. Discuss the Explanation.

❏ INFERRING THE MEANINGS OF METAPHORS

Blackline
Master Pages
139-140

Hand out copies of Blackline Master Pages 139-140. Read the instructions aloud and show students how to follow the four steps to infer the meaning of the first metaphor. Help them as necessary to infer the meanings of metaphors 2 and 3, then have them analyze the remaining metaphors independently. Elicit how they used the four steps to infer each metaphor.

Answers for Blackline Master Pages 139-140

1. Step 1: bulldozed his way
   Step 2: People do not bulldoze. A bulldozer is a machine.
   Step 3: bulldozer; its size, its strength, and its purpose.
   It was invented to push things around.
   Step 4: Deke was large, strong, and forceful.
2. Step 1: skyrocketing cost
   Step 2: The cost of living is not a skyrocket.
   Step 3: skyrocket, its speed and its upward movement in the sky
   Step 4: The cost of living is moving upward very fast.
3. Step 1: Life is a roller coaster.
   Step 2: Life is not a ride at an amusement park.
   Step 3: roller coaster, that it goes up and down, very fast, or thrills and scares the rider
   Step 4: My life is a fast-paced series of events that are both good and not so good (ups and downs).

4. Metaphor: exploded

   Characteristics: an explosion occurs quickly and with great force

   Meaning: The metaphor suggests that Tyrone went into action very quickly and with great force.

5. Metaphor: circus

   Characteristics: Acts in a circus are constantly changing; it is difficult to watch all the activities at the same time; it is sometimes chaotic and sometimes entertaining.

   Meaning: The metaphor suggests that so many activities are going on in the office that it is difficult to keep track of all of them.

6. Metaphor: jewel

   Characteristics: a jewel sparkles, is precious, and is an important possession

   Meaning: The metaphor suggests that the mother sees her child as being priceless as a jewel.

7. Meaning: The metaphor suggests that Elvira's lies were like a spider web; they trapped people as a spider's web traps insects.

8. Meaning: Alex closes his mind to everything he does not want to hear, just as someone closes or shuts a door to keep something out.

dditional Activities

☐ RECOGNIZING COMPARISONS

Remember that signal words are clue words. They alert you that a comparison is being made in a given sentence or a set of sentences.

To analyze a comparison, use the following strategy:

Step 1:   *Think*: This sentence contains a comparison signal word.

Step 2:   *Ask Yourself*: What is being compared?

Step 3:   *Ask Yourself*: How are they alike or different?

☐ RECOGNIZING COMPARISONS IN CONTEXT

☐ Read each sentence carefully and underline the signal word or words.
- Write **S** on the line provided if the sentence contains a similarity.
- Write **C** if the sentence contains a contrast. The first pair of sentences has been done for you as an example.

___S___   1. a. In "Rikki-Tikki-Tavi," by Rudyard Kipling, the mongoose and the snake are <u>both</u> animals.

___C___   b. The mongoose was a friend to the English family, <u>but</u> the snake was their enemy.

        Think: l. a. The word *both* is a similarity signal word. It shows that the two main characters are similar. They are both animals.

              b. The word *but* shows that the two animals are different in their relationship to the family.

_____   2. a. Tiger Woods and Tara Lipinski have something in common. They are both young athletes who have won major competitions.

_____   b. Tiger Woods is a golfer, while Tara Lipinski is a figure skater.

_____   3. a. In *The Pigman*, a novel by Paul Zindel, John was a cool and tough character in contrast to Lorraine, who was selfish but more mature.

_____   b. However, John and Lorraine felt the same about Mr. Pignati. They both understood that when they destroyed his treasured possession, they destroyed his will to live.

INSIGHTS: Reading as Thinking ©
Charlesbridge Publishing • (800) 225-3214

BLACKLINE MASTER

UNIT 3 – Comparisons
Additional Activities

135

_____ 4. a. Helen Keller became blind in early childhood and never regained her sight, whereas her teacher, Annie Sullivan, was only partially blind.

_____ b. Helen Keller, like Annie Sullivan, had violent temper tantrums when she was a child. (See the biography *Helen Keller's Teacher* by Margaret Davidson.)

_____ 5. a. Both Old Dan and Little Anne fought courageously to save Billy from the cougar in the novel *Where the Red Fern Grows* by Wilson Rawls.

_____ b. Although Little Anne was small compared to Old Dan, she was intelligent and quick and could hold her own in a fight.

EXPLAINED AND UNEXPLAINED COMPARISONS

It would be quite boring if authors explained everything, so they usually leave many statements unexplained. Thus, you have to infer their meaning.

This is also true of comparisons. An explained comparison is one in which the author tells you how two or more things are alike or different. In an unexplained comparison, you have to figure out the meaning for yourself.

Example

Explained Comparison   Unexplained Comparison

Explanation

In the picture on the left, the speaker states exactly how the hat looks like a moose (since a moose has antlers). In the picture on the right, the speaker suggests that the hat looks like a moose, but you have to infer that the decoration looks like the antlers of a moose.

BLACKLINE MASTER   *INSIGHTS: Reading as Thinking* ©
Charlesbridge Publishing • (800) 225-3214

TWO TYPES OF COMPARISONS

Read each pair of sentences.

    If the sentence contains an explained comparison, write **E** on the line.
    If the sentence contains an unexplained comparison, write **U** on the line. The first
        pair has been done for you as an example.

___E___   1. a. My cereal is as tasteless and as soggy as wet tissues.

___U___   b. I would rather eat wet tissues than my cereal.

_____   2. a. In Farrell's Ice Cream Parlor you can order mountains of ice cream
                  covered with different sauces.

_____   b. On special occasions, my brother likes to eat huge mounds of ice cream
                  shaped like mountains.

_____   3. a. Peter wolfed down his food before I could stop him.

_____   b. Peter ate his food as fast as a wolf pack devours its prey.

_____   4. a. I prefer to eat my steak the same way that the French eat steak — very
                  rare.

_____   b. When my uncle orders steak, he says, "Just put a saddle on it," to the
                  waiter or waitress.

_____   5. a. Being in some movie theaters is like being in a bus station.

_____   b. A bus station would be quieter than some movie theaters that are filled
                  with the noise of people running up and down the aisles, coughing and
                  talking, munching popcorn, and endlessly crackling candy bar wrappers.

COMPARISONS WITHOUT SIGNALS OR EXPLANATIONS: METAPHORS

If you have learned the signal words, finding comparisons with signal
words should be easy. Finding comparisons without signals and
interpreting their meaning is more difficult. You can recognize a
comparison without a signal word because its meaning cannot be true
in a literal sense. For example, in sentence 2a in the previous section,
you cannot literally order a *mountain* of ice cream. Nor does a boy
wolf down his food, as in sentence 3a. Thus, comparisons without
signal words may be recognized by their lack of literal truth.

Comparisons without signal words are metaphors and are always unexplained. To infer their meaning, you follow these steps:

Step 1: *Ask yourself*: What is the metaphor?
Step 2: *Ask yourself*: What does the metaphor describe? The subject of the metaphor.
Step 3: *Ask yourself*: What are the main characteristics of the metaphor?
Step 4: *Think*: These characteristics apply to the subject of the metaphor.

 Example

Metaphor: You can order mountains of ice cream covered with different sauces.

Step 1: The metaphor is *mountains of ice cream*.
Step 2: The metaphor describes a mountain. A dish of ice cream is not really a mountain.
Step 3: The main characteristics of a mountain are its size (huge) and its shape (cone-shaped).
Step 4: The metaphor suggests that you can order a mound of ice cream that is huge and cone-shaped.

Use the same steps to infer the meaning in the next Example.

 Example

Metaphor: Peter wolfed down his food before I could stop him.

Step 1: The metaphor is _____ .

Step 2: You know that this is a metaphor because _____ .

Step 3: The main characteristic of _____ is _____ .

Step 4: The metaphor suggests that _____ .

 Explanation

The metaphor is *wolfed down his food*. You know that it is a metaphor because people do not wolf food; they eat it. Wolves run in packs in search of food, which they eat, without chewing, very quickly. The metaphor suggests that Peter ate his food very quickly.

■ INFERRING THE MEANINGS OF METAPHORS

❏ Read each of the following sentences. Each sentence contains a metaphor.

• Explain the meaning of the metaphor.

1. Deke bulldozed his way through the opposing team.

    Step 1: The metaphor is _____ .

    Step 2: I know that this is a metaphor because_____

    _____ .

    Step 3: The main characteristics of a _____ are_____

    _____ .

    Step 4: The metaphor suggests that_____

    _____ .

2. The workers were on strike because of the skyrocketing cost of living.

    Step 1: The metaphor is _____ .

    Step 2: I know that this is a metaphor because_____

    _____ .

    Step 3: The main characteristics of a _____ are_____

    _____ .

    Step 4: The metaphor suggests that_____

    _____ .

3. My life is a roller coaster at the moment.

    Step 1: The metaphor is _____ .

    Step 2: I know that this is a metaphor because_____

    _____ .

    Step 3: The main characteristics of a _____ are_____

    _____ .

    Step 4: The metaphor suggests that_____

    _____ .

INSIGHTS: Reading as Thinking ©
Charlesbridge Publishing • (800) 225-3214

BLACKLINE MASTER

UNIT 3 – Comparisons
Additional Activities

139

4. Tyrone exploded into action.

   Metaphor: _____

   Main characteristics:_____

   _____ .

   Meaning: _____

   _____ .

5. The office that I work in is a circus most of the time.

   Metaphor: _____

   Main characteristics:_____

   _____

   _____ .

   Meaning: _____

   _____ .

6. "My precious jewel! How can I thank you for your thoughtful Mother's Day gift?"

   Hint—Sometimes people use metaphors to address people. That is, a metaphor may be used in place of a name for another person.

   Metaphor: _____ .

   Main characteristics:_____

   _____ .

   Meaning: _____

   _____ .

7. Elvira spun a web of lies to protect her true identity.

   Meaning: _____

   _____ .

8. Alex shuts his mind to anything he does not want to hear.

   Meaning: _____

   _____ .

Re-assessment

The Re-assessment uses the same format as the Assessment and asks the students to demonstrate the same understandings and strategies.

Blackline Master Pages 142-143

Hand out copies of Blackline Master Pages 142-143. Ask students to read the directions carefully. Answer any questions they have about what they are to do.

Answers for Blackline Master Pages 142-143.

Part 1
1. S
2. D
3. NC
4. S/D
5. D

Part 2
1. Accept any two of the following: They both campaigned. They both want to be president. They are both in the seventh grade. They are both girls.
2. Accept any two of the following: Ana is good at sports and her studies. Lynn is average in both. Lynn is a helpful person who is popular with people, Ana is not.
3. The two things compared are Lynn and a swan. The simile means that Lynn's movements are graceful as those of a swan.
4. The metaphor is *stars in her eyes*. The comparison suggests that Ana's eyes sparkled or shone like stars when she learned the good news.
5. Accept any two of the following: Lynn had a very active social life, Ana did not. Lynn worked after school, Ana did not. Lynn was a member of many clubs, Ana was not. Lynn had friends come to her home for dinner; Ana did not.
6. The metaphor is *iron out*. The metaphor suggests that just as an iron smoothes out wrinkles, Ana and Lynn could smooth out or solve the problems that sometimes occurred in their friendship because of different interests.

❑ SCORING:

Part 1: Score 1 point for each answer.

Part 2: Score 2 points for each answer.

Mastery Level: 14 out of 17 points.

Re-assessment

❏ **PART 1**

- Read each sentence.
  - Write **S** if the sentence contains a comparison showing a *similarity*.
  - Write **D** if the sentence contains a comparison showing a *difference*.
  - Write **S/D** if the sentence contains a similarity and a difference.
  - Write **NC** if the sentence contains no comparisons.

_____ 1. Lantern fish, like other luminous (glowing) sea creatures, have special body parts which glow.

_____ 2. Many luminous sea creatures stop glowing to protect themselves when they are in danger, whereas sea centipedes do just the opposite. They display a warning light in times of danger.

_____ 3. Luminous fish live in salt water as well as in fresh water.

_____ 4. The New Zealand glowworm and the railroad worm of Central and South America are similar in that they both glow. Unlike the New Zealand worm, however, the railroad worm has two different colored lights: a red "headlight" and glowing greenish lights along its side.

_____ 5. Some of these sea creatures blink their lights to find mates, but others do not.

❏ **PART 2**

- Read each comparison that follows.
  - Answer the questions in complete sentences. You may use a dictionary to look up any word that you do not know.

1. Ana and Lynn both campaigned to be president of the seventh grade.
   In what ways are Ana and Lynn alike? Give at least three similarities.

   _____

   _____

2. Ana was an excellent student and was good in sports, whereas Lynn had only average grades and was not good in sports. However, Lynn differed from Ana in that Lynn was always very helpful and was very popular with students and teachers.
   In what ways are Ana and Lynn different? Give at least two differences.

   _____

3. Lynn moves as gracefully as a swan.

   What is the simile? What does the comparison mean?

   _____

   _____

   _____

4. Ana had stars in her eyes when she learned she had won.

   What is the metaphor? What does the comparison mean?

   _____

   _____

   _____

5. Unlike Ana, Lynn had a very active social life: she worked after school, she was a member of several clubs, and she often had friends come to her house for dinner.

   In what ways are Ana and Lynn different? Give at least two differences.

   _____

   _____

   _____

6. In spite of their different interests, Ana and Lynn were friends because they were able to iron out their differences.

   What is the metaphor? What does the comparison mean?

   _____

   _____

   _____

UNIT 4

Analyzing Characters

Learning Objectives

The students will analyze characters by

- distinguishing between details that reveal character traits and other details
- identifying traits revealed through action, dialogue, and direct statement
- charting the similarities and differences between two characters
- comparing traits and predicting behavior by charting characters' responses to a particular situation
- inferring a character's motivation by charting reasons for specific actions and dialogue

Lesson 1: Charting character differences
Lesson 2: Making situation-response charts
Lesson 3: Using charts to infer motivation
Lesson 4: Analyzing fiction using more than one type of chart
Lesson 5: Comparing authors' points of view of a nonfiction character
Assessment: Blackline Master Pages 190-193
   Extension: Organizing information in a character differences chart
   Remediation: Additional Activities on Blackline Master Pages 200-210
Re-assessment: Blackline Master Pages 212-215
Special Writing Project on Page 216

Purpose of this Unit

Analyzing characters is a crucial part of understanding fiction. In order to fully process the story, the reader must be able to understand why a character does or says certain things. Inferring character traits also helps the reader to make plot predictions and actively construct meaning. In this unit, emphasis is placed on comparative analysis through the use of charts. Comparing different characters allows the reader to understand them not only as individuals, but also in relation to each other.

Activating Prior Knowledge

Before beginning the unit, ask the students what adjectives they would use to describe a character in a book the class is reading. Make a list of the words and save it so that the students can categorize the adjectives as character traits and other details after Strategy Lesson 1.

Prerequisites and Introduction

Strategy Lesson 1 develops a working definition of character traits so that students have a way to distinguish them from other details.

❏ WHAT ARE CHARACTER TRAITS?

Ask volunteers to read aloud the opening paragraphs and the definitions of character traits, action, dialogue, and direct statement.

Read the Example, which shows the difference between details and character traits. Have students read the Explanation. Then discuss the difference between character traits and details as defined in the Explanation.

PREREQUISITES AND INTRODUCTION

In this unit, you will analyze characters in a story to discover the reasons why the characters act as they do. This will involve identifying or inferring character traits.

▢ WHAT ARE CHARACTER TRAITS?

Character traits indicate how a person feels and acts. Character traits are generally stable or lasting. They are part of a character's nature over a long period of time. A character can be brave, cowardly, cheerful, or gloomy. In contrast, a character's mood may change from day to day or even hour to hour. A character can be in a happy or depressed mood, depending on what has happened.

Authors reveal the traits of their characters through **action**, **dialogue**, and **direct statement**.

> **Action:** Danica picked up the sick cat and cradled it in her arms.
>
> **Dialogue:** "Poor cat," she said.
>
> **Direct statement:** Danica felt sympathy for any animal that was hurt.

A reader can infer that Danica feels sympathy for injured animals from what she says and does. In the direct statement, the author tells the reader how the character feels.

Example

Jared, a tall, angular boy, was by nature very aggressive in playing sports and interacting with people.

Explanation

The author uses the phrase *tall, angular boy* to describe how Jared looks. Therefore, the phrase tells a **detail**. The phrase *was by nature very aggressive in playing sports and interacting with people* describes how Jared usually acts. Therefore, that phrase tells a **character trait**.

Traits show how the character usually feels or acts, whereas details tell how a character looks, where a character lives, what a character does for a living, and so forth. Details about a character usually do not reveal character traits.

Investigation **A**: IDENTIFYING TRAITS AND DETAILS

❏ The following paragraphs contain phrases that show both character traits and details about a character. The phrases have been underlined.
  • Write the trait phrases in Column 1.
  • Write the detail phrases in Column 2.

Delilah <u>has short black hair and shining eyes</u>. She <u>lives in a house in the Arizona desert</u>. Usually <u>she likes the peace and quiet</u> of the desert, but <u>she is often lonely</u>. Delilah <u>can strike up a conversation with anyone</u>. She is just about the <u>friendliest woman I know</u>. Next year she <u>plans to move to San Francisco</u>, where she <u>will work as a student activities coordinator</u> at a high school.

Column 1 — Traits	Column 2 — Details
1. _____	5. _____
2. _____	6. _____
3. _____	7. _____
4. _____	8. _____

Alex, <u>a tall, thin man who is nearly bald</u>, was painting a picture of the desert when Delilah came over to visit. "<u>I really enjoy painting</u>," he told her. "<u>I never get lonely when I'm working</u> in my studio." "You must be <u>the most patient man I know</u>," Delilah replied. Alex answered, "I'm <u>having fun trying to capture the desert's colors</u>."

Column 1 — Traits	Column 2 — Details
9. _____	12. _____
10. _____	13. _____
11. _____	_____

INSIGHTS: Reading as Thinking ©
Charlesbridge Publishing • (800) 225-3214

Investigation A: IDENTIFYING TRAITS AND DETAILS

Have the students read the directions and the first passage. Help them to evaluate the underlined phrases to determine which show character traits and which give other kinds of details. Discuss the entries for each column with the class. Have them read and analyze the second passage independently.

After the students have identified the traits and details, discuss their analyses.

Answer Key
Traits
  1. she likes the peace and quiet
  2. she is often lonely
  3. can strike up a conversation with anyone
  4. friendliest woman I know
Details
  5. has short black hair and shining eyes
  6. lives in a house in the Arizona desert
  7. plans to move to San Francisco
  8. will work as a student activities coordinator

Traits
  9. I really enjoy painting
  10. I never get lonely when I'm working
  11. the most patient man I know
Details
  12. a tall, thin man who is nearly bald
  13. having fun trying to capture the desert's colors

❑ OPPOSITE CHARACTER TRAITS

For each type of character trait, there is an opposite trait (honest – dishonest; patient – impatient). Delilah and Alex have at least one set of opposite character traits, because Delilah often feels lonely and Alex rarely does. Spotting differences like this often helps us understand a pair of characters better in relation to each other and as individuals.

Investigation B: IDENTIFYING OPPOSITE TRAITS

Have the students read the directions. As a class, use the *Think* statements to find the opposite of the first phrase in Column 1. Have the students find the remaining opposites on their own. Discuss their answers and elicit other opposites when appropriate.

Authors often give pairs of characters opposite character traits. Explain that a protagonist in a story can often have a *foil*, or a character that serves as a contrast for another. Illustrate the point with pairs such as Snow White and the Stepmother Queen, or the Wicked Witch of the West and Glinda the Good from L. Frank Baum's *The Wizard of Oz*. Discuss which traits make these characters "opposites."

Investigation **B**: IDENTIFYING OPPOSITE TRAITS

❑ Read each character trait phrase in Column 1.
  • *Think:* What trait does each phrase show?
  • *Think:* What trait is the opposite of that trait?
  • Choose the opposite trait from the choices in Column 3.
  • Write your choice in Column 2.

Column 1 – Phrases	Column 2 – Opposites	Column 3 – Choices
1. liked to make things *Think:* What is the *opposite* of making things?	_____	sly, cheerful, destructive
2. doubted people's motives *Think:* What is the *opposite* of doubting people?	_____	mean, trusting, cheerful
3. loved everybody *Think:* What is the *opposite* of loving?	_____	hateful, modest, pushy
4. usually felt happy	_____	sad, responsible, honest
5. didn't do a bit of work	_____	hardworking, brave, friendly
6. bragged often	_____	messy, cowardly, modest
7. often spilled things	_____	neat, bragging, patient
8. smiled whenever she saw you	_____	independent, gloomy, spoiled
9. responded politely	_____	trusting, happy, rude
10. afraid of the dark	_____	creative, brave, cheerful
11. was rough and pushy	_____	gentle, sad, honest
12. told the truth	_____	angry, dishonest, depressed

INSIGHTS: Reading as Thinking ©
Charlesbridge Publishing • (800) 225-3214

UNIT 4 – Analyzing Characters **97**

Answer Key

1. destructive	7. neat
2. trusting	8. gloomy
3. hateful	9. rude
4. sad	10. brave
5. hardworking	11. gentle
6. modest	12. dishonest

⬛ MAKING CHARACTER DIFFERENCES CHARTS

In this lesson, the stories and passages have two main characters. You can do two important things to analyze the characters:

- Find the character traits (as revealed through action, dialogue, and direct statement).

- Compare the traits of the characters to find out how they are **similar to** or **different from** each other.

Investigation : COMPARING CHARACTERS

❑ Read the following paragraphs. Pay attention to the underlined character trait phrases. They show how the two characters are different from each other.
  • Write the character trait phrases for Dave in Column 1.
  • Write the character trait phrases for Amit in Column 2. Be sure to list the opposite traits directly across from each other.

Dave sits next to me in my life science class, but I don't like him much. He <u>gets angry often</u>, and he <u>complains a lot</u>. He <u>loudly contradicts (disagrees with) anything anyone else says</u>. Dave <u>does not get along with people</u>.

Amit hangs out with me in the computer lab, and we often eat lunch together. He <u>rarely becomes angry</u>, and <u>never complains</u>. He <u>listens carefully to other people's opinions</u>. Amit <u>gets along with people</u> better than anyone I know.

Column 1 — Dave	Column 2 — Amit
_____	_____
_____	_____
_____	_____
_____	_____

You just made a character differences chart. It should look like this:

Dave	Amit
gets angry often	rarely becomes angry
complains a lot	never complains
loudly contradicts anything anyone else says	listens carefully to other people's opinions
does not get along with people	gets along with people

INSIGHTS: Reading as Thinking ©
Charlesbridge Publishing • (800) 225-3214

❑ MAKING CHARACTER DIFFERENCES CHARTS

Have a volunteer read aloud the two goals of this lesson. Discuss why it is important to identify the traits of characters in a story and to compare the traits of different characters.

Investigation A: COMPARING CHARACTERS

Have students complete the character differences chart and check their answers with the completed chart at the bottom of the page.

Investigation A: COMPARING CHARACTERS *continued*

Have students answer the question comparing Dave and Amit. Discuss the layout of the chart and why a chart is a useful graphic device for organizing character traits. (You can list related traits next to each other so they are easy to see and remember.)

Ask the students to predict what would happen if Dave and Amit were assigned to work on a science project together. What would they say? How would they act?

Answer Key
1. Amit
2. Dave
3. Amit
4. Dave

Investigation B: ORDERING TRAITS IN PAIRS

To show students how confusing it is to have a chart with unpaired traits, have them make an accordion fold down the middle of page 99 to bring the column labeled Traits next to Column 1.
1. Fold the right edge of the page to the left edge.
2. Fold the top edge back toward the right so that all of Column 3 shows next to Column 1.

Have students read the directions and complete the chart. Discuss how much more useful paired traits in the chart are.

❑ Answer the following questions, using information in your character differences chart.

1. Who is more friendly, Dave or Amit?_____
   Think: A friendly person gets along with people. Which person gets along with people?
2. Which person is often angry? _____
3. Which person has a more cheerful attitude?_____
4. Which person is not happy most of the time? _____

The phrases in your character differences chart show character traits. Notice the following two things about your chart:

- For each trait for Dave, there is an opposite trait for Amit.
- These opposite traits are listed directly across from each other in the character differences chart.

Investigation B: ORDERING TRAITS IN PAIRS

In the character comparison chart below, the trait phrases are listed in the wrong order. The opposing traits are not opposite each other. Your task is to put them in order.

❑ Read each trait in Column 1.
  • Find its opposite in the Traits column.
  • Write the opposing traits in Column 2.

Column 1 — Skylar	Column 2 — Elise	Traits
usually has fun	_____	punctual (on time)
rarely feels lonely	_____	dislikes crowds
likes crowds	_____	usually feels lonely
frequently late	_____	often does not enjoy things

Column 1 — Jerry	Column 2 — Andrew	
saves his money	_____	is easily excited
clumsy	_____	usually feels good
is bored most of the time	_____	agile
usually feels bad	_____	spends his money

INSIGHTS: Reading as Thinking ©
Charlesbridge Publishing • (800) 225-3214   **UNIT 4 – Analyzing Characters** | **99**

Answer Key

Elise	Andrew
often does not enjoy things	spends his money
usually feels lonely	agile
dislikes crowds	is easily excited
punctual (on time)	usually feels good

Investigation C: CHARTING CHARACTER DIFFERENCES

❏ Read each description and underline the phrases describing character traits.
  • Write opposite character traits directly across from each other in the chart.
  • Answer the questions that follow each chart.

Tamika and Josh

Tamika likes to go places by herself. She learned to ride the bus on her own when she was in the sixth grade. Nobody ever has to tell her to clean up her room or do her homework. Tamika keeps her room neat and always has her homework done on time. Every morning she wakes up early and helps her mother make breakfast. She never complains about having to do work. Usually, she is in a good mood and looks on the bright side of things.

Josh does not go anywhere on his own. He will not even catch the bus into town without someone to keep him company. He will not clean his room unless someone insists that he do it, so it is no surprise that his room is usually a mess. He hardly ever does his homework on time and he sleeps late every morning. His parents practically have to drag him out of bed in time for school. He complains a lot. Sometimes he is very grumpy. He rarely smiles, and he tends to see the dark side of everything.

Tamika	Josh
1. _____	_____
2. _____	_____
3. _____	_____
4. _____	_____
5. _____	_____
6. _____	_____

7. Who is more independent, Tamika or Josh? _____

8. Who has a gloomy outlook on life? _____

9. Who is a better student? _____

10. Who seems happier? _____

100   UNIT 4 – Analyzing Characters   INSIGHTS: *Reading as Thinking* ©
                                                    Charlesbridge Publishing • (800) 225-3214

 ## Writing Connection

Tamika and Josh would be more realistic characters if they had more developed personalities and character traits. Suggest that students expand Tamika and Josh into fully developed characters. Ask them to facilitate their writing by first making a character chart with additional traits.

Investigation C: CHARTING CHARACTER DIFFERENCES

Have the students read the directions. Answer any questions they may have. Identify and list the first pair of opposite traits as a class activity. After students have completed the chart and answered the questions that follow it, discuss their answers. Elicit the idea that it is easier to answer reading comprehension questions when you have focused notes.

Answer Key

Accept alternate wordings and ideas that are supported by the passage.

Tamika
  1. likes to go places by herself
  2. keeps her room neat
  3. always has her homework done on time
  4. never complains
  5. usually, she is in a good mood
  6. looks on the bright side of things

Josh
  1. does not go anywhere on his own
  2. his room is usually a mess
  3. hardly ever does his homework on time
  4. complains a lot
  5. Sometimes he is very grumpy.
  6. tends to see the dark side of everything
  7. Tamika
  8. Josh
  9. Tamika
  10. Tamika

Investigation C: CHARTING CHARACTER DIFFERENCES
continued

Have the students use the same reading comprehension strategy – read, underline, and make a chart – for the passage about Mrs. Flores and Mrs. Gomez.

Point out that although Mrs. Flores and Mrs. Gomez have opposite character traits, the same is not necessarily true for all pairs of characters. This passage includes character traits that are opposites because they are easier to chart. A chart can also be constructed to compare the similarities and differences between characters.

Answer Key

Mrs. Flores
1. does not mind waiting
2. easy to get along with
3. hardly ever angry
4. loves to have people come to her house
5. greets people cheerfully
6. loves to laugh
7. loves to have a good time

Mrs. Gomez
1. does not like to wait
2. hard to get along with
3. always seems angry
4. will not invite anyone to her house
5. greets people unpleasantly
6. never seen Mrs. Gomez smile or laugh
7. doesn't enjoy anything
8. Mrs. Flores is more patient.
9. Mrs. Gomez is unfriendly.
10. Mrs. Flores is willing to help others.

 Mrs. Flores and Mrs. Gomez

Mrs. Flores does not mind waiting for things. Even being stuck in traffic jams does not bother her. She just turns up the radio and sings along with the music. She is easy to get along with and is hardly ever angry. She loves to have people come to her house. When I visit her for help with my Spanish, she greets me with a bright smile. Mrs. Flores loves to laugh and have a good time.

Our neighbor Mrs. Gomez does not like to wait for anything. She will not stand in line to see a movie, even if it is a short line. She is hard to get along with and always seems angry. She does not invite anyone to her house. She wouldn't even let me interview her for my school project. Whenever I say hello to her in the hall, she asks, "Who are you?" in a mean, crackly voice. I have never seen Mrs. Gomez smile or laugh or enjoy anything.

	Mrs. Flores	Mrs. Gomez
1.	_____	_____
2.	_____	_____
3.	_____	_____
4.	_____	_____
5.	_____	_____
6.	_____	_____
7.	_____	_____

8. Which woman is more patient? _____
9. Which woman is unfriendly? _____
10. Which woman is willing to help others? _____

INSIGHTS: Reading as Thinking ©
Charlesbridge Publishing • (800) 225-3214

 ### Literature Connection

Have the students analyze two main characters in a book of fiction that they are reading or have read recently. Have each student make a character differences chart for the two characters, listing at least five differences.

Character Responses

CHARACTER RESPONSES

In Strategy Lesson 1, you made character trait charts. In this lesson, you will see how an author can reveal a character's traits through the character's responses.

☐ SITUATIONS AND RESPONSES

One way that an author reveals a character's traits is by showing how the character responds to situations, especially situations that put the character under a lot of pressure. For example, imagine this situation:

Your teacher asks you a question, and you do not know the answer.

Do you—

1. Become nervous and embarrassed, and not say anything? or

2. Calmly admit that you do not know the answer? or

3. Say what you know about the topic, trying to include information that answers at least part of the question? or

4. Ask a question to focus attention on another topic or person? or

5. Claim that you know the answer but it's stuck on the tip of your tongue?

Write what character trait each response would show.

Trait 1: _____

Trait 2: _____

Trait 3: _____

Trait 4: _____

Trait 5: _____

When you read about a character in a particular situation, it is often useful to picture yourself in the same situation. (If the character is very different from you, think of someone you know or have seen in a similar situation.) Your own knowledge of how a person in that situation would feel and act is very useful when you are reading.

In this strategy lesson, students chart characters' responses to particular situations. This will help them to infer and compare the characters' traits and to predict behavior.

❏ SITUATIONS AND RESPONSES

Ask students to read the introductory paragraph. Discuss the hypothetical situation and the possible traits each response reveals. Point out that it takes many responses to reveal a character trait. When a reader makes inferences during reading, the reader may have to revise those inferences if new information reveals different character traits.

INSIGHTS: Reading as Thinking ©
Charlesbridge Publishing • (800) 225-3214

Investigation A: CHARTING SITUATIONS AND RESPONSES

Students read four stories and compare the main characters in each one. Have the students read "Eavie and Tess." Tell them they may underline the traits of the animals if they wish.

Before the students complete the chart and questions about Eavie and Tess, ask the following questions: **What does Eavie do when company knocks on the door?** (She runs to greet the company, wags her tail, and jumps.) **Why does she do this? What traits does her action show?** (She is sociable and friendly.) **How do you know this? The author doesn't say so.** (Accept answers expressing prior knowledge of dog behavior.) Ask similar questions regarding Tess's response.

Explain that the narrator is *anthropomorphizing* the animals, interpreting their actions in terms of human characteristics. Explain that students may infer certain character traits from the animals' actions, but that they must be careful in assuming the truth of those inferences, since we do not know what or how animals think.

Investigation : **CHARTING SITUATIONS AND RESPONSES**

Each of the following stories has two main characters. Each story is followed by a situation-response chart and questions to answer from the chart. You will compare how the two characters respond to the situations in each story and what traits these responses reveal. This is another way to analyze characters. To help you do this, the Situations column has been completed throughout.

❑ Read each story and complete each situation-response chart.
  • Write each character's responses and what traits they reveal.

 Eavie and Tess

Personally, I need pets like a submarine needs a screen door, but my friend Manuela has two of the most delightful pets I have ever met. Although they are different animals, they both have round faces and big eyes — just like Manuela. It is strange how pets often resemble their owners. Anyway, Eavie is a cheerful, undersized Shih tzu,* and Tess is a rather gloomy Persian cat.**

Eavie is a sociable, friendly dog. She has long, silky hair and a cute pug nose, and weighs about seven pounds. A knock on the door always sends Eavie yapping happily to greet the company. Then she jumps for joy and wags her tail as she is being petted. Tess, meanwhile, takes the knock on the door as a cue to head for the hills to enjoy her privacy.

Tess is a very neat cat and spends hours cleaning her honey-colored coat. You can imagine Tess's displeasure when Manuela calls her pets for dinner and Eavie dives face-first into her food dish. Not wanting to participate in a food shower, Tess always waits at a dignified distance until Eavie takes her food-matted face to another part of the house.

Eavie has a favorite toy. One day after eating, Eavie bounced up to Tess bearing the toy, more or less inviting Tess to play. Tess took one look at that hairy little face, hissed, and swiped at Eavie with her paw. As Tess stalked away, you could just imagine her wondering why that fur-covered kidney bean would expect a full-grown cat to play. What nerve!

* Shih tzu — a 5 to 7 lb. dog with long, silky hair and gentle, intelligent behavior
** Persian cat — a species of cat with a flat face and long hair

INSIGHTS: Reading as Thinking ©
Charlesbridge Publishing • (800) 225-3214   UNIT 4 – Analyzing Characters   **103**

Situations	Eavie's Responses	Tess's Responses
1. Company knocks on the door	_____ _____ _____ Traits: _____	_____ _____ _____ Traits: _____
2. Mealtime	_____ _____ _____ Traits: _____	_____ _____ _____ Traits: _____
3. Playtime	_____ _____ _____ _____ Traits: _____	_____ _____ _____ _____ Traits: _____

❑ Use your chart to answer these questions.

4. What three things did Eavie do that show she is sociable?

_____

_____

_____

5. What two things did Tess do that show she likes to be alone?

_____

_____

_____

INSIGHTS: Reading as Thinking ©
Charlesbridge Publishing • (800) 225-3214

Investigation A: CHARTING SITUATIONS AND RESPONSES
continued

Answer Key

Accept all reasonable inferred traits.

Eavie's Responses
1. runs to greet company, wags tail, jumps for joy
   Traits: sociable, friendly, likes people
2. dives face-first into food
   Traits: messy, sloppy, untidy, eager, good appetite
3. bounced up to Tess with a toy
   Traits: eager, playful

Tess's Responses
1. heads for the hills to enjoy privacy
   Traits: anti-social, unfriendly, private
2. waits at a dignified distance
   Traits: neat, tidy, picky eater, aloof
3. hissed, swiped at Eavie, stalked away
   Traits: not playful, unfriendly
4. Answers may include: happily greeted company, jumped for joy, wagged tail, invited Tess to play
5. Answers may include: headed for the hills when company arrived, waited at distance while Eavie ate, wouldn't play

Curriculum Connection

Science: Have the students make a differences chart comparing mammals and birds or two species, microbes, or even plants with which they are familiar. The class might discuss how these differences might result in character traits if an author were using these animals as two main characters in a story.

Investigation A: CHARTING SITUATIONS AND RESPONSES
continued

Have students read "Best Friends," and discuss it in small groups in order to complete the chart on the following page.

When they have completed the chart, ask the following types of questions.

What is the situation at the beginning? (After practicing for weeks, Jennifer and Cara wait nervously to audition.)

How does Jennifer behave while waiting to audition? (She says she can't hit the high notes and doesn't think she can get the part. She doesn't know how she would have prepared for the audition without Cara's help.)

What does this reveal about Jennifer? (She is nervous, unsure, and not confident. She is also grateful to Cara for her help and reassurance.)

Discuss the traits students listed in their charts and how they used a character's responses to infer traits.

 Best Friends

The sun blazed down on the buildings of McKinley High School. Most students had already gone home, and the hallways were empty. In the auditorium, however, students clustered in the aisles. This afternoon, the drama club was holding tryouts for the school production of *Qualifying Catherine of Canobie Creek*.

Two students waited nervously backstage. One girl was very well dressed; the other was not. Jennifer had jet black hair and smooth, clear skin; she wore beads in her hair and sat up straight. Cara was wearing clothes that didn't go together well and looked messy. She resembled a poorly packed sack of groceries, but she had bright eyes and a warm smile. Both girls wanted the part of Catherine, the local Olympic hero who learned to swim in Canobie Creek, or the part of Zola, her headstrong and witty coach.

Jennifer shook her head. "I just can't hit those high notes."

Cara tried to cheer her up. "You can, Jen. Just open your mouth and let them come out."

"Then why do I always feel so bad when I sing 'It's Only a Crawdad'?"

"Remember what I told you about taking deep breaths," Cara told her.

"I don't think I can," Jen said.

"Jen, just act confidently, like we practiced. You're the one person in the junior class who has a good chance to play Catherine."

"Me? Really? Well, I hope you're right. I don't know what I'd do without you, Cara. I'm so disorganized. I don't know how I would have prepared for this audition without you."

"You don't mean you *liked* working on songs every day, while I plunked them out on the piano and pointed out everything you did wrong?" Cara asked wryly.

Jennifer grinned. "You know I loved it — thanks, Cara. Here goes, it's my turn. Wish me luck."

Jennifer strode out on stage to the opening notes of "Water'll We Do?" She smiled and held her head proudly, just as they had practiced.

When she finished singing, Mr. Mariki, the club advisor, called her over and said something to her. Jen pointed toward Cara and smiled.

Cara sank down into her chair as if she were trying to hide. Her face turned red. It was Cara's turn to audition. Cara thought, "I can't, not now. I'd look silly singing right after Jen." She reminded herself how much she had practiced and forced herself to get up. As Cara walked slowly onto the stage, she froze. She imagined all those seats filled and all those eyes staring at her.

"Come on, Cara," Jen said from the wings. "Show them you can sing."

Cara's mouth was dry as she answered. "Never mind. I've decided not to try out."

(Continued on following page)

INSIGHTS: *Reading as Thinking* ©
Charlesbridge Publishing • (800) 225-3214

(Continued from previous page)

Jen and Mr. Mariki whispered some more. "Come over here, Cara," Jen called. "Mr. Mariki wants to talk to you. Trust me. He has a great plan."

The opening night of *Qualifying Catherine of Canobie Creek* was a great success. Jen sang the part of Catherine to loud applause, and the audience laughed and clapped when they were supposed to. At the end of the play, lighting, costume, and stage crews, and the actors came out on stage and bowed. The loudest round of applause was for the proud pianist and singing coach, Cara.

Situations	Jen's Responses	Cara's Responses
1. Jen and Cara wait to audition	_____ _____ _____ Traits: _____	_____ _____ _____ Traits: _____
2. Jen tries out	_____ _____ _____ Traits: _____	_____ _____ _____ Traits: _____
3. Cara's turn comes	_____ _____ _____ Traits: _____	_____ _____ _____ Traits: _____
4. Mr. Mariki has a plan	_____ _____ _____ Traits: _____	_____ _____ _____ Traits: _____

INSIGHTS: Reading as Thinking ©
Charlesbridge Publishing • (800) 225-3214

After discussing their charts, have students take out paper and write a paragraph in answer to each of the following questions.

1. What does Jennifer do for Cara that shows friendship?
2. What does Cara do for Jennifer that shows friendship?

Answer Key

1. Answers may include: thanks Cara for her help; encourages Cara to take her turn and show everyone how she can sing; convinces Mr. Mariki that Cara has the skills to be a musical coach
2. Answers may include: practices every day with Jennifer; reassures Jen that she can make it; reminds her to act confidently

Jen's Responses
1. worries about high notes,
   Trait: lacks confidence, nervous
2. smiles and holds head proudly
   Trait: confident
3. encourages Cara
   Trait: supportive
4. tells Mr. Mariki about Cara's talents
   Trait: caring

Cara's Responses
1. encourages Jen to do her best
   Trait: supportive
2. Cara watches and feels less talented than Jen
   Trait: lacks self-confidence, shy
3. sinks down, freezes on stage, decides not to try out
   Trait: frightened, not confident
4. uses musical talents to coach performers
   Trait: agreeable, flexible, resourceful

Investigation A: CHARTING SITUATIONS AND RESPONSES
continued

Have students read "The Choice." The space station commander in the story must choose between two likely successors. After students have completed the charts, you may want to discuss the character traits of such popular fictional leaders as the various captains of *Star Trek* or of real military leaders. Discuss desirable character traits in military and civilian leaders.

Literature Connection

Have students review the character differences chart they made in the Literature Connection on page 152. Have them also make an action-reason chart listing at least six important things that the characters did and the reasons why they did them.

Ask volunteers to explain and discuss their charts with the class.

The Choice

The Commander's brow furrowed as he read the message that had just come over the telecommunicator. It was not unexpected, but he had hoped for a little more time to decide on the right person for a very tough job.

Selecting the next person to command the station had become a very difficult task. He had two excellent choices — Lieutenant Colonel Arion Brink and Lieutenant Colonel Whitney Jackson. Both wanted the position. Both were young, ambitious, and intelligent. Both had earned outstanding grades at the Space Training Academy, and both had graduated with high honors. They were alike in so many ways, but they were different, too. Just how, the Commander was not yet sure, but it was imperative (very important) that the right person be given the job.

Of all the space stations, Rosaic (ro-sā′ik) was the most crucial one. This station alone stood between Earth and Cycand. In order to attack Earth, the Cycanders would first have to eliminate Rosaic. So far, the Cycanders had been afraid to try.

Cycand was a warring planet. Its goal was to conquer every planet in the galaxy, and Earth was its main target. With its natural resources and billions of inhabitants, Earth would be a valuable prize for the Cycanders.

A cadet interrupted his thoughts. "Commander, sir, the space shuttle is ready to depart." Ah, yes, the shuttle back to Earth; he had almost forgotten. The Commander was supposed to be on that shuttle, but he could not leave, not just yet, not until he had made his decision. "Thank you, Cadet. Tell them they have my permission to take off, and wish them all a safe and pleasant journey for me." He walked to the side window that allowed a view of the launching pad. He watched thoughtfully as the space shuttle blasted off into the void. He stood there long after the craft had been swallowed up in a mass of blue and silver stars. "What a magnificent sight," he thought as he studied the heavens around him.

Lieutenant Colonel Brink invaded (entered abruptly) his peaceful meditation. "Commander Lee," he exploded, his voice on the verge of pure panic, "we're being attacked by the Cycanders!"

The Commander could not believe his ears. They certainly hadn't wasted any time. They probably thought he had left on the shuttle, and that Rosaic was weak without an experienced defender. Wouldn't they be surprised!

(Continued on following page)

INSIGHTS: Reading as Thinking ©
Charlesbridge Publishing • (800) 225-3214

(Continued from previous page)

"What shall we do?" Brink's voice quavered. The Commander stared at Brink intently. Lee had never seen him like this; he was wild-eyed and almost shaking.

"What direction are they attacking from, Lieutenant?"

"I don't know, sir," Brink gulped as he nervously twisted his hands.

"How many battleships show up on the scanner?"

"I don't know, sir. I didn't take time to look. I just came here to inform you, sir," said Brink in an uneven voice.

"Has the general alarm been sounded?" asked the Commander.

"I forgot to do that," cried Brink in despair. "Oh, Commander, what should we do? We're all going to be annihilated (completely destroyed)!"

"Don't just stand there; assemble the crew!" the commander shouted.

"The crew has been assembled, sir, and they are standing ready at their battle stations." The Commander whirled around to find Lieutenant Colonel Jackson standing calmly behind him. Her steady hands held some papers; both her feet were planted firmly and securely, but she was ready to spring into action at the first order. Her eyes were as clear as the job ahead. "From what direction are they attacking?" asked Lee.

"They are approaching from the starboard (right) side," replied Jackson.

"How many battleships?"

"I counted ninety on the scanner, sir."

"I take it for granted that you sounded the alarm, Lieutenant?"

"Yes, sir," replied the Lieutenant in a strong voice.

"Good; I want a full damage report."

"It's right here, sir," responded Jackson. "The Cycanders almost caught us by surprise, sir. But it occurred to me as I watched the space shuttle take off that they might think you were aboard and would attack, thinking our defenses were down. I was calling the weapons room to alert them when the first blast hit us. I ordered our protective shields up and deployed (sent out) 200 of our battleships. I ordered them to attack at warp 2. At that speed, they should intercept the Cycanders and send them home to count meteors. I hope you approve of my actions, sir. There was no time to confer (talk) with you first."

Commander Lee looked decisively at Lieutenant Colonel Jackson. "Not only do I approve, but I commend you for your quick thinking and initiative. Your take-charge attitude saved our station, but, more importantly, Earth was saved. Congratulations, Commander Jackson of Rosaic Space Station," beamed former Commander Lee.

INSIGHTS: Reading as Thinking ©
Charlesbridge Publishing • (800) 225-3214

Investigation A: CHARTING SITUATIONS AND RESPONSES
continued

This is a continuation of the story, "The Choice." After students have completed the situation-response chart and answered the questions on the next page, you may want to do the following activity with them.

Discuss the qualities Commander Lee was looking for in a successor (ability to think quickly, initiative, bravery, decisiveness, intelligence). Explain that teachers, coaches, and employers likewise look not only for specific skills, but also for certain personality traits in future employees. Bring in examples of classified ads that illustrate this.

Type up or print several "job listings" on index cards. These listings can be ones you find in the newspaper or ones you make up. If you are writing the listings, include fun, fictional, or strange jobs like "dinosaur cloner," "lion tamer," and "special effects designer." Include the company name, the contact name, the position offered, the duties involved, and the specific skills and traits desired.

Post these job listings on the bulletin board. Have students choose a listing that interests them and write a job application explaining why the student wants the job and how he or she is qualified for it in terms of skills and traits. Explain that if the students were actually applying for the job, they would include a résumé with the letter.

Investigation A: CHARTING SITUATIONS AND RESPONSES
continued

Have students complete the chart and answer the question.

Answer Key
Accept all reasonable variations.
Brink's Responses
1. attended Space Training Academy, had good grades, graduated with high honors
   Traits: ambitious, brave, intelligent
2. didn't take time to look at telescreen
   Traits: easily scared, panicked
3. forgot to sound alarm
   Traits: nervous, could not follow routine in a crisis
4. too panicked to think of what to do
   Traits: unable to take charge, insecure

Jackson's Responses
1. attended Space Training Academy, had good grades, graduated with high honors
   Traits: ambitious, brave, intelligent
2. counted battleships on telescreen
   Traits: responsible, calm, cool, collected
3. sounded the alarm
   Traits: resourceful, calm
4. took charge, organized defenses
   Traits: commanding, confident, responsible
5. Answers may include: Jackson was calm and responsible, followed correct procedures, and showed leadership qualities; Brink was panic-stricken, nervous, and unable to act.

Situations	Brink's Responses	Jackson's Responses
1. Background	_____ _____ _____ Traits: _____	_____ _____ _____ Traits: _____
2. Enemy battleships approach	_____ _____ Traits: _____	_____ _____ Traits: _____
3. Enemy attacks	_____ _____ _____ Traits: _____	_____ _____ _____ Traits: _____
4. Need to organize defense	_____ _____ _____ Traits: _____ _____	_____ _____ _____ Traits: _____ _____

❑ Use your chart to answer this question.

5. What are three things about Jackson's actions that are different from Brink's actions?

_____

_____

_____

INSIGHTS: Reading as Thinking ©
Charlesbridge Publishing • (800) 225-3214

Camping

Munroe had waited a lifetime for this trip, even though he was just thirteen years old. Daniel, his older brother, had finally agreed to take him on a canoe trip. This was a wonderful opportunity for someone who had lived in the city all his life, and he knew he would do well.

For years, Munroe had read everything he could about animals, plants, rivers, and forests. Then he pored over books about backpacking and survival in the wilderness. This trip would be the first real test of his skills — he could almost feel the cool mountain air. Abruptly, the call of the wild was rudely interrupted.

"Munroe!" It was Daniel, shouting angrily. "Hurry up! The car's packed except for your stuff! Get moving!"

That was all Munroe needed. He swiftly finished packing his frame backpack, efficiently distributing weight and adjusting the straps. Within minutes, he was perched on the front seat of Daniel's car and headed for the woods.

The drive was uneventful except for Daniel's long-winded account of his first canoe trip. Daniel told him the story because he was determined to give Munroe the full benefit of his experience. His report detailed everything from wild animal sounds to the patterns of wind on the water.

Munroe endured his brother's story patiently.

"After all," he thought, "he's my brother, he means well, and he's responsible for my going on this trip."

Mercifully, Daniel's tale ended when they arrived at the ranger station. With a few "hurry-ups" from you-know-who, the canoe was taken off the car, loaded, and launched. It took quite a while for them to get the knack of paddling together. Daniel had a fit every time Munroe accidentally splashed him.

They paddled all day. Every so often they caught sight of a water bird, either flying overhead or swimming, and they saw small animals that came down to the water's edge to drink. Once they saw a huge bull moose, which really made Munroe's day.

That night they camped on a tiny island and slept out under the stars. They had to; Daniel had forgotten the tent. It was exciting though, and neither regretted it. Morning arrived with a drizzling rain, so they ate a soggy breakfast and headed out once again.

Around noon, the rain ended and so did the lake. They had to portage* about a half mile to the next lake. This meant two trips: one with their gear and one with the canoe. Daniel decided that they should carry their gear first, and he led the way down the muddy trail.

Suddenly, ten minutes down the trail, Daniel slipped. By the time Munroe reached him, he was on his back, his face twisted in pain.

*portage — to carry things (canoes, boats, goods) overland from one body of water to another

INSIGHTS: Reading as Thinking ©
Charlesbridge Publishing • (800) 225-3214

Investigation A: CHARTING SITUATIONS AND RESPONSES
continued

In the fourth story, "Camping," two brothers reveal their character traits when caught in a perilous situation. Have students read the story and complete the chart and questions on the following pages.

You may wish to use this story as a starting point for a discussion of how responses based on knowledge or experience can reveal traits. Munroe had knowledge from reading but Daniel had knowledge from experience. Usually, a character's actions, dialogue, and motivation depend to a large extent on the character's experience. The surprise in this story is that with no experience, but the self-confidence that comes from knowledge, Munroe saves the day.

Investigation A: CHARTING SITUATIONS AND RESPONSES
continued

This is the conclusion of the story "Camping." Have students complete the chart and answer the questions on the next page.

Answer Key

Accept all reasonable variations.

Munroe's Responses
1. prepared by reading books
   Traits: eager, enthusiastic, smart
2. listened to Daniel
   Traits: patient, grateful, polite
3. performed first aid, made Daniel comfortable
   Traits: resourceful, confident, cool

Daniel's Responses
1. yelled at Munroe
   Traits: impatient
2. talked about earlier trip
   Traits: boastful, talkative
3. didn't complain
   Traits: respectful, thankful, stoic

"It's my ankle. I think it's broken." Sure enough, Daniel's ankle was turned at an unnatural angle and had already begun to swell.

"Don't move, Daniel. I know what to do." Munroe disappeared into the woods and returned with some soft leaves and small branches.

"I'm back, Daniel. Let me make you more comfortable." Then Munroe proceeded to put cold cloths on the swollen ankle and to make a splint for Daniel's leg. Daniel made no sound.

Then Munroe built a shelter, placed pine boughs on the ground, and put a sleeping bag over them. He helped Daniel onto the sleeping bag, propped up his foot, and covered him with the other sleeping bag. After making a fire and placing food and water near his brother, Munroe said he was going for help. As Munroe left, Daniel managed a weak smile and waved. "I'll be back in about two hours," Munroe called over his shoulder as he waved back.

True to his word, Munroe came back. He had made the trip in record time and returned with two forest rangers. In no time at all, Daniel was on a stretcher in the rangers' plane, flying to a hospital. Munroe had really come through.

"Munroe, thanks a lot. Why didn't you tell me you could do all those things?" Daniel asked with new respect.

Munroe grinned. "You never asked."

Situations	Munroe's Responses	Daniel's Responses
1. Munroe and Daniel prepare for the canoe trip	_____ _____ Traits: _____	_____ _____ Traits: _____
2. The boys drive to the woods.	_____ _____ Traits: _____	_____ _____ Traits: _____
3. Daniel breaks his ankle.	_____ _____ Traits: _____	_____ _____ Traits: _____

INSIGHTS: Reading as Thinking ©
Charlesbridge Publishing • (800) 225-3214

UNIT 4 – Analyzing Characters   **111**

☐ Use your chart to answer these questions.

4. Which of the characters was not thoughtful and did not think things out carefully?

_____

5. What are two things that he said or did that show this?

_____

_____

_____

6. Which of the characters was more thoughtful and thought things out very carefully?

_____

7. What are two things that he said or did that show this?

_____

_____

_____

INSIGHTS: *Reading as Thinking* ©
Charlesbridge Publishing • (800) 225-3214

Investigation A: CHARTING SITUATIONS AND RESPONSES
continued

Students use their Situation-Response charts to answer questions about the characters' traits as revealed by action and dialogue.

Answer Key
4. Daniel
5. Daniel was impatient with Munroe's packing; he forgot to pack the tent; and he had a fit when Munroe splashed him.
6. Munroe
7. He was patient when Daniel spoke. He was calm and resourceful after the accident.

After you have discussed the answers with the students, you may want to do the following improvisation activity called "Who's on the Bus?" These character trait improvisations will give the students an opportunity to infer traits from actions.

Arrange a row of chairs for the passengers and one facing forward for the driver. On strips of paper, write different character traits such as *shy*, *bold*, *honest*, and *unfriendly*, then place the folded slips in a box. Have ten students pick a trait from the box. Ask for a volunteer to be the driver.

When you give the signal, each student gets on the bus as a character with the chosen trait. The rest of the class takes notes on their observations to try to infer the traits.

Characters' Reasons

In this lesson, students make Action/Reason charts to infer a character's motivation.

❏ ACTIONS AND REASONS

Ask volunteers to read aloud the opening paragraphs. Students have, of course, been deducing characters' motivation since they began listening to and reading stories on their own. The goal of this lesson is to help sensitize readers to the author's use of action and dialogue as clues to a character's motivation.

Investigation A: INFERRING REASONS

Have students read the instructions and read the first story part. Discuss the first question and complete the first chart with the students.

Answer Key
Accept all reasonable answers.
1. She did not want to play; Tess did not like Eavie; Tess liked to spend her time alone.
2. She did not want to play.

 Strategy Lesson

CHARACTERS' REASONS

In Strategy Lesson 2, you learned how an author can use a character's response to a situation to show character traits. In this lesson, you will learn how characters' behavior, including their speech, tells us about their reasons or motives.

■ ACTIONS AND REASONS

People are curious; we all are. That is why we attend school — to learn why things happen and why people do what they do. That is also why we read stories. A good story presents characters who do things, and shows us why they do them. In this lesson, you will learn to deduce (figure out) why different characters do what they do and say what they say.

Investigation **A: INFERRING REASONS**

❏ Read the parts of the stories from Strategy Lesson 2.
  • Answer each question by asking yourself why and finding clues in the story part.
  • Use the information in your answer to complete each reason chart.

From "Eavie and Tess"

Tess took one look at that hairy little face, hissed, and swiped at Eavie with her paw. As Tess stalked away, you could just imagine her wondering why that fur-covered kidney bean would expect a full-grown cat to play. What nerve!

1. Why did Tess take a swipe at Eavie? _____

_____

2.

Character	Action/Dialogue	Reason Why
Tess	swiped at Eavie	_____ _____

INSIGHTS: *Reading as Thinking* ©
 Charlesbridge Publishing • (800) 225-3214   UNIT 4 – Analyzing Characters **113**

From "Best Friends"

Cara sank down into her chair as if she were trying to hide. Her face turned red. It was Cara's turn to audition.

3. Why did Cara turn red? _____

_____

4.

Character	Action/Dialogue	Reason Why
Cara	turned red	

From "The Choice"

Commander Lee looked decisively at Lieutenant Colonel Jackson. "Not only do I approve, but I commend you for your quick thinking and initiative. Your take-charge attitude saved our station, but, more importantly, Earth was saved. Congratulations, Commander Jackson of Rosaic Space Station," beamed former Commander Lee.

5. Why did Commander Lee call Jackson "Commander Jackson"?

_____

_____

6.

Character	Action/Dialogue	Reason Why
Commander Lee	called Jackson "Commander Jackson"	

INSIGHTS: Reading as Thinking ©
Charlesbridge Publishing • (800) 225-3214

Investigation A: INFERRING REASONS *continued*

Have students work independently or in pairs to answer the inference questions and complete the charts. Discuss their ideas, emphasizing that, although inferences must be based on text clues, they also require the reader to use his or her knowledge of similar situations or emotions. Ask students to explain prior knowledge they used to infer the reason for the dialogue excerpt from "The Choice."

Answer Key

Accept all reasonable answers.

3. She was nervous, embarrassed, afraid of performing in front of people, or afraid she would not do well.

4. was nervous, embarrassed, self-conscious, not confident

5. Commander Lee had decided to give Jackson the job of commanding the space station.

6. Jackson would be the new commander of the space station.

Investigation A: INFERRING REASONS *continued*

Have students infer reasons for the excerpt from "Camping."

Answer Key

Accept all reasonable answers.

7. Daniel was too interested in his own experiences to find out what Munroe already knew.
8. Munroe showed his brother how much he knew about survival in the wilderness.
9. He was too interested in his own experiences.

❏ ASKING WHY

Have a volunteer read aloud the introductory paragraph and the three strategy steps for inferring reasons.

Discuss how making a correct inference is not possible unless a reader pays careful attention to step 2: finding the author's clues.

From "Camping"

For years, Munroe had read everything he could about animals, plants, rivers, and forests. Then he pored over books about backpacking and survival in the wilderness. This trip would be the first real test of his skills.

[end of story] "Munroe, thanks a lot. Why didn't you tell me you could do all those things?". . ..

"You never asked."

7. Why didn't Daniel know about Munroe's knowledge and interest in the wilderness? _____

_____

8. Besides wanting to help his brother, why is it important for Munroe to take care of Daniel? _____

_____

9.

Character	Action/Dialogue	Reason Why
Daniel	never asked about his brother's interests	_____ _____

◻ ASKING WHY

You have discovered the reasons for characters' actions by asking yourself, *Why did the characters do what they did?* and then looking for the answer in the passage. Now you will read longer stories, and you will have more clues to use to infer the reasons for the characters' actions. To infer the reason for the characters' actions in longer stories, you should do the following:

1. Look for the place in the story where the action happens.

2. Find the clues given by the author.

3. Use your knowledge of similar situations to interpret the clues and infer the reasons.

INSIGHTS: Reading as Thinking ©
Charlesbridge Publishing • (800) 225-3214

Investigation A: COMPLETING REASON CHARTS

Students read two stories and use the strategy to infer the reasons for the main characters' actions.

Investigation **A**: COMPLETING REASON CHARTS

❑ Read each story and *ask yourself:* Why did the character act this way?
  • Complete the reason chart that follows each story.

Clay Goes Ape

Clay had a problem; he also had a headache. His band, The Deetsie Sub-Woofer Express, had become very popular following a summer tour. A large record company heard of the band's growing popularity and asked them to record a single. This meant the band needed a new song. The band's future success would depend on this new song because, if it were a hit, every radio station in the country would be playing it. Then people would rush to buy it, the song would soar on the charts, and the band would be another rock-and-roll success story.

Clay, overly confident, announced that he would write the new song. After all, he could not let the group think that he had lost his creative touch. This promise had turned into a headache because he had not had an idea in three days. Time was running out.

During those three days, Clay did not sleep much, which made him irritable. When someone played a wrong chord or missed a cue in rehearsal, Clay lost his temper. Sometimes he insulted the person, and once he stormed out. Everyone was concerned about Clay's strange behavior. Akiba, the drummer, suggested that perhaps it was time to

break up the group despite the recording offer. Laura, the guitarist, complained that she was tired of being insulted. Clay was losing his friends and his future — fast. Finally, Katya, the bass player, caught on. She knew what his problem was. She suggested that if Clay went somewhere and relaxed, he would have a better chance of coming up with an idea for the song.

Clay decided to go to the library and browse. Perhaps he might find an idea in a book. The quiet of the library had a calming effect, but, unfortunately, inspiration did not come to him. Then Clay decided to go to the zoo.

The zoo was not crowded because it was Tuesday. This allowed him to take his time observing the animals. Clay felt completely relaxed. Being in the open air surrounded by the trees and animals on a sunny day made him feel like his old self. It was wonderful!

Suddenly screams shattered the calm. People began streaming towards the exit. Clay stood still. He was torn between joining the fleeing crowd and finding out what they were running from. He did not have to wait long.

A huge lowland gorilla burst through the bushes to his right. Clay turned pale. He did not know whether to run, shout, or stand absolutely still and act like a tree.

Investigation A: COMPLETING REASON CHARTS *continued*

When students have read the story, "Clay Goes Ape," use the strategy to discuss and complete the first two items in the chart. Note that the chart continues on the next page.

Answer Key
Accept all reasonable answers.
Reasons Why
1. He didn't want the group to think he'd lost his touch.
2. He was tired, frustrated, and irritable.

The gorilla had found that freedom was not all fun. Munching celery back in the confines of the compound was better than being around these noisy humans. The outside world was interesting, but the humans screamed and ran around. The gorilla's normally peaceful nature turned first to irritation, then to rage. Then the gorilla saw Clay.

Clay remembered reading an article about ape behavior by Jane Goodall. He knew gorillas were not normally dangerous, but that when they are confused, they become unpredictable.

Clay's instinct when he saw the gorilla looking at him was to run, but his legs wouldn't do what his brain instructed. Then, as if in a fog, he heard a zookeeper talking in a very calm voice. Clay realized that he and the gorilla were surrounded by zookeepers holding nets and other rescue equipment.

Clay heard one zookeeper talking to the animal in a soothing manner. "Don't worry, we're going to get you home in a minute. We're not going to let anyone hurt you." And then, in the same tone,

he said to Clay, "Don't worry, young man. Just don't do anything the gorilla might mistake for an attack. My partner is getting ready to inject the gorilla with a tranquilizer* shot that will take effect in about ten seconds."

Those ten seconds seemed like ten years to Clay. But then, as suddenly as it had started, the excitement was all over. The now calm gorilla was led peacefully back to the compound. Clay breathed a sigh of relief and hoped his legs would stop shaking long enough for him to make it over to a bench. In the meantime, activity at the zoo returned to normal. Clay decided he'd had enough adventure for a while, and headed home.

A few months later, the great zoo escape was history, but a new song was on the radio. The Deetsie Sub-Woofer Express was on its way to the top of the charts with a new hit single, "Gorilla of My Dreams." People were going bananas over it.

*tranquilizer — a drug that calms without putting to sleep

Character	Action/Dialogue	Reason Why
1. Clay	announced he would write the new song	_____ _____ _____
2. Clay	lost his temper	_____ _____ _____

Character	Action/Dialogue	Reason Why
3. Akiba	wanted to break up the group	_____ _____ _____
4. Katya	told Clay to go somewhere and relax	_____ _____ _____
5. Clay	went to the library and the zoo	_____ _____ _____
6. Clay	wanted to find out why people were running	_____ _____ _____ _____
7. Clay	turned pale	_____ _____ _____
8. Gorilla	was irritated and in a rage	_____ _____ _____ _____
9. Clay	didn't run	_____ _____
10. Zookeeper	spoke to Clay	_____ _____ _____
11. Gorilla	went back to the compound peacefully	_____ _____ _____
12. Clay	left the zoo	_____ _____

INSIGHTS: Reading as Thinking ©
Charlesbridge Publishing • (800) 225-3214

Investigation A: COMPLETING REASON CHARTS *continued*

Have the students infer the reasons for the remaining actions and dialogue in the chart. Discuss variations in answers and how reasonable or unreasonable each is.

Answer Key

3. Clay's behavior was strange; he was angry at Clay or disappointed in him.
4. She was concerned; she understood what was bothering Clay.
5. He wanted to relax, or to find inspiration.
6. He was curious.
7. He was frightened of the gorilla.
8. The gorilla was unhappy out of its compound with noisy humans all around.
9. He was too scared to move.
10. He wanted to calm down the gorilla and to let Clay know the plan.
11. The gorilla had been tranquilized.
12. He'd had enough adventure.

Investigation A: COMPLETING REASON CHARTS *continued*

The second passage is an excerpt from *Tom Sawyer* by Mark Twain. Before students read "The Glorious Whitewasher," explain the context to them. Explain that *Tom Sawyer* is a classic, and it is full of colloquial language such as the word *ain't* for *am not* and *warn't* for *were not*. Be sure that the students know that these words are not acceptable in formal speech and writing. You may wish to discuss how colloquial language, when used by a skilled creative writer, can reflect the way people really speak and may lend credibility and color to written dialogue.

Mark Twain's work also contains phrases such as *honest injun* and other terms and characterizations of racial stereotypes that are offensive. Explain that this story and other works by Mark Twain continue to be read and appreciated today because they have a great deal to offer us despite their use of informal language and unacceptable racial stereotypes. Tell students that these works are a part of American culture and that they give us an opportunity to examine and discuss beliefs that were commonly held in the past.

The following story is from the classic book *Tom Sawyer* by Mark Twain. (Mark Twain is the pen name of Samuel L. Clemens.)

 The Glorious Whitewasher

Saturday morning had come, and all the summer world was bright and fresh, and brimming with life. There was a song in every heart; and if the heart was young the music issued at the lips. There was cheer in every face and a spring in every step. The locust trees were in bloom and the fragrance of blossoms filled the air.

Tom appeared on the sidewalk with a bucket of whitewash and a long-handled brush. He surveyed the fence, and all gladness left him and a deep melancholy settled down upon his spirit. Thirty yards of board fence, nine feet high. Life to him seemed hollow, and existence but a burden. Sighing, he dipped his brush and passed it along the topmost plank; repeated the operation, did it again, compared the insignificant whitewashed streak with the far-reaching continent of un-whitewashed fence, and sat down on a tree-box, discouraged.

He began to think of the fun he had planned for this day, and his sorrows multiplied. Soon the boys would come tripping along on all sorts of expeditions, and they would make a world of fun of his having to work — the very thought of it burnt him like fire.

¹straitened means — limited wealth
²tranquilly — calmly
³ranged — roamed freely over

He got out his worldly wealth and examined it — bits of toys, marbles, and trash; enough to buy an exchange for work maybe, but not half enough to buy so much as half an hour of pure freedom. So he returned his straitened means¹ to his pockets, and gave up the idea of trying to buy the boys. At this dark and hopeless moment an inspiration burst upon him! Nothing less than a great, magnificent inspiration.

He took up his brush and went tranquilly² to work. Ben Rogers came in sight presently — the very boy, of all boys, whose ridicule he had been dreading. Ben's gait was the hop-skip-and-jump, proof enough that his heart was light and his anticipation high. He was eating an apple, and giving a long, melodious whoop, at intervals, followed by a deep-toned ding-dong-dong, ding-dong-dong, for he was impersonating a steamboat.

Tom went on whitewashing — paid no attention to the steamboat. Ben stared a moment and then said: "Hi-yi! You're in bad, ain't you!"

No answer. Tom surveyed his last touch with the eye of an artist, then he gave his brush another gentle sweep and surveyed the result as before. Ben ranged³ up alongside of him. Tom's mouth watered for the apple, but he stuck to his work. Ben said: "Hello, old chap, you got to work, hey?"

(Continued on following page)

INSIGHTS: Reading as Thinking ©
Charlesbridge Publishing • (800) 225-3214

(Continued from previous page)

Tom wheeled suddenly and said: "Why, it's you, Ben! I warn't noticing."

"Say — I'm going in a-swimming, I am. Don't you wish you could? But of course you'd druther[4] work — wouldn't you? Course you would!"

Tom contemplated[5] the boy a bit, and said: "What do you call work?"

"Why, ain't that work?"

Tom resumed his whitewashing, and answered carelessly: "Well, maybe it is, maybe it ain't. All I know is, it suits Tom Sawyer."

"Oh come now, you don't mean to let on that you like it?"

The brush continued to move.

"Like it? Well, I don't see why I oughtn't to like it. Does a boy get a chance to whitewash a fence every day?"

That put the thing in a new light. Ben stopped nibbling his apple. Tom swept his brush daintily back and forth — stepped back to note the effect — added a touch here and there — criticized the effect again — Ben watching every move and getting more and more interested, more and more absorbed. Presently he said: "Say, Tom, let me whitewash a little."

Tom considered, was about to consent; but he altered his mind: "No — no — I reckon it wouldn't hardly do, Ben. You see, Aunt Polly's awful particular about this fence — right there

[4]druther — slang for "would rather"
[5]contemplated — looked at
[6]afeared — slang for "afraid"
[7]alacrity — cheerful readiness, promptness

on the street, you know — but if it was the back fence I wouldn't mind and she wouldn't mind. Yes, she's awful particular about this fence; it's got to be done very careful; I reckon there ain't one boy in a thousand, maybe two thousand, that can do it the way it's got to be done."

"No — is that so? Oh come, now — lemme just try. Only just a little — I'd let you, if it was me, Tom."

"Ben, I'd like to, honest injun; but Aunt Polly — well, Jim wanted to do it, but she wouldn't let him; Sid wanted to do it and she wouldn't let Sid. Now don't you see how I'm fixed? If you was to tackle this fence and anything was to happen to it —"

"Oh shucks, I'll be just as careful. Now lemme try. Say — I'll give you the core of my apple."

"Well, here — No, Ben, now don't. I'm afeared[6] — "

"I'll give you all of it!"

Tom gave up the brush with reluctance in his face, but alacrity[7] in his heart. And while the late [former] steamer worked and sweated in the sun, the retired artist sat on a barrel in the shade close by, dangled his legs, munched his apple, and planned the slaughter of more innocents. There was no lack of material; boys happened along every little while; they came to jeer, but remained to whitewash. By the time Ben was fagged [worn] out, Tom had traded the next chance to Billy Fisher for a kite, in good repair; and when he played

(Continued on following page)

INSIGHTS: Reading as Thinking ©
Charlesbridge Publishing • (800) 225-3214

Investigation A: COMPLETING REASON CHARTS *continued*

This is a continuation of the story, "The Glorious Whitewasher."

 ## Literature Connection

If students enjoy this passage, suggest they read all of *Tom Sawyer*, which is full of lively characters and wit. Other titles by Mark Twain include the following:
A Connecticut Yankee in King Arthur's Court,
Huckleberry Finn, and
The Prince and the Pauper.
Some more recent examples of strong characterization can be found in E.L. Konisburg's Newbury-winning *The View from Saturday,* Patricia Kindl's *Owl in Love,* and Karen Cushman's *Catherine Called Birdy.*

Investigation A: COMPLETING REASON CHARTS *continued*

This is the end of the story, "The Glorious Whitewasher," by Mark Twain.

Have students use the three-step strategy to complete the chart. Discuss students' inferences and accept any that are supported by clues in the story. Make sure students realize that the chart continues on a second page.

Answer Key

1. wanted to play, but had to whitewash fence
2. wanted Ben to think he was enjoying himself
3. wanted to hide his plan from Ben
4. wanted to tease Tom because Tom couldn't go swimming

(Continued from previous page)

out, Johnny Miller bought in for a dead rat and a string to swing it with — and so on and so on, hour after hour. And when the middle of the afternoon came, from being a poor poverty-stricken boy in the morning, Tom was literally rolling in wealth. He had besides the things before mentioned, twelve marbles, a piece of blue bottle-glass to look through, a spool cannon, a key that wouldn't unlock anything, a fragment of chalk, a tin soldier, a couple of tadpoles, six firecrackers, a kitten with only one eye, a brass doorknob, a dog-collar — but no dog — the handle of a knife, four pieces of orange peel, and a dilapidated[8] old window sash.

He had had a nice, good, idle time all the while — plenty of company — and the fence had three coats of whitewash on it! If he hadn't run out of whitewash, he would have bankrupted every boy in the village.

Tom said to himself that it was not such a hollow world, after all. He had discovered a great law of human action, without knowing it — namely that in order to make a man or boy covet[9] a thing, it is only necessary to make the thing difficult to attain.

[8]dilapidated — falling to pieces
[9]covet — desire eagerly a thing that belongs to another

Character	Action/Dialogue	Reason Why
1. Tom	thought that life was hollow	_____ _____
2. Tom	took up his brush and went tranquilly to work; surveyed his work with the eye of an artist	_____ _____ _____
3. Tom	"Why, it's you, Ben! I warn't noticing."	_____ _____
4. Ben	"Say — I'm going in a-swimming, I am. Don't you wish you could? But of course you'd druther work."	_____ _____ _____

INSIGHTS: Reading as Thinking ©
Charlesbridge Publishing • (800) 225-3214

UNIT 4 – Analyzing Characters | **121**

Character	Action/Dialogue	Reason Why
5. Tom	"No — no — I reckon it wouldn't hardly do, Ben. You see, Aunt Polly's awful particular about this fence. . . ."	_____ _____ _____ _____
6. Ben	"I'll give you all of it [his apple]!"	_____ _____ _____
7. Tom	said to himself that it was not such a hollow world, after all	_____ _____ _____

8. The last line of the story is: "He [Tom] had discovered a great law of human action, without knowing it — namely that in order to make a man or boy covet a thing, it is only necessary to make the thing difficult to attain." What does this mean?

_____

_____

_____

9. When Ben first asked Tom to let him paint the fence, Tom responded, "Ben, I'd like to, honest injun; but Aunt Polly — well, Jim wanted to do it, but she wouldn't let him. . . ." Do you think Tom was being honest? Explain.

_____

_____

10. What are three of Tom's character traits?

_____

_____

_____

INSIGHTS: Reading as Thinking ©
Charlesbridge Publishing • (800) 225-3214

Investigation A: COMPLETING REASON CHARTS *continued*

Discuss students' inferences about why the characters spoke and behaved as they did.

Answer Key

5. He wanted to make Ben think whitewashing took special talent and skill.
6. Ben wanted Tom to let him whitewash the fence in exchange for the apple.
7. He discovered a way of getting other boys to whitewash the fence for him.
8. People always want things that are hard to get. Tom found out that he could get the other boys to do his work by making it seem special.
9. Probably not. Tom just wanted to make whitewashing the fence seem very difficult and special.
10. Answers may include: Tom is clever, sly, cunning, lazy, greedy, and fun-loving.

Using Character Analysis Charts

Have students read the introductory sentence. Ask the following questions:

What are the three types of character analysis charts that you have made? (character differences, situation-response, action-reason)

What does a Character Differences Chart do? (It shows how the character is similar to or different from other characters.)

What does a Situation-Response Chart do? (It shows how the character behaves in response to a situation and what this reveals about him or her.)

What does an Action-Reason Chart do? (It shows the reasons behind the character's actions or words.)

Elicit from the students a list of memorable fictional characters. You might want to make all three charts on the chalkboard for an especially popular character. Discuss which chart is the most revealing of the character's traits.

Point out that enjoyable books, television shows, or movies often have characters with strongly delineated personalities. Whether the students identify with them, dislike them, or have mixed feelings about them, the characters are usually powerful and believable.

Investigation A: ANALYZING CHARACTERS WITH CHARTS

Have students read the story, "Gone Fishing." In this story, the first-person narrator tries to convince his daughter, Sarah, to go fishing with him.

Strategy Lesson **4**

USING CHARACTER CHARTS

In this lesson you will use all three types of character analysis charts to infer traits.

Investigation **A**: ANALYZING CHARACTERS WITH CHARTS

❏ Read the following story and complete the charts that follow.

Gone Fishing

Teenagers are so busy having a good time that they sometimes miss out on the best of times. Take my daughter, Sarah, for example. She is your average fun-loving kid — you know, the kind who dances around with headphones in her ears, paints her nails a new color every other month, and shoots baskets out in the driveway for hours. She plays on both the basketball and volleyball teams. She would live in a movie theater if she could. She is very outgoing and loves crowds. She is not at all like me. I do not like sports, and I am not too crazy about some of the movies that are out these days. I love solitude (privacy) and big, open spaces. That is probably why I love to fish. Fishing is what I call having a really great time. Not being a selfish man, I wanted Sarah to share this enjoyable experience with me.

"Fishing?" laughed Sarah. "You're joking!"

"Try it," I urged. "You'll love it."

"The only thing I love about fish is how good it tastes with french fries and cole slaw," teased Sarah.

"Think how good that fish will taste if you catch it yourself," I said encitingly (invitingly). "It'll be great!"

"It'll be boring," said Sarah with a grin. "Besides, I don't think I can sit still that long unless I'm tied down. I really don't want to go, Dad," she said, more seriously.

I was never bored. I could sit in the boat on the peaceful lake for hours, waiting patiently for the fish to bite. But Sarah, I knew, found it hard to wait quietly for anything. "That's okay, Sarah; you don't have to go," I said, disappointed but not wanting to force her into anything.

My disappointment must have shown on my face, however, because only a few seconds passed before Sarah said, 'Well, maybe I'll try fishing once."

I knew Sarah was doing this for me. What a kid! I was so pleased and proud of her, and I wanted to do something special for her, too. "Then let's get going," I said, "so we can get back in time to catch the new movie playing in town."

"Now you're talking!" said Sarah enthusiastically and ran out to begin packing the car.

INSIGHTS: Reading as Thinking ©
Charlesbridge Publishing • (800) 225-3214

Dad's Character Traits

1. _____
2. _____
3. _____
4. _____
5. _____

Sarah's Character Traits

_____
_____
_____
_____
_____

Situation	Dad's Response	Sarah's Response
1. Sarah has never been fishing.	_____ _____ Traits: _____	_____ _____ Traits: _____
2. Sarah says she does not want to go fishing.	_____ _____ Traits: _____	_____ _____ Traits: _____

Character	Action/Dialogue	Reason Why
1. Dad	wanted to take daughter Sarah fishing	_____
2. Sarah	refused to go at first	_____
3. Dad	was disappointed but accepted Sarah's refusal	_____
4. Sarah	changed her mind and said she would go	_____
5. Dad	said they should go to a movie, too	_____

INSIGHTS: Reading as Thinking ©
Charlesbridge Publishing • (800) 225-3214

Investigation A: ANALYZING CHARACTERS WITH CHARTS
continued

Have students complete the three charts for the story "Gone Fishing." Discuss their answers.

Answer Key
Character Differences Chart
Dad's Character Traits
1. does not like sports
2. does not like movies
3. likes solitude (privacy)
4. loves fishing
5. patient

Sarah's Character Traits
1. loves sports
2. loves movies
3. likes crowds, outgoing
4. doesn't like fishing
5. impatient

Situation-Response Chart
Dad's Response
1. wants to take Sarah fishing
   Traits: caring, unselfish, fatherly, loving
2. disappointed, says Sarah does not have to go
   Traits: understanding, accepting

Sarah's Response
1. doesn't want to go, jokes about it
   Traits: sense of humor, mind of her own
2. sees Dad's disappointment so agrees to go fishing
   Traits: dutiful, kind, caring

Action-Reason Chart
1. wanted to introduce Sarah to a new experience, wanted to share an experience that he loves.
2. not interested, thought fishing would be boring

(Answer Key continues on page 176.)

3. did not want to force daughter to go fishing, was understanding and thoughtful
4. did not want to disappoint her father, wanted to make her father feel better
5. wanted to do something Sarah would like

Discuss the similarities between a Situation-Response Chart and an Action-Reason Chart. Sometimes, the two charts can give slightly different traits. In the Situation-Response Chart, the father's response to Sarah's refusal reveals that he is understanding and accepting. In the Action-Reason Chart, the reason he accepts Sarah's refusal is that he is understanding and thoughtful.

Investigation B: COMPLETING ANALYSIS CHARTS

Students read the story "The Emerald Ring." In the first part of the story, the main characters are introduced. Have students complete the character differences chart before moving on to Part 2.

When students have read all three parts, you may want to discuss the author's use of a nameless first-person narrator.

Explain that although we do not know the first-person narrator's name, we do know certain things about her. Elicit the following details: She is a female student at Central High; she is a friend of both Trina and Stephanie. She describes Trina's negative traits honestly, but defends her. She

 Investigation **B**: COMPLETING CHARACTER ANALYSIS CHARTS

❑ Read the story, "The Emerald Ring"
  • Complete the chart that follows each part.

 The Emerald Ring
Part 1

Central High is like any other high school, I guess. We have a good football team, a number of clubs you can join, and some really good teachers and counselors. Of course, a school could not be a school without students, and we sure have enough of them. We have those who are happy and those who are not so happy. We have those who are smart, and those who are not so smart. It doesn't matter who or what you are, you can still claim Central High as your school, and you can feel that you are part of it. It's a great place to be most of the time. Sometimes, however, problems come up, and then it's not such a nice place to be — like the time Trina's ring was stolen.

How can I describe Trina? You would actually have to meet her to understand how she really is — inside, I mean. Trina comes from a wealthy family and is the youngest child. This may explain why she is spoiled and tends to expect things her way. Some of the students call her snobbish, but I don't think she is; she just doesn't associate with a lot of people. Some students also think she is a big show-off. I must admit that at

times she does act like that, but I guess she just wants to show us some of her beautiful things. For her birthday, her parents gave her an elegant, green, emerald ring with a gold band. Her father even had her initials engraved (carved) inside the band.

Trina couldn't wait until all the girls in our homeroom arrived so she could exhibit it. "Where's Stephanie?" she asked. "I have something to show all of you, but I want everyone to see it at the same time. It's my birthday present, and it's the best present I've ever had."

"What is it?" we all asked, almost at the same time. "Come on, don't keep us in suspense!"

"You'll see, just as soon as Stephanie comes. Where is she?" Trina asked, keeping her hands behind her back.

For some strange reason, Trina is always interested in what Stephanie thinks about her. She is not a friend of Stephanie's — they don't even hang out in the same group. As a matter of fact, I'm not sure if Trina even likes Stephanie. I think she is a little envious (jealous) of Stephanie, and I find that very strange. Stephanie's family is not wealthy like Trina's. In fact, they have very little money.

(Continued on following page)

INSIGHTS: Reading as Thinking ©
Charlesbridge Publishing • (800) 225-3214

thinks that Stephanie did not steal the ring and defends her before Ms. Mapps.

We can infer that the narrator is loyal, understanding, and willing to give people the benefit of the doubt. She feels that the accusations are unfair. Discuss the two major principles in the story: It is wrong to jump to conclusions without adequate evidence, and good reputation is important.

(Continued from previous page)

Stephanie does not have fancy clothes or jewelry like Trina. She is rich in personality, brains, and friends. Lately, though, she has been running around with some girls who seem to always be in trouble, and we haven't been talking as much. Anyway, whenever Trina comes to school with a new treasure, she tries to make sure that Stephanie sees it. Stephanie is always very polite, but she never makes a fuss over Trina's things like the rest of us do. She tells Trina how nice her belongings are, then goes about her business. Maybe that's what bothers Trina; she loves attention.

Trina's Character Traits	Stephanie's Character Traits
1. _____	_____
2. _____	_____
3. _____	_____

Hint: Some character traits may be the same for both girls.

Part 2

"It's about time you got here," exclaimed Trina, as Stephanie entered our homeroom.

"You're holding up the show," squealed Jin. "Trina is going to show us what she received for a birthday present. Come on, Trina, let's see it!"

Trina began bringing her hands slowly in front of her. With an exaggerated flip of her right hand, she displayed a fantastic, exquisite ring. You could have heard the screams of surprise and admiration all the way downtown. That was some ring!

The ring even caught Stephanie's complete attention. "Oh, Trina," she sighed, "it's such a gorgeous ring. I've never seen anything like it. It must have cost a small fortune. What I wouldn't do to have a ring like this!" She turned Trina's finger from side to side, admiring the ring. I have never known Stephanie to be so attracted to anything like that before. It was truly a beautiful ring.

(Continued on following page)

INSIGHTS: Reading as Thinking ©
Charlesbridge Publishing • (800) 225-3214

Investigation B: COMPLETING CHARACTER ANALYSIS CHARTS *continued*

Have students complete the Character Differences Chart. Discuss students' answers and make sure that correlating traits are recorded across from each other.

Answer Key

Accept all reasonable answers.
Trina's Character Traits
1. spoiled, snobbish
2. shows off, brags
3. gets along with others

Stephanie's Character Traits
1. not spoiled, not snobbish
2. does not show off or brag
3. gets along with others

Have students read Part 2 of the story, in which Trina shows off her ring, then loses it. Seemingly incriminating evidence against Stephanie is also planted in this part of the story.

Investigation B: COMPLETING CHARACTER ANALYSIS CHARTS *continued*

This is a continuation of "The Emerald Ring." After students have completed the action-reason chart, discuss their reasons. You may want to talk about the relationship of motivation to character traits. Not all of the reasons show character traits. During discussion, ask the following questions:

Why did Trina display her ring? (She wanted to show off; she was proud or boastful.)

Are these character traits? Why or why not? (Yes, because they tell how Trina acts or feels most of the time.)

Why did Trina take off her ring? (She wanted to wash her hands or avoid dulling her ring with soap.)

Are these character traits? Why or why not? (Yes, they could be. She is careful about taking care of the things she values, or she is proud of her possessions and wants to take good care of them.)

Discuss the other actions and reasons in a similar manner.

Answer Key

Reason Why

4. She wanted to show off. She was proud or boastful.
5. She was proud and careful not to ruin her valuables.
6. She had made plans to meet her friends.
7. She was responsible for clearing the area during a fire drill.

(Continued from previous page)

Trina stood there, beaming with the knowledge that she really had something special — something that no one else in the whole school had. The bell rang, and we headed for class, agreeing to meet before lunch in the third-floor bathroom, which was our meeting place every day.

"Hurry up and wash your hands, so we can go eat. I'm starving," complained Nadia to Trina.

"Hold your horses; I'm hurrying as fast as I can. I have to take my ring off so soap won't get on it. I heard somewhere that soap will dull a precious stone," replied Trina, as she removed her ring and placed it on the corner of the sink. At that moment, Stephanie came in.

"Want to go to Harry's Hamburger Hut with us?" I asked, even though I knew what the answer would be.

"No. Thanks, anyway," Stephanie responded. "I have to meet my friends."

Just then the fire alarm bell went off. Ms. Mapps, the counselor, stuck her head in the door.

"Clear this place right away," she said firmly. Ms. Mapps is a terrific counselor. You can talk to her as if she were your sister. All the students like her. She always makes time for you no matter how busy she is. She's the kind of person you can trust with a secret or share a joke with. She is firm, but fair. When she says something, you listen; when she says "Move," you move. And we moved!

"Hurry up and get out of here," I yelled over my shoulder to Stephanie, who was still washing her hands.

"I'm coming, I'm coming," she said.

Character	Action/Dialogue	Reason Why
4. Trina	displayed her ring	_____
5. Trina	took her ring off	_____
6. Stephanie	would not join the girls for lunch	_____
7. Ms. Mapps	told girls to clear room	_____

INSIGHTS: Reading as Thinking ©
Charlesbridge Publishing • (800) 225-3214

Part 3

Your school has fire drills, so you know what they are like. We were standing outside when Trina let out a loud gasp.

"Oh, no!" she cried in panic. "I ran out and left my ring on the sink."

"You didn't," groaned Nadia. "How could you be so careless?"

"When Ms. Mapps told us to leave the building, I ran out with the rest of you. What'll I do?" She was near tears.

"Hey, Stephanie was still in there," remembered Nadia. "She probably saw it and picked it up for you. Don't worry; when the 'all-clear' signal goes off, we'll find Stephanie and your ring. She's probably looking for you right now."

"Yes," we all agreed.

For what seemed like forever, we waited for the "all-clear" signal. It finally came, and we all headed back toward the building.

"There she is," said Jin, as she spotted Stephanie by the cafeteria. "Am I glad to find you," Trina exclaimed.

"Why?" asked Stephanie, with a puzzled look on her face.

"Don't you have my ring?" asked Trina.

"Of course not. Why would I have your ring? The last time I saw it, it was on your finger," said Stephanie.

"Maybe it's still on the sink in the bathroom," I said.

All of us, except Stephanie, dashed up to the third floor. It was not there!

Trina stood, rooted to the spot, staring at the sink where she had placed her ring. Suddenly she burst into tears.

"It's gone," she wailed. "Someone found it, and it's gone! I'll never see that ring again." We tried to console her, but what can you say at a time like that?

"I know who has your ring," said Nadia suddenly.

"Who?" we all asked.

"Stephanie!" said Nadia with certainty. "She was the last one in the bathroom. No one else could have gone in because Ms. Mapps was moving everyone out. And you saw how Stephanie admired the ring this morning. She never liked anything else of Trina's the way she liked that ring. The only way she could ever have a ring like that would be to steal it. You all heard her say she would do anything to have a ring like that. Look at the people she hangs around with — they're always being accused of taking things. She has it; I just know it. She's nothing but a thief." With that, Nadia stalked out with the others following.

I thought, "I know Stephanie really liked that ring, but she would never take anything that didn't belong to her. I've got to talk to Ms. Mapps; she'll know how to handle this mess."

When I reached her office, Trina, Lisa, and Stephanie were already there. Ms. Mapps was listening to Nadia accuse Stephanie of stealing the ring.

"I don't know what the truth is," I stated, "but I just know that Stephanie wouldn't have stolen that ring."

INSIGHTS: Reading as Thinking ©
Charlesbridge Publishing • (800) 225-3214

Investigation B: COMPLETING CHARACTER ANALYSIS CHARTS *continued*

This is the conclusion of the story, "The Emerald Ring." In Part 3, Nadia accuses Stephanie of stealing the ring, a confrontation occurs, and Ms. Mapps explains all.

Writing Connection

Analyzing People's Behavior: Have students use a newspaper or magazine article to make an action-reason chart. The charts should list at least five important actions described in the article, who took part in those actions, and why. Students then use their charts to write a character monologue in which the character explains and justifies his or her behavior.

Investigation B: COMPLETING CHARACTER ANALYSIS CHARTS *continued*

Have students complete the action-reason chart. Discuss the reasons the students inferred.

Answer Key

Answers may include:

8. Her ring was missing; she was frightened, upset, or surprised.
9. She thought Stephanie took the ring because she was last to leave the bathroom and she had admired it; Nadia didn't like Stephanie's friends.
10. She wanted to keep the ring safe.
11. Stephanie had been unjustly accused, and Ms. Mapps thought an apology would be fair or just.
12. She knew she was innocent and felt she should be judged for herself.

 Writing Connection

Discuss the character traits of the protagonist in a novel or short story the students have recently read. Draw a character differences chart on the board. As a group, analyze the traits of the antagonist in the same novel or the protagonist in a different novel. Model for the students how you use this information to write a compare/ contrast paragraph or essay.

Have students make a Situation-Response Chart, Character Differences Chart and an Action-Reason Chart to do one of the following assignments:

(Continued from previous page)

"Girls," said Ms. Mapps soothingly, "I know you are all upset about Trina's ring. You haven't given me a chance to say a word since you flew in here. Stephanie does not have the ring; I do. After I chased you out of the bathroom, I went back to make sure everyone was gone and I spotted the ring on the sink. I knew such a valuable ring would be missed soon, so I locked it up for safekeeping until the owner claimed it.

"I think you owe Stephanie an apology. You jumped to conclusions and made some very serious charges against her. You could have ruined her reputation, simply because you thought she had the ring. Next time, stop and think about the consequences of what you are saying." Ms. Mapps returned

* Guilt by association — judging someone guilty because of that person's friends or associates

Trina's ring to her.

Nadia apologized to Stephanie quickly, then sat down. Trina, for once, looked embarrassed. She apologized to Stephanie for jumping to conclusions without evidence. Ms. Mapps turned to Stephanie and said, "Do you have any idea why Nadia and the others thought you had the ring?"

"No, I don't," said Stephanie. "Is it because of my new friends?"

"Well, perhaps it is. They have a reputation for making trouble," replied Ms. Mapps. "That is called guilt by association."*

"But that's not fair," said Stephanie, "I should be judged for myself."

In the end, we all agreed that someone is innocent until proven guilty, and someone's reputation is more valuable than anything else.

Character	Action/Dialogue	Reason Why
8. Trina	let out a gasp	_____
9. Nadia	accused Stephanie of taking the ring	_____ _____
10. Ms. Mapps	took the ring	_____ _____
11. Ms. Mapps	wanted the girls to apologize to Stephanie	_____ _____
12. Stephanie	wondered why the others were so quick to accuse her	_____ _____

INSIGHTS: Reading as Thinking ©
Charlesbridge Publishing • (800) 225-3214

1. Write an essay comparing yourself to the main character in the book you have read most recently.
2. Write an essay comparing two characters from different books in a situation that you invent. (For this type of essay, generic situations such as family life, a school experience, a social activity, or a problem work best.)

 COMPARING POINTS OF VIEW

TWO POINTS OF VIEW ABOUT THE SAME CHARACTER

So far, you have been analyzing fictional characters. In this lesson, you will read excerpts from an autobiography and a biography of a real person, Admiral R.E. Byrd.

An **autobiography** is the story of a person's life written by the person himself or herself. A **biography** is the story of a person's life written by someone else. Frequently, an autobiography and a biography have different points of view about the same person or event. A biographer is likely to see a person in a different way than the person sees himself or herself. That is the case in the passages in this lesson.

Admiral Byrd was a famous explorer who was the first person to reach the North and South Poles by air. He established Little America, a settlement on the Antarctic continent. He was an adventurous person throughout his life (1888-1957). According to many accounts, he was once told that he could never become a pilot because of an injury to his leg, but he managed to convince the Navy doctors to let him try anyway, and he became a famous aviator.

In the passages that follow, you will read two different points of view about Admiral Byrd's first trip to the South Pole. It is useful for you to be able to analyze the same person from different points of view, because biographers frequently disagree with each other and sometimes with an autobiographer.

Authors often give readers two or more points of view about the same character in a novel or play. When you read these different points of view about the same character, it is useful to make a reasons chart or a chart that shows similarities and differences. Using the chart, you can clearly see what each point of view is.

Investigation : USING CHARTS TO COMPARE

❏ Read the passages from the autobiography and the biography of Admiral Byrd.
   • Complete the charts that follow the passages.

TWO POINTS OF VIEW ABOUT THE SAME CHARACTER

In this lesson, students will analyze authors' points of view. They read a biography and an autobiography with two different views of R.E. Byrd's character.

Have volunteers each read aloud a paragraph of the introduction. Discuss the fact that two different authors may have varying opinions about the same person. Editorials in magazines or newspapers, for instance, may describe the same person in very different ways.

Point out that writers of history are always influenced by their culture, their time period, and their beliefs about what is important.

Investigation A: USING CHARTS TO COMPARE

Have the students read the instructions for comparing the excerpts from the biography and autobiography of R.E. Byrd.

INSIGHTS: Reading as Thinking ©
Charlesbridge Publishing • (800) 225-3214

Investigation A: USING CHARTS TO COMPARE

continued

The author of the biography of Byrd is critical of Byrd's actions at Advance Base in Antarctica.

Have students read both excerpts before discussing them. Then, point out that we cannot accept Byrd's autobiography as the truth just because he wrote it. People often have different opinions of us than we ourselves do. A biographer can also believe that an autobiographer was mistaken, withholding information, tailoring the truth, or lying. Also, Byrd or the biographer might have had a personal reason for writing the story – to glorify or defame Byrd, for instance.

The same story can be told from many different angles. Discuss reasons why biographies might differ.

 Literature Connection

Autobiographies and Biographies: If students enjoy reading about history from a personal point of view, suggest the following.

Bode, Janet. *New Kids on the Block: Oral Histories of Immigrant Teens*. Eleven teens from different countries tell their stories.

Carle, Eric. *The Art of Eric Carle*. New York: Philomel/Putnam, 1997. The life and art of Eric Carle, the creator of *The Very Hungry Caterpillar* and other children's classics.

Excerpt from a Biography of Admiral Byrd

It was important to set up the Advance Base, a base nearer the South Pole than Little America, to make the necessary measurements. However, it is not at all clear that any one person should have gone there alone, or that Byrd should have been the one to go. The dangers of the Antarctic weather and of failure of the equipment were great. One person alone had almost no chance of surviving if anything went wrong.

Byrd was the leader of the scientific mission to the Antarctic. In choosing to go to the Advance Base, he was really turning his back on his group. It was his responsibility to care for his men and direct their research. Instead, he went off on what was really a personal adventure. What would have happened if something had gone wrong? Did Byrd consider that his men might have lost their lives trying to rescue him? It is hard to justify his decision to live in the Advance Base himself — and alone.

He started his solitary life at the end of March. On April 1, he radioed Little America for the first time. Two members of his group, Dyer and Waite, reported that he sounded cheerful and self-confident. All was going well. He did not seem to be suffering from the cold.

Indeed, everything had been done to keep the cold from being a problem. The one-room house at the Advance Base was buried in snow and ice to keep it warm, and opened into a tunnel, so that the weather could not beat on its door. The house had a good stove, and Byrd had the warmest sleeping bag then invented. He also had a good supply of warm clothes. Unless some accident happened, he was likely to be fairly comfortable. An accident, however, could have occurred at any time. Byrd must have spent many hours worrying about such an event.

Excerpts from *Alone* by Richard E. Byrd*

During the four and a half months I occupied Advance Base alone, I kept a fairly complete diary. Nearly every night, before turning in, I sat down and wrote a thoroughgoing account of the day's doings.

April 1

April came in on Easter Sunday. It came in blowing and snowing, with a wind which shot the temperature up from -48° to -25° before the day was done. Not a pleasant day, but decidedly on the warmish side, after March's cold.

(Continued on following page)

*Reprinted by permission of G.P. Putnam and Sons. Copyright 1938 by R.E. Byrd.

INSIGHTS: Reading as Thinking ©
Charlesbridge Publishing • (800) 225-3214

Cleary, Beverly. *My Own Two Feet: A Memoir*. New York: Morrow, 1995. The author of the *Ramona* books and *Dear Mr. Henshaw* tells of her life.

Filipovic, Zlata. *Zlata's Diary: A Child's Life in Sarajevo*. Trans. Christina Pribichevich-Zoric. New York: Viking, 1994. A teen's experience of war.

(Continued from previous page)

In the morning at 10 o'clock, I attempted the first radio contact with Little America. Considering my inexperience, the fact that I was successful — at least in that I managed to make myself understood — pleased me very much.

For if any possibility truly disturbed me, it was the chance of my losing radio contact with Little America. Not on my account, but on the expedition's account generally. In spite of the orders I had given that nobody was to try to rescue me, I knew in my own heart that my order might be ignored if Little America was out of touch with me for long.

Realizing how much depended upon my ability to hold communication, I was worried by the thought I might fail through sheer ignorance. Dyer had shown me how to make repairs, and Waite had coached me in operating the set; but, whenever I looked at the complications of tubes, switches, and coils, my heart sank. I scarcely knew the Morse code. Fortunately, Little America could talk to me by radio telephone. So I didn't have to try to understand quickly tapped dots and dashes from skillful operators. But I had to reply in dots and dashes, and that I doubted I could do.

April 8

The shack was always freezing cold in the morning. I slept with the door open. When I arose, the inside temperature (depending upon the surface weather) might be anywhere from 10 to 40 below zero. Frost coated the sleeping bag where my breath had condensed during the night; my socks and boots, when I picked them up, were so stiff with frozen sweat that I first had to work them between my hands. A pair of silk gloves hung from a nail over the bunk, where I could grab them first thing. Yet, even with their protection, my fingers would sting and burn from the touch of the lamp and stove as I lighted them. The old flesh had worn off the tips, and the new flesh for a while was painfully tender. So I had my troubles.

Some came from my own stupidities. At first I had a devil of a time with the weather instruments. The graphs became horribly blotched, the pens stuck, and the instruments themselves stopped without rhyme or reason. But, one way or another, I usually managed to find a cure. I learned how to thin the ink with glycerin to keep it from freezing, and to thin the oil in the instruments with gasoline and rub the delicate parts with graphite, which wasn't affected so much by the cold.

INSIGHTS: Reading as Thinking ©
Charlesbridge Publishing • (800) 225-3214

Investigation A: USING CHARTS TO COMPARE
continued

This is the conclusion of Byrd's autobiography. In it, Byrd gives his point of view concerning his occupation of Advance Base.

Literature Connection
continued

Jones, Hettie. *Big Star Fallin' Mama: Five Women in Black Music.* New York: Viking, 1995. Biographies of Ma Rainey, Bessie Smith, Mahalia Jackson, Billie Holiday, and Aretha Franklin.

Lyons, Mary E. *Keeping Secrets: The Girlhood Diaries of Seven Women Writers.* New York: Holt, 1995. The public and private lives of Louisa May Alcott, Kate Chopin, Ida B. Wells, Charlotte Perkins Gilman, and other women writers.

Meltzer, Milton, ed. *Frederick Douglass: In His Own Words.* New York: Harcourt, 1995. Selections from autobiographies of Frederick Douglass.

Thwaite, Ann. *The Brilliant Career of Winnie-the-Pooh: The Definitive History of the Best Bear in All the World.* New York: Dutton, 1994. This "biography" includes articles, letters, interviews, and illustrations documenting the life of that famous bear.

Wilder, Laura Ingalls. *West from Home: Letters of Laura Ingalls Wilder, San Francisco, 1915.* HarperCollins, 1994. The beloved author of the Little House books wrote letters to her husband while on a trip to visit her daughter.

Investigation A: USING CHARTS TO COMPARE *continued*

Have students complete the action-reason chart and the attitude comparison chart for Byrd's biography and autobiography. Discuss their responses and accept all reasonable variations.

Answer Key

Reason Why
1. He was off on a personal adventure; he did not care about their lives.
2. a. His expedition might suffer.
   b. People from Little America might try to rescue him.
3. He did not know how to make repairs or use Morse Code.

Byrd – biography
4. He must have worried about having an accident.
5. He turned his back on his men; he did not care about their lives.

Byrd – autobiography
4. He was worried about accidents and equipment failure.
5. He says he was worried that his men might try to rescue him.

Discuss other books or movies in which different points of view about the same character are given. Ask, **Why might an author give more than one point of view about a character?** (to imitate life, to expand our perspective, to explore the way people interact, to show different sides of an issue)

Character	Action/Dialogue	Reason Why
1. Byrd in the biography	turned his back on his group by choosing to go to the Advance Base alone	_____ _____ _____ _____
2. Byrd in the autobiography	was worried about losing communication with Little America (Give two reasons.)	a. _____ _____ b. _____ _____
3. Byrd in the autobiography	thought he might fail through sheer ignorance	_____ _____ _____

	Byrd in the biography	Byrd in the autobiography
4. attitude concerning an accident	_____ _____ _____ _____	_____ _____ _____ _____
5. attitude toward others	_____ _____ _____ _____	_____ _____ _____ _____

Ask yourself: What does the biographer say about Byrd's attitude toward his men?

INSIGHTS: Reading as Thinking ©
Charlesbridge Publishing • (800) 225-3214

UNIT 4 – Analyzing Characters **133**

❏ IMPLIED CHARACTERS

Sometimes an author will develop the character of a person or group who does not really exist in the story. An **implied character** is a person or group whose views or actions are considered as if they are real, although they are never detailed in the story.

In the story that follows, there are really only three characters: the two grandparents and the narrator. They talk about two things: self-confidence and the positive philosophy of the grandparents, who always "see the glass as half full." That is, they realize that life (the glass) is not always perfect, but that one should be thankful for what one has.

In contrast, the opposite point of view is taken by "others," who always see the glass as half empty. Such people focus on what they do not have. These "others" are never named and are not characters in the story, but their point of view is expressed by a character (the narrator). Thus, it is possible to compare two *different* points of view even though the characters in the story actually have only one point of view.

 Investigation **A**: CHARTING IMPLIED CHARACTER DIFFERENCES

❏ Read the following story and complete the charts that follow it.

Half Full

The sun grinned down at me as I walked along whistling. Some robins had organized a chorus, and they began competing with my song. The sky reminded me of my grandparents' powder-blue bedspread covered with dazzling white lilies. I always felt so safe lying on top of that spread, talking. At least with my grandparents, I could really discuss my problems.

I am so lucky to have grandparents like Granddad and Gransy. They know the true meaning of generosity; they know it means more than just giving presents when what you really need is attention and love. They are wiser and more understanding than most people.

They always see the bright side of things and believe that whatever happens, happens for the best. One day, as Gransy was doing the laundry, the washing machine went on the blink. Water was everywhere — all over the basement floor. Gransy simply said the floor was long overdue for a good mopping anyway. Granddad agreed and said that he now had enough water to do the mopping. Why can't everyone be like them?

(Continued on following page)

INSIGHTS: Reading as Thinking ©
Charlesbridge Publishing • (800) 225-3214

❏ IMPLIED CHARACTERS

Have a student read aloud the introductory paragraphs. Discuss implied characters in books that students have read in your class.

Investigation A: CHARTING IMPLIED CHARACTER DIFFERENCES

Have students read the story, "Half Full."

Investigation A: CHARTING IMPLIED CHARACTER DIFFERENCES *continued*

Have the students read the directions for the character differences chart. Discuss the first set of traits as a class. Then have students complete the chart.

Have students read the directions for the situation-response chart and complete it.

Discuss student responses and accept all reasonable variations.

Answer Key

Character Differences Chart
Grandad and Gransy
1. easy to talk to
2. generous
3. see the bright side of things
Other People
1. not easy to talk to
2. stingy
3. see the negative side of things
Situation-Response Chart
Grandparents' Response
1. They would listen with patience and understanding.
   Traits: patient, helpful, or understanding
2. They would give their time.
   Traits: loving or caring
3. They did not get upset.
   Traits: cool, calm, optimistic, cheerful
Implied "Others'" Response
1. They would not listen or would not understand.
   Traits: impatient
2. They would buy presents.
   Traits: unwise, don't understand
3. They probably would have become upset.
   Traits: angry, frustrated

They love to use the example about the glass of water. According to Granddad and Gransy, there are two ways of looking at a glass partly filled with water. If you are a person who really feels positive about yourself, then you will view the glass as being half full. But if you are a person who does not feel good about yourself, then you will see the glass as being half empty.

It is funny how a picture of that glass came into my mind as the names of the science fair winners were announced. My name was not one of them, but for some strange reason I didn't feel too disappointed. I had worked hard on my project, and I really wanted to win, but I knew I had done my best. As my grandparents always say, when you have done your best, you cannot do any more. Besides, I enjoyed doing the project, and I had learned a lot. As I walked home, I thought about how good it feels to drink from a glass that is half full.

❏ List implied differences between the grandparents and other people in the character differences chart.

Granddad and Gransy	Other People
1. _____	_____
2. _____	_____
3. _____	_____

❏ Complete the situation-response chart below. Determine the response of the implied person or generalized "others."

Situation	Grandparents' Response	Implied "Others'" Response
1. narrator has problems	_____ _____ Traits: _____	_____ _____ Traits: _____
2. narrator needs attention	_____ _____ Traits: _____	_____ _____ Traits: _____
3. washing machine flooded floor	_____ _____ Traits: _____	_____ _____ Traits: _____

INSIGHTS: Reading as Thinking © Charlesbridge Publishing • (800) 225-3214

Self-evaluation

Have the students complete the Self-evaluation. Encourage them to use the Self-evaluation to identify areas in which they need further preparation. Discuss any areas of concern with students before conducting the unit Assessment.

1. What strategy did you learn in this unit?

_____

_____

2. What part of the unit was easiest?

_____

_____

3. What part of the unit was the most difficult? Why?

_____

_____

4. When can you use the unit strategy?

_____

_____

_____

5. Write one question you think should be on a test of this unit.

_____

_____

_____

6. Circle the number that shows how much you learned in this unit.

1	2	3	4	5	6	7	8	9	10
DIDN'T LEARN		LEARNED A LITTLE		LEARNED SOME		LEARNED MOST		LEARNED ALL	

INSIGHTS: Reading as Thinking ©
Charlesbridge Publishing • (800) 225-3214

Assessment

A student's performance is rated against a predetermined level of mastery. The Assessment is used as a diagnostic tool to provide feedback on the learner's progress.

Blackline Master Pages 190-193

Hand out copies of Blackline Master Pages 190-193. Tell students that the Assessment has two parts. Ask the students to read the instructions carefully.

Collect, score, and record the Assessments before returning them and discussing them with the students. Accept all reasonable answers.

PART 1
Answers for Blackline Master Page 190
Jessica's Character Traits
   1. tries hard to make friends, but it is not easy
   2. has no really close friends
   3. has no one to talk to
   4. spends free time alone
   5. nervous when she meets people

Nomsa's Character Traits
   1. makes friends easily
   2. has many close friends
   3. always has someone to talk to
   4. spends free time with club
   5. likes meeting new people

PART 2
Answers for Blackline Master Page 192
Nicole's Responses
   1. thinks he probably just wandered off
      Trait(s): calm, optimistic, not worried
   2. a. happy they found him
      b. tells Fernando how to get out
      Trait(s): responsible

Sergio's Responses
1. thinks he might be hurt or in trouble
   Trait(s): concerned, worried, panicked
2. a. happy they found him
   b. wants to break into garage
   Trait(s): impulsive, thoughtless

Answers for Blackline Master Page 193
1. thought it was the best way to find Fernando
2. thought it was the best way to figure out where Fernando would have gone
3. was concerned that Fernando was hurt
4. thought they would find Fernando soon
5. thought Fernando had probably followed the sounds also
6. could not find another way to get in

❑ SCORING

Part 1: For scoring the Character Differences Chart, characteristics may be listed in any order, but each must be paired with its opposite. Each pair of traits has a value of 1 point.

Part 2: Score 1 point for each response or trait in the Situation-Response Chart. Responses a and b are worth a half point each. Score 1 point for each reason in the Action-Reason Chart.

Mastery Level: 15 out of 19 points.

 ## Conditional Knowledge

To help students apply the strategies in this unit, it is important to discuss the conditions under which each strategy is best used. Conduct the following discussions with the entire class after the Assessment has been completed.

Have students form small groups to discuss and report when they would use any or all three of the charts in this unit. After each group reports its ideas, elicit careers that involve character analysis: psychiatrist, social worker, novelist, public relations specialist, personnel department administrator, school principal, actor, advertising executive, TV producer, journalist, detective, etc. Discuss when each of the careers requires a person to use character analysis.

Assessment

☐ PART 1

- Read the passage.
- Complete the chart to show five differences between the two characters. Be sure to list opposite character traits directly across from each other in the chart.

Jessica and Nomsa

Jessica has lived in many different places: San Francisco, Dallas, Chicago, New York, and other cities. Wherever Jessica lives, she tries hard to make friends, but it is not easy because she does not stay in one place long enough. Her family moves every six months or so. She does not have any really close friends, so she does not have anyone to talk to about her problems. Her mother works, and her older brother, Taylor, is too busy to pay much attention to her. So Jessica spends most of her free time alone, reading, or walking around and watching other people. When she meets someone for the first time, she is usually nervous and does not know quite what to say.

Nomsa has lived in the same city her whole life. Because Nomsa's family knows almost everyone in their neighborhood, it is easy for her to make friends. She has many close friends and always has someone to talk to. Wherever she goes, people say hello and ask her how she is feeling. She spends her free time with a club that tutors elementary school children and works on community projects, so she is usually out with people doing something. Last winter, she helped collect used coats and distribute them to people who couldn't afford new ones, and last summer, her club took 40 children hiking in a state park outside of the city. Nomsa likes meeting new people and always knows just what to say to them.

Jessica's Character Traits	Nomsa's Character Traits
1. _____	_____
2. _____	_____
3. _____	_____
4. _____	_____
5. _____	_____

BLACKLINE MASTER

INSIGHTS: *Reading as Thinking* ©
Charlesbridge Publishing • (800) 225-3214

• Read the story and complete the Situation-Response Chart and the Action-Reason Chart.

The Search

The late afternoon sun was warm and pleasant. Sergio Ellis and his best friend, Nicole Wang, were sitting on the front porch talking to Sergio's grandfather about the things that happened at school that day. They were just about to amuse him with another story when Sergio caught sight of Mrs. Alvarez hurrying toward them with a worried look on her face. "Have you seen Fernando?" she asked, somewhat out of breath. "He was playing in the backyard a few minutes ago, but now he's nowhere to be seen. I've looked all over the house and searched the playground, but I just can't find him."

"Hey, I wonder if he's hurt or in trouble," Sergio thought out loud, a little panic creeping into his voice.

"Don't worry, Serge. Fernando has probably just wandered off to play," Nicole stated with her usual self-confidence. "Little kids often stray when something has caught their attention. Mrs. Alvarez will probably find him playing somewhere. There's nothing to be concerned about yet."

"I don't know how you can be so certain, Nic. I think we should start a house-to-house search right away. We can use Grandpa as an information center," Sergio said. He continued, "Mrs. Alvarez can cover everything east of here, and you and I will search the area to the west. Sure, he's most likely to be nearby, but it's getting late." He jumped off of the porch.

"Hold on a minute, Serge," said Nicole unhurriedly. "We've got to think about this from Fernando's point of view. Where would I go if I were Fernando? What could have caught his attention enough to cause him to leave the yard? Let's start our search near his yard."

Nicole and Sergio started for Fernando's house. After a quick survey of the yard, they concluded that he probably wandered out by the gate, but they could not find any clues as to which direction he might have taken. "I'll bet he went to the playground; he's been begging me to take him there," said Nicole.

"I wouldn't be surprised if he went there! But, isn't there a huge ditch near the playground?" Sergio chattered nervously. "He could be hurt; we'd better hurry."

"That's true if he's there, but let's not think the worst yet."

When Nicole and Sergio reached the playground, their attention was immediately drawn to a jacket caught on the fence. Sergio raced over to examine it and found that it was newly torn. "It looks as if he might have been hurt. We'd better call the police. It's getting late. They need daylight to search for him, Nic," he said worriedly.

"I know what you mean, but we seem to be hot on his trail. He may be nearby," Nicole reasoned. "Let's look around."

Just then both friends heard some meows and scratching noises. They followed the sounds to a nearby garage. Nicole and Sergio exchanged glances. Both ran to the door, but it was locked. Next they ran to the window of the garage in an attempt to look inside, but the window was boarded up, and no one was home. Sergio sounded discouraged as he panted, "I don't think we have any

INSIGHTS: *Reading as Thinking* ©
Charlesbridge Publishing • (800) 225-3214

BLACKLINE MASTER

UNIT 4 – Analyzing Characters
Assessment

191

choice but to pry the boards off the window; I'm sure he's in there.

"Before we do anything drastic, let's find out if he's okay. Fernando! Can you hear me? It's me, Nic — Nic and Serge. Are you in there?" Nicole shouted.

"Nic," came a weak cry from within. "It's dark in here, and I can't see. I'm hungry and scared! Help me, Nic!"

"Let's see if we can pull a board or two loose, just enough to get him out," said Nicole anxiously. Nicole and Sergio found a hammer and began to pry the boards loose. Eventually, two of the boards came free at once. Fernando's tear-streaked face was pressed against the window, smiling from ear to ear. Nicole told him how to unlock the window and crawl out. Fernando gratefully did everything Nicole said, beaming with relief.

"Wait, Nic. We have to rescue the kitten, too. That's why I got locked in there," Fernando said breathlessly. "I heard the kitten and walked in, and the door slammed shut behind me. The kitten's still in there. He'll starve to death if we leave him!"

"Okay, but hurry. It's late. Your mom's worried about you, and so were we. You know you shouldn't wander off without telling anyone, Fernando. That's dangerous," said Nicole.

"We were frantic. We almost called the police! Are you okay?" Sergio asked, stroking Fernando's hair to soothe him.

"Yes," said Fernando. Sergio helped Fernando back through the window, instructing him to be careful. Fernando disappeared into the garage, then reappeared bearing a small grey and white, mewing bundle of fur.

Fernando looked at them both happily. He gave the kitten to Sergio as he took Nicole's hand. Together they began to walk toward Fernando's house. Nicole and Sergio looked at each other over Fernando's head, unconvinced that he understood what he had done wrong.

Situation	Nicole's Responses	Sergio's Responses
1. Mrs. Alvarez says that Fernando is lost.	_____ _____ Trait(s): _____ _____	_____ _____ Trait(s): _____ _____
2. Nicole and Sergio find Fernando.	a. _____ b._____ _____ Trait(s): _____ _____	a. _____ b._____ _____ Trait(s): _____ _____

BLACKLINE MASTER

INSIGHTS: Reading as Thinking © Charlesbridge Publishing • (800) 225-3214

Character	Action/Dialogue	Reason Why
1. Sergio	wanted to organize a house-to-house search	_____ _____ _____
2. Nicole	wanted to start looking for Fernando at his house	_____ _____ _____
3. Sergio	wanted to call police when they found the jacket	_____ _____ _____
4. Nicole	did not want to call police when they found the jacket	_____ _____ _____
5. Nicole and Sergio	followed the sounds of the cat's meows	_____ _____ _____
6. Nicole and Sergio	pried the boards on the garage window loose	_____ _____ _____

INSIGHTS: Reading as Thinking ©
Charlesbridge Publishing • (800) 225-3214

BLACKLINE MASTER

UNIT 4 – **Analyzing Characters**
Assessment

193

Extension

Students who achieved mastery on the Assessment may do the Extension or read a book of their choice.

The Extension involves organizing information in a character differences chart, then using the chart as a basis for writing a story or essay. This method of writing – first putting character traits in a chart to compare and contrast, then using that chart as a basis for writing – is very useful for preparing both biographical reports and creative stories.

Encourage students to share what they have written. Ask volunteers to present their essays or stories, demonstrating how they used character differences charts in their writing.

Extension

This activity will give you an opportunity to take a closer look at your best qualities, talents, interests, ambitions, and so on, and to compare them with those of another student. You will make a character differences chart in which you and a classmate describe these aspects of yourselves, and then you will both use that chart as the basis for writing a story about the two of you. To do the activity, follow the steps below:

1. Pick a classmate to be your partner. Try to pick someone whom you don't know very well — this will make the activity more interesting!

2. Discuss with your partner some of the obvious differences between you. Work together to make a character differences chart with four or five categories describing the two of you. Each person should describe himself or herself in the chart. Try to include areas in which you differ. Some possibilities include
   a. best qualities
   b. talents
   c. interests (what you do in your free time)
   d. favorite things (CDs, TV shows, books, movies, foods)
   e. ambitions

3. Each of you will now write your own essay or story based on the character differences chart. You may write an essay describing you and your partner, or you may write a story describing you and your partner in an imaginary situation. Possible situations include
   a. You are members of a neighborhood committee that is starting an urban garden.
   b. You are shipwrecked on a desert island with nothing to eat but coconuts.
   c. You are assigned to work together to raise money for a local charity by having a yard sale.
   d. You are co-pilots for a space exploration vehicle that is about to run out of fuel.

   Have fun writing your story, and be sure to include the differences between you and your partner that were listed in your character differences chart.

4. Exchange your completed stories with your partner to read and enjoy.

Additional Activities

The Additional Activities are designed as the remediation for those students who did not achieve mastery on the Assessment. In this unit the Additional Activities provide visual aid in comparing opposite character traits, practice turning charts into stories, and several *Ask yourself* prompts.

❏ CHARTING CHARACTER DIFFERENCES

Make sure the students understand the difference between a character trait and a detail. Read aloud the following list and discuss how you tell whether each item is a character trait or a detail:

on the fund-raising committee (detail)
as shy as they come (trait)
rarely spoke at committee meetings (trait)
not very witty (trait)
liked by Leslie (detail)
dependable (trait)
generous (trait).

> Blackline
> Master Page
> **200**

Hand out copies of Blackline Master Pages 200. Have the students read the two Examples and ask them to verbalize what the two charts show: (1) traits out of order and (2) opposite traits across from each other. Drawing arrows to show the relationship of traits in each chart will help students visualize the mental process of organizing charts.

❏ IDENTIFYING CHARACTER TRAITS

> Blackline
> Master Page
> **201**

Have students read "Martin and Jamil" and underline the character traits in the passage. Discuss the traits they find. The traits are shown in parallel order as they will appear after students have rewritten them.

Answers for Blackline Master page 201

Martin	Jamil
as shy as they come	not the least bit shy
not very witty	very witty
dependable	an undependable person
very generous	never had time for anybody

❏ COMPLETING CHARACTER DIFFERENCES CHARTS

Tell the students to use the underlined phrases to complete the character differences chart. Call their attention to the *Think* prompts. The purpose of the arrows is to emphasize the parallel organization of opposite traits.

Ask students to compare their completed charts to the chart in the second Example on page 200. Discuss any differences.

❏ CHARTING DIFFERENCES

Write the following two sentences on the board.

1. Jared was by nature very aggressive in playing sports and interacting with people.
2. Caitlin had a strong individualistic streak and hated dressing like other people.

Identify these sentences as direct statements about Caitlin and Jared's traits. Ask students to reword each direct statement as dialogue and as an action that reveal the same character trait.

You may wish to refer students to the paragraphs about Delilah and Alex on student page 96 to discuss reasons for the characters' statements or behavior. Ask discussion questions such as the following.
   Why is Delilah lonely? (She enjoys being with people, but the desert is a quiet, relatively unpopulated place.)
   Why would a job as a student activities coordinator be particularly suited to Delilah? (She is friendly and gets along with people.)
   Why does Delilah call Alex patient? (He can work alone, painting the quiet, seemingly empty desert.)

Point out that Alex and Delilah have opposite character traits, and this can be seen in the reasons why they do or say things.

Blackline
Master Pages
202-203

Hand out copies of Blackline Master Page 202. Have students read the story, "Vic and Ramon," and underline the phrases that show opposite character traits. Help them find the first set of opposing traits to write in the chart. Have them complete the chart independently, providing help as necessary. Discuss their completed charts.

Continue with the second story, "Monica and Yannis."

Answers for Blackline Master Page 202

Vic	Ramon
1. not happy the season was over	glad the season was finally over
2. good at taking and giving advice	never listened to anyone's advice
3. You always knew exactly what he was talking about.	Everyone had a hard time finding out what was on his mind.
4. would usually tell you anything you wanted to know about his life	hardly ever talked about himself

If there still seems to be confusion, write each of the traits on a slip of paper. Give pairs of students an empty character chart. Mix up each group of slips, then have the student pairs arrange the traits so that opposite traits are across from each other.

Answers for Blackline Master Page 203

Monica	Yannis
1. disliked riding the subway	enjoyed riding the subway
2. an efficient person	not an efficient person
3. almost always in a serious mood	almost always in a good mood
4. did not like herself	liked himself

❏ WRITING WITH A CHARACTER CHART

Blackline Master Page 204

Hand out copies of Blackline Master Page 204. Explain that the phrases in the chart were taken from the paragraph about Tasha. Have students read the paragraph on Tasha and find details that are examples of each phrase in the chart. Help the students to write sentences that support the first trait given for Alice – "had a mind of her own." Then ask the students to complete the paragraph independently.

Accept all paragraphs that include each of the given traits. Encourage volunteers to explain how they used the chart to write their paragraph.

❏ DEDUCING REASONS

Blackline Master Pages 205-207

Hand out copies of Blackline Master Pages 205-207. Ask a volunteer to read the introductory paragraph on Blackline Master Page 205 aloud. Discuss the first Example and Explanation with the students, using the *Ask yourself* prompt. Ask students if the reason for a character's action is always stated directly in the passage. Elicit that they may need to infer the reason from clues in the text and their own experiences.

Ask a student to imagine a scene and complete a reason chart for each of the following actions:
   1. Liana tore down the street gasping for breath.
   2. Hiro pounded on Mr. Sumida's door.

Have each student think of a reason for one of the actions.

❏ CREATING REASON CHARTS

Students read two stories and complete reason charts for them. Call their attention to the *Ask yourself* prompts with the chart for the first story, "Teeth Marks on the Ham." Tell them to continue asking themselves *Why?* as they fill out the chart for the second story, "Fire!" Accept all reasonable answers.

Answers for Blackline Master Page 206
   1. he smelled the ham
   2. to protect his hands when taking the ham from the hot oven
   3. to take a taste of the ham
   4. to hear if his mother was still on the telephone
   5. the ham was hot
   6. to cool her burned mouth

Answers for Blackline Master Page 207
   1. to keep the house from catching fire
   2. thought firefighters would take care of it
   3. because Ellen was hosing down her roof
   4. busy hosing down roof
   5. to look for hose
   6. didn't want to see Pete's house burn

❏ SITUATION-RESPONSE CHARTS

Blackline
Master Pages
208-210

Hand out copies of Blackline Master Pages 208-210. Have students read the introductory paragraph.

Explain that *The Iliad* and *The Odyssey* are both classics by Homer. In *The Iliad*, Agamemnon leads the Greeks in a war against the Trojans. In *The Odyssey*, Odysseus and his men try to return home from the Trojan War, only to be lost at sea for ten years. Despite the war and violence in both works, the main characters often defeat their enemies through trickery and cleverness, as shown in "Odysseus in the Land of the Cyclops."

❏ CREATING SITUATION-RESPONSE CHARTS

Have the students read the story, "Odysseus in the Land of the Cyclops," and look over the two charts that follow it. Ask them what type of chart each one is (situation-response, action-reason). Discuss the first item of the situation-response chart with the class, then have students complete both charts as independently as possible. Discuss the responses and traits that the students chart and address any variations.

Answers for Blackline Master Page 209-210
Accept all reasonable inferred traits.
Odysseus's Responses
 1. hid in a corner and cowered
  Trait(s): afraid
 2. watched and trembled
  Trait(s): afraid, worried
 3. makes a plan to save his men
  Trait(s): clever, responsible
 4. hid in back of cave to wait until dawn
  Trait(s): clever
 5. had his men hide under rams' bellies
  Trait(s): shrewd, clever
Cyclops's Responses
 1. roared and sneered
  Trait(s): rude and nasty
 2. ate two sailors
  Trait(s): cruel, monstrous, barbaric
 3. blocks door with boulder so men can't escape while he is out
  Trait(s): cruel, mean
 4. staggered to entrance of cave to escape his attackers
  Trait(s): afraid
 5. checked backs of rams
  Trait(s): not clever, careful

Answers for Blackline Master Page 210
Accept all plausible reasons.
Reason Why
 6. curious to know more about who lives on island
 7. to prevent Greeks from escaping
 8. to put Polyphemus to sleep
 9. to get a chance to escape
 10. to escape; so Polyphemus can't tell they're escaping

Additional Activities

CHARTING CHARACTER DIFFERENCES

A character differences chart lists the differences between two characters opposite each other so that you read across the chart to see the differences. What is wrong with the chart in the Example below?

Example

Martin	Jamil
1. not very witty	1. never had time for anybody
2. as shy as they come	2. undependable
3. dependable	3. not the least bit shy
4. very generous	4. very witty

Explanation

Did you notice that the differences between Martin and Jamil are *not* listed across from each other in the chart? This makes comparing the two characters more difficult. Draw arrows [↔] between the opposite traits. For a chart of different traits to be useful, the opposite traits must be listed across from each other, as in the Example below.

Example

Martin	Jamil
1. not very witty ⟵	⟶ 1. very witty
2. as shy as they come	2. not the least bit shy
3. dependable	3. undependable
4. very generous	4. never had time for anybody

Explanation

In this chart, the differences between Martin and Jamil are listed across from each other. The four character differences in the chart are made up of phrases taken or inferred from a passage about the two characters. You will now read the passage about Martin and Jamil.

☐ IDENTIFYING CHARACTER TRAITS

❑ Underline the eight phrases that show the character traits listed in the Example you just read.

 Martin and Jamil

Martin and Jamil were on the fund-raising committee. Leslie, the committee chairperson, liked working with them both, even though they were very different from each other. Although Martin got along with individuals, he was as shy as they come when he was in a group. He rarely spoke at meetings, and Leslie had to ask him again and again for his ideas. Martin was also not very witty. While he laughed at everyone else's jokes, he never had a funny story of his own to tell. Leslie liked Martin, however, because he was dependable. He came to every meeting and always finished his reports on time. Leslie knew that Martin would be there until the deadline, even if he had to work until midnight. Martin was very generous with his time and knowledge. He showed other committee members how to use computer spreadsheets.

Jamil, on the other hand, never had time for anybody. When Leslie asked Jamil to help other committee members, he would say, "Let them figure it out themselves. I have work to do." Jamil was undependable. One day he would work for four hours straight, and another day he wouldn't even show up. Yet Jamil certainly made life interesting whenever he was there. He was not the least bit shy, and he always told the best jokes. Jamil was very witty.

☐ COMPLETING CHARACTER DIFFERENCES CHARTS

❑ Write the eight phrases you underlined in the chart. Remember to list the traits *opposite each other* in the chart.
  • Draw arrows between the opposite trait pairs.

Martin	Jamil
1. _____	_____

Think: Do the two phrases show opposite traits?

| 2. _____ | _____ |

Think: Do the two phrases show opposite traits?

| 3. _____ | _____ |

Think: Do the two phrases show opposite traits?

| 4. _____ | _____ |

Think: Do the two phrases show opposite traits?

◼ CHARTING DIFFERENCES

Now make a chart of character differences from the following passages. The passages are about two people who are very different from each other.

❏ Read each set of paragraphs. Pay special attention to the differences between the characters in each set.
- Underline the phrases that show how they are different from each other.
- Write the phrases in the charts that follow the paragraphs. Be sure to list the differences directly opposite each other.
- Draw arrows between the opposite trait pairs.

Vic and Ramon

Vic was not happy that the season was over, even though it had been a losing season. He remembered all the times his coach had told him not to take losing so seriously, and it seemed like good advice to Vic, who was good at both taking and giving advice. Vic had a soft, soothing voice that made you want to listen to whatever he had to say. He thought he might like to be a disc jockey some day. You always knew exactly what he was talking about. One of his favorite subjects was himself. Vic would usually tell you anything you wanted to know about his life, even his deepest feelings.

Ramon was glad that the season was finally over. His team had lost nearly all their games. His coach had tried to convince Ramon that losing a basketball game was not the end of the world, but Ramon never listened to anyone's advice. Even his best friends had a hard time convincing him of anything. Everyone had a hard time finding out what was on his mind. Ramon hardly ever talked about himself. Some people called him a walking secret. And when he did talk, he rarely could make himself understood. Ramon had a hard time getting through to people.

Vic	Ramon
1. _____	_____
2. _____	_____
3. _____	_____
_____	_____
4. _____	_____
_____	_____

INSIGHTS: Reading as Thinking ©
Charlesbridge Publishing • (800) 225-3214

Monica and Yannis

Monica disliked riding the subway to work. Every day she got on at Jefferson Park station, transferred at Belmont, and got off at Grand. Two blocks away was the office building where she worked as a computer programmer. Monica was an efficient person both on and off the job, and that was why she disliked riding the subway. It was not efficient; it was often late and sometimes broke down in cold weather. At the office, Monica worked with a graphic designer named Yannis. Yannis was always joking, and Monica did not like that because she was almost always in a serious mood. When Yannis would kid her about being so serious, she would frown at him and look away. Secretly, however, Monica liked talking to Yannis because he was not at all like her. The truth was that most of the time Monica did not like herself, so it was hard for other people to like her.

Whenever Yannis looked in the mirror, he smiled because he liked what he saw. Yannis liked himself, and he wondered why people like Monica did not like themselves. Yannis wished that she could loosen up and laugh a little. Yannis was almost always in a good mood, even when things were not going quite right, like the morning when the subway broke down, and he had to wait out in the cold for forty-five minutes. Yannis was not happy about it, of course, but he was not angry either. He knew that things had to break down once in a while. Things could not always be efficient, and neither could people. Yannis was not an efficient person himself, and maybe that is why he enjoyed riding the subway to work, even when it broke down.

Monica	Yannis
1. _____	_____
2. _____	_____
3. _____	_____
_____	_____
4. _____	_____
_____	_____

◼ WRITING WITH A CHARACTER CHART

Now that you've worked with character differences paragraphs and charts, you are ready to write a paragraph of your own. Have fun with it and be as creative as you like.

INSIGHTS: *Reading as Thinking* ©
Charlesbridge Publishing • (800) 225-3214

BLACKLINE MASTER

UNIT 4 – Analyzing Characters
Additional Activities

203

❑ Read the chart and paragraph about Tasha.

• Write a paragraph about Alice, using the four phrases in the chart that describe her.

Tasha	Alice
1. always did exactly as she was told	had a mind of her own
2. thought she was the nicest person	was modest about herself
3. careless of her pets	loved animals
4. only cared about herself	liked to help others

 Tasha and Alice

Tasha always did exactly as she was told. She never talked back in class, and she always followed Ms. Knott's instructions to the letter. Tasha's projects in her classes were neat, nicely printed, and just like the examples in the book. When Ms. Knott returned papers, Tasha always smiled at her grade and showed it to everyone sitting next to her. During recess, she would tell funny stories about her weekend and give advice to all of her friends. She thought she was the nicest person in the world. Tasha, however, did not always act this way. At home, she was careless of her pets, forgetting to feed them and rarely playing with them. Once she didn't clean her fish tank for a month and the fish almost died. Tasha never did anything for her pets or for other people on her own. She never volunteered to help her father clean the house or help with the laundry. She never made new juice when the pitcher was empty, replaced the paper towel roll when it was used up, or took out the garbage when it was full. Tasha only cared about herself.

Alice was someone who _____

_____

_____

_____

_____

_____

_____

_____

_____

_____

_____

_____

_____

_____

_____

_____

DEDUCING REASONS

We usually have reasons for our actions. So do the characters in stories. Now you will be analyzing paragraphs to figure out why characters do what they do and say what they say. Making a chart helps you do this kind of analysis.

Example

Passage: Kip smelled the ham. His mouth watered. He bent down and watched the ham cooking in the oven.

Chart:

Character	Action (or Dialogue)	Reason Why
Kip	mouth watered	_____
		_____

Ask yourself: Why did Kip's mouth water?

Explanation

Kip is the *character* in the passage. His mouth waters: that is the *action*. These two pieces of information are already written in the chart. *Why* does his mouth water? To learn why, ask yourself, "Why did Kip's mouth water?" Then think about what makes a person's mouth water and look back in the passage to find clues. Write your answer in the chart.

Check your answer: You should have written something resembling "He smelled the ham" or "because he smelled the ham cooking."

To complete a reason chart, you must follow three steps:

1. Find the place in the story where the action happens.
2. *Ask yourself*: Why did the character do this?
3. Think about what you know of similar situations and look back in the passage for clues. Use the clues to answer the question. Your answer is the reason, so you can write it in the reason column of the chart.

CREATING REASON CHARTS

The passage in the example is the beginning of the story "Teeth Marks on the Ham." As you create your reason chart, remember to follow the steps listed above.

❏ Read the following stories.
   • Complete the reason charts. Use the *Ask yourself* questions to help you.

Teeth Marks on the Ham

Kip smelled the ham. His mouth watered. He bent down and watched the ham cooking in the oven. His dog, Sydney, was with him, and Sydney's mouth was watering, too. But they would not be eating for another hour. Kip's mother was in the living room talking on the phone to Mr. Abdallah. Kip put on an oven mitt to protect his hand. He opened the oven and reached inside. He lifted the ham out and set it on the open oven door. The ham looked good, and very hot. Kip told Sydney to stay right where she was while he went to get a knife and fork. On the way, Kip listened at the door

— his mother was still talking on the phone. Then Kip heard a clatter and a plop. Quickly, he turned.

The ham was on the kitchen floor, sizzling. Sydney had knocked it down. Before Kip could stop her, Sydney bit into the sizzling ham. Sydney yelped in pain and jumped back from the ham. From the living room, Kip's mother asked what was the matter. "Don't worry, Mom, everything's all right," Kip said, picking up the ham and quickly putting it back in the oven. Sydney was at her water dish, drinking the cool water as fast as she could.

Later, at the dinner table, Kip's mother noticed teeth marks on the ham, and wondered where in the world they came from.

Character	Action	Reason Why
1. Kip	mouth watered	_____

Ask yourself: Why would Kip's mouth water?

| 2. Kip | put on an oven mitt | _____ |
| | | _____ |

Ask yourself: Why would Kip put on an oven mitt?

| 3. Kip | went to get a knife and fork | _____ |

Ask yourself: Why would Kip go to get a knife and fork?

| 4. Kip | listened at the door | _____ |
| | | _____ |

Ask yourself: Why would Kip listen at the door?

| 5. Sydney | yelped in pain | _____ |

Ask yourself: Why would Sydney yelp in pain?

| 6. Sydney | drank water as fast as she could | _____ |

Ask yourself: Why would Sydney drink water as fast as she could?

BLACKLINE MASTER

INSIGHTS: *Reading as Thinking* ©
Charlesbridge Publishing • (800) 225-3214

Fire!

Ellen Ahadzie lived in California among the dry hills above Malibu Beach. On one of those hills a fire had started, and the fire was coming her way. That was why she was out on her roof wetting it down with a hose. Meanwhile, her next-door neighbor, Pete Johnson, was out on his back porch watching a hockey game on TV. Pete had not even bothered to look at the fire; he was too busy relaxing. He called up to Ellen: "Hey, neighbor, trying to grow grass on your roof?" Ellen called back: "Your house might burn if you don't wet it down." Pete said: "You're a fool, Ellen. Leave it to the firefighters and come down here and watch the game." Ellen, however, remained on her roof. "What a character," Pete thought. "Why bother with that when the firefighters always stop the flames on time?"

Then, however, the game was interrupted by a news flash, and suddenly the TV screen showed a burning hill. Houses on the hill were going up in flames. The announcer, who was riding in a helicopter with the TV camera, said that the fire was raging out of control. Pete gasped, ran out in his yard, and looked up at the hill. There was the TV news helicopter — and there were the flames. Pete dashed to his garage and pulled out his hose. It was full of holes; he had not bothered to buy a new one.

Pete called up to Ellen for help. Ellen looked down at the frantic man. Pete Johnson had called her a fool, and she did not like that one bit. But she did not want to see her neighbor lose his house, so she told Pete that she had an extra hose and to go ahead and use it. Three minutes later, Pete was up on his roof wetting it down with Ellen's hose and telling his neighbor what a great person she was.

Character	Action	Reason Why
1. Ellen	wet her roof down	_____
2. Pete	watched TV and ignored the fire	_____
3. Pete	called Ellen a fool	_____
4. Ellen	did not come down to watch the game	_____
5. Pete	dashed to his garage	_____
6. Ellen	let Pete use her hose	_____

INSIGHTS: Reading as Thinking ©
Charlesbridge Publishing • (800) 225-3214

BLACKLINE MASTER

UNIT 4 – Analyzing Characters
Additional Activities

207

SITUATION-RESPONSE CHARTS

Characters in stories often do what they do in **response** to a **situation**, or something that happens in the story. What the characters do often tells you about their character traits. We use situation-response charts to help us understand more clearly what characters' responses to situations can tell us about them.

CREATING SITUATION-RESPONSE CHARTS

❑ Read the story, "Odysseus in the Land of the Cyclops," which is adapted from the classic *The Odyssey* by the Greek bard, Homer.
  • Complete the situation-response chart.
  • Complete the action-reason chart.

 Odysseus in the
Land of the Cyclops

As Odysseus and his men sailed across the sea, they came to the land of the Cyclops, a race of vicious giants who had only one eye, located in the center of their foreheads. The land was fertile and lush, full of flocks and herds. From their ships, the Greeks could see smoke rising softly from homes in the hills.

Curious to know more about the creatures who lived there, Odysseus went ashore with twelve of his crew. As they explored the land, they came to the cave of Polyphemus, (Pol•i•fee'•mus). He was a Cyclops who lived by himself as a shepherd. His cave was huge, big enough to house both the giant and all his flocks. Polyphemus was away grazing his herds when Odysseus and his crew entered the cave. Inside the cavern they found many lambs and rams (male sheep) and large supplies of tasty cheeses and rich cream. They immediately lit a fire and began to feast on the food they had found.

Suddenly, a great, dark shadow fell across the cave, and the Greeks looked up to see the Cyclops returning with his flocks. They quickly ran to the darkest corner of the cave and hid. The Cyclops drove his flocks into their pens and rolled a huge boulder across the mouth of the cave. As he stirred up the fire, he noticed the Greeks cowering in the corner. "Who are you?" he roared. "Robbers? Pirates?"

"We are the army of Agamemnon, protected by Zeus, king of the gods," Odysseus answered. "We sailed off our course and are lost. We have come to you for help."

"You are a fool to think I will help you," sneered Polyphemus. "I only help myself and do what I please. But, tell me, where is your boat?"

"It sank in a storm at sea," the crafty Odysseus replied. "Only my crew and I survived."

Polyphemus, who had been watching them with his one eye, seized two of the sailors and ate them, while the rest of the crew trembled with fear. When he finished his evening meal, the Cyclops lay down on the floor of the cave and slept.

(Continued on following page)

(Continued from previous page)

No sleep came to the wretched sailors, who were powerless to move the huge boulder from the door and escape.

The Cyclops awoke at dawn, ate two more of the men, and drove his flocks out of the cave, turning back to block the door with the boulder. As soon as he was gone, Odysseus and his men took a long pole from one of the sheep pens and sharpened it to a point. Odysseus and his men hid it in the back of the cave and waited for their chance to escape. When Polyphemus returned at sundown, Odysseus gave him a goblet of the wine the Greeks had brought with them from their ship. The Cyclops tasted the wine and laughed with delight. "This is a wonderful drink. Give me more."

Odysseus gave the giant a potion (drink), which he drank quickly. The potion soon clouded the wits of the Cyclops, and he sank heavily to the floor in a deep sleep. The sailors brought the sharpened pole from the corner of the cave and blinded the Cyclops.

Polyphemus staggered to the door of the cave to escape his attackers. He removed the boulder, and sat in the entrance. He stretched out his hands to prevent any of the sailors from escaping. The sailors hid in the back of the cave until the rams awoke at dawn. As the rams hurried to the door of the cave, eager to graze in the pasture, the sailors stopped them, and each sailor hid himself under the belly of one of the shaggy creatures, clinging to the long, woolly fleece.

As the rams passed through the door of the cave, the Cyclops felt their backs to make sure the sailors were not riding them to freedom. He never suspected that the clever Odysseus and his men clung to the bellies of the beasts. Once the rams had carried them to safety, the sailors loosened their grasps and ran back to their ship, which set sail without delay.

Situations	Odysseus's Responses	Cyclops's Responses
1. Cyclops discovers Odysseus and his sailors.	_____ _____ Trait(s):_____	_____ _____ Trait(s):_____
2. Cyclops gets hungry.	_____ _____ Trait(s):_____	_____ _____ Trait(s):_____

INSIGHTS: Reading as Thinking ©
Charlesbridge Publishing • (800) 225-3214

BLACKLINE MASTER

UNIT 4 – Analyzing Characters
Additional Activities

209

Situations	Odysseus's Responses	Cyclops's Responses
3. Odysseus and his crew are trapped in cave.	_____ _____ _____ Trait(s):_____	_____ _____ _____ Trait(s):_____
4. The Cyclops is blinded.	_____ _____ _____ Trait(s):_____	_____ _____ _____ Trait(s):_____
5. Sailors need to get past the Cyclops's hands.	_____ _____ _____ Trait(s):_____	_____ _____ _____ Trait(s):_____

Character	Action	Reason Why
6. Odysseus	decides to go ashore and finds cave	_____ _____
7. Cyclops	covers doorway with the boulder	_____ _____
8. Odysseus	gives the Cyclops potion of wine	_____ _____
9. Odysseus	blinds the Cyclops	_____ _____
10. The sailors	ride under the bellies of the rams	_____ _____

UNIT 4 – Analyzing Characters
Additional Activities

BLACKLINE MASTER

INSIGHTS: Reading as Thinking ©
Charlesbridge Publishing • (800) 225-3214

Re-assessment

The Re-assessment uses the same format as the Assessment and asks the students to demonstrate the same understandings.

Blackline Master Pages 212-215

Hand out copies of Blackline Master Pages 212-215. Ask the students to read the instructions carefully.

Collect, score, and record the Re-assessments before returning them and discussing them with the students. Accept all reasonable variations.

Answers for Blackline Master Pages 212-215

PART 1

Margot's Character Traits	Laurie's Character Traits
1. happy to graduate	sorry to graduate
2. liked being around a lot of people	never liked a lot of people around
3. had no fears	afraid of many aspects of city living
4. dressed in loud and bright colors	wore muted, plain colors
5. always laughing and talking loudly	a quiet person

PART 2

Elton's Responses	Nia's Responses
1. yells at Nia to stop, wants to get turtle out Trait(s): concerned, sympathetic	keeps vacuuming Trait(s): unconcerned, practical
2. imagines how it must feel, wants to get him out right away Trait(s): caring, imaginative, sympathetic	knows turtle is okay, wants to finish cleaning up Trait(s): practical, responsible, dutiful

1. liked food and being together with family
2. two weeks since they cleaned; wanted to take care of pets
3. she was hungry
4. curious to see what the turtles were up to
5. to clean wood shavings on rug that spilled from turtle tank
6. he was starving; wanted to eat sandwich first

❑ SCORING

Part 1: For scoring the Character Differences Chart, characteristics may be listed in any order, but each must be paired with its opposite. Each pair of traits has a value of 1 point.

Part 2: Score 1 point for each correct response or trait in the Situation-Response Chart and in the Action-Reason Chart.

Mastery Level: 15 out of 19 points.

Re-assessment

PART 1

- Read the passage.
- Complete the chart to show five differences between the two characters. Be sure to list opposite character traits directly across from each other in the chart.

Margot and Laurie

Margot was so happy to graduate. The years had just flown by. Margot, who had always liked being around a lot of people, had decided to move to New York City. She craved the excitement of a big city. Margot's parents feared for her safety in New York, but Margot had no fears. Margot's taste in clothes might be called extreme, too. Almost every time you saw her, she was dressed in loud and bright colors. Sometimes she looked like a patchwork quilt walking down the street. If you did not see Margot, you certainly could hear her. Wherever she was, she was always laughing and talking loudly. If volume were a way to measure intelligence, then Margot would have been a genius.

Laurie, on the other hand, was sorry to graduate. She had enjoyed school, and now it was over. Laurie was a quiet person. She often spent her weekends hiking alone, observing the plants and animals in respectful silence. Laurie usually wore practical clothes in muted, plain colors, the better to blend in with the trees. Laurie was happy to find a job in a small town. She preferred living in a small town because she never liked being around a lot of strangers. She said that crowds made her feel nervous. Laurie was afraid of many aspects of city living. She worried about the pollution and crime in big cities. She also feared confrontations with hurried, unsympathetic strangers. In a small town, she hoped to be on a first-name basis with most of the people.

Margot's Character Traits	Laurie's Character Traits
1. _____	_____
2. _____	_____
3. _____	_____
4. _____	_____
5. _____	_____

- Read the story, "The Clean-Up."
- Complete the situation-response chart and the action-reason chart

The Clean-Up

Saturday was Elton's favorite day of the week. It always started with the good smells of breakfast drifting into his bedroom from the kitchen. He would go into the kitchen to find his father at the stove, frying eggs and popping bread into the toaster. His older sister, Nia, was usually up before him, and Elton would join her at the table.

When their mother joined them, they all enjoyed the huge, hot breakfast their father had cooked. They laughed and talked as they ate, and all of them helped do the dishes when they had finished their meal.

This Saturday, after his parents left for work at the store they owned on Madison Street, Nia said, "I think we should take care of our pets. It's been two weeks since we worked on the cages and cleaned the filters in the fish tanks."

Elton nodded in agreement. Both Nia and Elton loved animals, and their collection of pets was large enough to be considered a small zoo. Besides a dog and two cats, they had three kinds of fish, hamsters, birds, and a family of turtles. Nia spread newspaper on the floor in the living room while Elton went to their bedroom and got the hamster cage. Elton cleaned the fish tank while Nia tackled the hamster cage. Both attacked the bird cages; that took a

seemingly endless amount of time.

As Elton came into the living room with the aquarium where the family of turtles lived, Nia said, "I'm hungry. While you clean up the turtle tank, I'll fix some lunch. After we eat, we'll clean the house so it looks nice when Mom and Dad come home."

"OK," Elton said, not really wanting to clean the house, but eager to eat. "I'm starving."

Nia grinned and went into the kitchen. Elton began to clean the turtle tank. He smiled as he worked. The turtles were his favorite animals. When he finished, he picked up the baby, Rapido, and tried to pet his head. Rapido looked worried and pulled his head back into his shell. Elton laughed, put him back in the aquarium, and went to the kitchen.

As Nia and Elton ate, Growls, their dog, came up from the basement and went into the living room. Noticing the aquarium in the middle of the floor, Growls began to sniff at the bottom of the tank, curious to see what the turtles were up to. One of the turtles resented Growls's wet nose sniffing at it, and the turtle bit the dog's nose. Growls jumped back, knocking the tank over. The turtles began to crawl all over the living room. Growls chased after them, knocking the wood shavings, charcoal, and sand from the newspaper onto the rug.

(Continued on following page)

INSIGHTS: Reading as Thinking ©
Charlesbridge Publishing • (800) 225-3214

BLACKLINE MASTER

UNIT 4 – Analyzing Characters
Re-assessment

213

(Continued from previous page)

Nia and Elton ran in from the kitchen, chased Growls back to the basement, and retrieved the turtles from the floor. When they had finished, Elton started for the kitchen. "Where are you going?" Nia asked.

"To finish eating."

"No, you aren't. We've got to clean this up before it stains the rug."

"It can wait until I finish my sandwich. I'm starving," Elton moaned.

"You pick up the papers," Nia said harshly as she took out the vacuum cleaner. "Hurry up, so I can vacuum."

Elton made a face, got down on his knees, and slowly began to crumple the newspapers. Nia turned on the vacuum cleaner and began to move it quickly back and forth over the rug. Elton looked up just as Rapido, who had been hiding under a chair and was scared by the noise of the vacuum, tried to crawl across the rug to safety under the sofa. Elton watched in horror as the vacuum rolled over Rapido, and the baby turtle disappeared. "Turn it off, turn it off!" Elton yelled. Nia ignored him and kept on vacuuming. "Turn it off, Nia! Rapido's inside, buried alive in all that dirt."

Nia turned off the vacuum cleaner, annoyed by the panic in Elton's voice. "It won't hurt him, Elton. Rapido's tucked up inside his shell. We'll take him out when I'm done."

"But he might be hurt. To Rapido, it must be like being sucked up by a tornado."

"Don't worry so much. Turtles never get hurt. Besides, I have to clean up this mess," Nia argued.

"Let me take him out," Elton demanded. "He must be scared to death. With all that dirt blowing around in the bag, it must be like a hurricane in there."

"I can see I'm not going to get anything vacuumed until you take the turtle out, so go ahead and get him," Nia said, handing him the vacuum cleaner.

Elton quickly opened the bag and found Rapido at the bottom. Unfortunately, there was no way for Elton to tell if Rapido was dead or alive. He tried knocking on the shell, but Rapido would not stick his head out. Then he tried listening for a heartbeat, but heard nothing. Nor could he pull out a foot to feel for a pulse. Finally, he had it! He ran to the bathroom sink and rinsed the dusty creature off. Delighted to be in his home element again, Rapido stuck his head out of his shell to see what was going on.

Situations	Elton's Responses	Nia's Responses
1. Nia vacuums up the turtle.	_____ _____ Trait(s):_____ _____	_____ _____ Trait(s):_____ _____
2. The turtle is stuck in the vacuum cleaner.	_____ _____ Trait(s):_____ _____	_____ _____ Trait(s):_____ _____

Character	Action	Reason Why
1. Elton	enjoyed Saturday breakfast	_____ _____ _____
2. Nia	decided to clean the cages	_____ _____
3. Nia	fixed lunch	_____ _____
4. Growls	sniffed bottom of turtle tank	_____ _____
5. Nia	got the vacuum	_____ _____
6. Elton	wanted to wait to finish cleaning	_____ _____ _____

INSIGHTS: Reading as Thinking ©
Charlesbridge Publishing • (800) 225-3214

BLACKLINE MASTER

UNIT 4 – **Analyzing Characters**
Re-assessment

215

Writing Connection

Making a Movie: Have small groups of students create plots for movies. Each group needs to decide on answers for the following questions and write them down.

1. Where does the movie take place? Some possibilities: in a large city, on an airplane, in a small town on another continent, in outer space.
2. What is the goal of the adventure? Some possibilities: rumors of a lost treasure, the need to rescue someone, an invasion from outer space, a shortage of an essential item (food, fuel, water, etc.).
3. What happens during the adventure? Make up at least three incidents.

Then each group member writes the following:

1. Describe one character including his or her name, age, and occupation.
2. Decide how the character first gets involved in the plot.
3. In a situation-response chart, list how the character reacts to each incident in the plot.
4. In an action-response chart, record why the character responds as he or she does.

Have each group read what they have created to the class. One student can begin by reading the basic plot for his or her group. Each student can then describe the character he or she has created.

If you wish, the groups may then put their plots and characters together into plays and perform them. If you have access to video equipment, you may want to let the students film their movies.

UNIT 5

Comprehending Complex Information

Learning Objectives

In this unit the student will analyze complex information commonly found in textbooks by

- identifying three basic grammatical structures of sentences: simple, compound, and complex

- recognizing how different sentence structures typically express condensed information about the 5W's plus How

- identifying sequential information about signal words showing simultaneous events and chronological order

- placing out-of-order events in chronological order

- comparing subjects and their attributes

- writing plot summaries

Lesson 1: Recognizing simple, compound, and complex sentences
Lesson 2: Analyzing a sequence of events
Lesson 3: Making sequence charts
Lesson 4: Comparing information
Lesson 5: Comprehending condensed information
Assessment: Blackline Master Pages 258-260
   Extension: Comparing characters, or
   Remediation: Additional Activities on Blackline Master Pages 269-280
Re-assessment: Blackline Master Pages 283-285

Purpose of this Unit

For the students to understand the important elements in complex text, it is essential for them to understand basic types of sentence structure. Condensed, sequential, or comparative information is used to express different types of information.

Activating Prior Knowledge

Ask students if they take notes when they read. If some do, ask them how they know what to look for and how they organize their notes. List their responses on the board and discuss them with the class. Tell students that this unit will help them take notes for three types of information.

Prerequisites and Introduction

❏ COMPLEX INFORMATION

Have the students read the introductory paragraphs. Write on the chalkboard the title of a story or play with which most students are familiar. Ask a volunteer to answer each of the 5W's plus How questions for the piece you have chosen.

Point out that the first lesson will focus on basic grammatical structures. Tell the students they will need to use their knowledge of the basic structure of simple sentences to understand more complex sentences in this unit.

Investigation A: REVIEWING THE 5W'S PLUS HOW

Give students a few minutes to reread the six questions. Then, ask them to cover the list and write the questions.

Answer Key

1. Who or what is the sentence about?
2. What happened?
3. Where did the events take place?
4. When did the events take place?
5. Why did something happen?
6. How did something happen?

PREREQUISITES AND INTRODUCTION

❏ COMPLEX INFORMATION

Textbook information is often presented in a complex manner. Frequently, an author will write a single sentence that contains all or most of the 5W's plus How: *who, what, when, where, why,* and *how.* When this happens, the 5W's plus How are usually given in different parts of the sentence. *Who,* for example, is usually the subject of a sentence, whereas *when* and *where* usually do not function as subjects in the sentence. Thus, understanding the grammatical structure of the sentence helps you understand how to identify the 5W's plus How information.

The purposes of this unit are:

1. To review basic grammatical structures of sentences
2. To identify three types of complex information
   a. sequential information
   b. comparative information
   c. condensed 5W's plus How
3. To give you some strategies to help you organize your notes and better understand what you read.

First, here are the 5W's plus How questions which you should ask yourself as you read.

1. Who or what is it about?   4. When did the events take place?

2. What happened?   5. Why did something happen?

3. Where did it take place?   6. How did something happen?

Investigation A: REVIEWING THE 5W'S PLUS HOW

❏ Think about the list of questions above. Then cover the list with your hand, and write the questions you should ask yourself when you read complex information.

1. Who _____

2. What _____

3. Where _____

4. When _____

5. Why _____

6. How _____

SIMPLE SENTENCES: A REVIEW OF BASIC TERMS

Any sentence, however short or long, that contains one subject and one predicate, expresses a complete thought, and can stand alone is called a *simple sentence*.

The **subject** of a sentence is usually a noun (a person, place, thing, or event) or pronoun (a word used in place of one or more nouns; for example, <u>I</u>, <u>you</u>, <u>he</u>, <u>she</u>, <u>it</u>, <u>we</u>, <u>they</u>). The subject tells you *who* or *what* the sentence is about.

Example

Subjects

    1. <u>The children</u> played baseball.
    2. <u>They</u> played baseball.

Explanation

<u>The children</u> in sentence 1, and <u>they</u> in sentence 2, are the subjects because these words tell *who* each sentence is about.

The **predicate** consists of the verb and whatever other words tell something about the subject: *what, where, when, why,* and *how* something happened.

Example

Predicates

    1. The children <u>played</u>.
    2. The children <u>played baseball</u>.
    3. The children <u>played baseball with their friends last night</u>.

Explanation

In sentence 1, the predicate consists only of the verb <u>played</u>. In sentence 2, the predicate consists of the verb <u>played</u> and the word <u>baseball</u> which tells you what the subject — <u>the children</u> — did. In sentence 3, the predicate consists of the verb <u>played</u> plus all the other words in the sentence. The predicate usually tells you *what* the subject did, *where* the subject did it, *when* the subject did it, and/or *how* the subject did it.

INSIGHTS: Reading as Thinking ©
Charlesbridge Publishing • (800) 225-3214

❏ SIMPLE SENTENCES: A REVIEW OF BASIC TERMS

Ask a student to read the first paragraph aloud. You may wish to have volunteers write the characteristics of a simple sentence on the chalkboard. They should include:

- contains one subject

- contains one predicate

- expresses a complete thought

- can stand alone

- length does not matter

Ask another student to read the paragraph that defines *subject*. Have the class read the first example. Write the two sentences on the board and read aloud the Explanation. Point out that the underlined words in each sentence can be replaced with other *who* words. Ask the students to suggest substitutions, such as <u>The team</u> or <u>We</u>.

Ask another volunteer to read the paragraph that defines *predicate*. Write the three predicate examples on the chalkboard. Have students identify the same verb in each sentence, and elicit the idea that all three have one predicate, despite the differences in length.

Have students read the Example and the first paragraph of the Explanation. Have students read the second paragraph of the Explanation. Explain that a *complete subject* includes the simple subject and all its modifiers, and that a *complete predicate* includes the verb and all its modifiers. Ask the students to notice that the underline shows the *complete subject* and the brackets enclose the *complete predicate*.

Investigation A: RECOGNIZING SUBJECTS AND PREDICATES

Have students read the directions, underline the complete subject, and bracket the complete predicate. Do the first one with them. Ask them:

• Who or what is the sentence about?
• What is the verb?
• What are the modifiers?
• What do they modify?

Answer Key

1. <u>Noisy and excited teams</u> [lined up to play baseball].
2. <u>The sun</u> [rises].
3. <u>The brilliant ball of orange fire</u> [rises every morning to create a beautiful dawn].
4. <u>The ferocious pack of angry wolf-like dogs</u> [barks loudly and noisily outside the peaceful village every night].
5. <u>The students</u> [read].
6. <u>All the students in the school</u> [read their books quietly and thoughtfully].
7. <u>The quarterback</u> [threw the ball].

 Example

Simple Sentences

Simple Sentence = Subject + Predicate and expresses a complete thought

1. <u>Campers</u> [marched]. = <u>subject</u> + [predicate]
2. <u>The tired, dirty, and footsore campers</u> [marched wearily over the hill, through the woods, across the creaky old bridge, and, finally, into the camp beyond the pine forest.] = <u>subject</u> + [predicate]

Explanation

Both sentences are simple sentences with a subject, a predicate, and a complete thought. Sentence 1 has only <u>campers</u> as a subject and [marched] as a predicate (noun + verb). Sentence 2 is very descriptive, but it is still a simple sentence.

In sentence 2, "The tired, dirty, and footsore" modifies <u>campers</u>, so it is part of the subject. In sentence 2, "wearily over the hill, through the woods, across the creaky old bridge, and, finally, into the camp beyond the pine forest" modifies the verb <u>marched</u>, so it is part of the predicate.

Investigation : RECOGNIZING SUBJECTS AND PREDICATES

❑ In each of the following sentences underline the subject, including its modifiers.
  • Put brackets [ ] around the predicate, including its modifiers.

1. Noisy and excited teams lined up to play baseball.
2. The sun rises.
3. The brilliant ball of orange fire rises every morning to create a beautiful dawn.
4. The ferocious pack of angry wolf-like dogs barks loudly and noisily outside the peaceful village every night.
5. The students read.
6. All the students in the school read their books quietly and thoughtfully.
7. The quarterback threw the ball.
8. The tall, athletic quarterback for the high school football team threw the ball quickly to avoid the oncoming tacklers.
9. The United States space shuttle, the *Columbia*, landed successfully after completing its historic mission.

8. <u>The tall, athletic quarterback for the high school football team</u> [threw the ball quickly to avoid the oncoming tacklers].
9. <u>The United States space shuttle, the *Columbia*</u> [landed successfully after completing its historic mission].

COMPOUND SUBJECTS IN SIMPLE SENTENCES

A simple subject consists of one noun or pronoun. However, a sentence may have a **compound subject** with two or more nouns or pronouns. Compound subjects are generally connected by the **conjunctions** *and* and *or*. Both simple and compound subjects tell you *who* or *what* the sentence is about.

Example

Simple and Compound Subjects

1. <u>Basketball</u> is an exciting sport.
2. <u>Basketball</u> and <u>football</u> are exciting sports.
3. <u>Basketball</u>, <u>football</u>, and <u>hockey</u> are exciting sports.

Explanation

The three sentences provide increasingly more information in the subject. The first sentence is a simple sentence with a simple subject. The second and third sentences are simple sentences with compound subjects. In the second sentence, the conjunction *and* separates the two nouns. In the third sentence, the series of three nouns is separated by commas and the conjunction *and*.

Investigation **A: RECOGNIZING COMPOUND SUBJECTS**

❏ In each of the following sentences, underline the complete compound subject.

1. The doctor and the specialist examined the sick patient.

2. The tall boy sitting at the end of the row and the girl sitting beside him were chosen to play the leads in the school play.

3. The ambitious young woman and her new boss considered the ways the work could be finished most quickly.

4. The American and Canadian governments have been friendly neighbors for years.

5. Alaska and Texas are the two largest states in the nation.

INSIGHTS: Reading as Thinking ©
Charlesbridge Publishing • (800) 225-3214

Answer Key
1. The doctor and the specialist
2. The tall boy sitting at the end of the row and the girl sitting beside him
3. The ambitious young woman and her new boss
4. The American and Canadian governments
5. Alaska and Texas

COMPOUND SUBJECTS IN SIMPLE SENTENCES

Explain that while a sentence must have at least one subject, it may have more than one subject. Ask a volunteer to read the introductory paragraph aloud. Ask another student to read aloud the three sentences in the Example. Have students read the Explanation. Ask them to point out the compound subjects in the second and third sentences. Help students distinguish between *complete subjects* and *compound subjects*. Elicit the idea that a complete subject has one noun with modifiers, whereas a compound subject has more than one noun, as in Example sentences 2 and 3. Have students think of other examples of compound subjects, using conjunctions to join the nouns.

Investigation A: RECOGNIZING COMPOUND SUBJECTS

Tell students that the following sentences may have more than one subject and the subjects may have modifiers. Ask the students to underline the complete compound subject in each sentence. Read the first sentence aloud and elicit the compound subject: <u>The doctor and the specialist</u>. Have the students identify the complete compound subject in sentences 2-5. Discuss the subjects and modifiers they found.

❏ COMPOUND PREDICATES IN SIMPLE SENTENCES

Have students read the introductory paragraph, the Example, and the Explanation. Ask a volunteer to read the three Example sentences aloud. Discuss the difference between a complete predicate and a compound predicate. Point out the use of conjunctions and commas to separate the verbs in sentences 2 and 3.

Investigation A: RECOGNIZING COMPOUND PREDICATES

Have students read the instructions. Remind them that complete compound predicates may contain multiple verbs as well as modifiers. Discuss the predicates they underlined and why they are complete and compound.

Answer Key

1. mowed the lawn
2. mowed and raked the lawn after lunch
3. was singing patriotic songs
4. was standing in the middle of the civic center and singing patriotic songs
5. stood patiently in the rain for two hours and waited for the box office to open

❑ COMPOUND PREDICATES IN SIMPLE SENTENCES

A simple predicate consists of one verb plus all its modifiers. However, a sentence may have a **compound predicate** with two or more verbs with modifiers. In sentences with compound predicates, two or more actions are stated. The compound predicates or actions are generally connected by the conjunctions *and* or *but*. The most important thing to keep in mind when you read sentences with compound predicates is that both simple and compound predicates tell you *what* happened, *why* something happened, or *how* something happened.

Example

Simple and Compound Predicates

1. Calvin <u>washed the dishes</u>.
2. Calvin <u>washed and dried the dishes</u>.
3. Calvin <u>washed, dried, and put away the dishes</u>.

Explanation

The first sentence is a simple sentence with a simple predicate. Sentences 2 and 3 are simple sentences with compound predicates. In the second sentence, the conjunction *and* separates the two verbs. In the third sentence, the series of verbs is separated by commas and the conjunction *and*. In all three sentences, the actions are related to doing something with the dishes.

Investigation **A**: RECOGNIZING COMPOUND PREDICATES

❑ Read each of the following sentences and underline the complete compound predicate.

1. Asma mowed the lawn.
2. Asma mowed and raked the lawn after lunch.
3. The boys' chorus was singing patriotic songs.
4. The boys' chorus from the Madison School was standing in the middle of the civic center and singing patriotic songs.
5. The crowd of loyal fans stood patiently in the rain for two hours and waited for the box office to open.

INSIGHTS: Reading as Thinking ©
Charlesbridge Publishing • (800) 225-3214

UNIT 5 – Comprehending Complex Information **143**

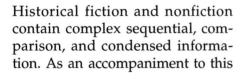

Literature Connection

Historical fiction and nonfiction contain complex sequential, comparison, and condensed information. As an accompaniment to this unit, ask students to read a book. Three well-written nonfiction books are:

Meyer, Carolyn, *In a Different Light: Growing Up in a Yup'ik Eskimo Village in Alaska.*

Finklestein, Norman H., *Thirteen Days / Ninety Miles: The Cuban Missile Crisis.*

Fisch, Robert O., *Light from the Yellow Star: A Lesson of Love from the Holocaust.*

❑ COMPOUND SENTENCES

When you read a passage or textbook that has detailed information, you will find many **compound sentences**. A compound sentence consists of two or more sentences joined by *and, or,* or *but.**
Compound sentences contain two or more complete thoughts; because of this, they are sometimes difficult to understand. It is important to identify the subject of each part of a compound sentence. The second part of a compound sentence may use a pronoun to refer to a noun in the first part. So, when you read a compound sentence, make sure you check to see which nouns the pronouns replace.

Example

Compound Sentence

Carl's [bat] connected cleanly with the ball, (and) [it] sailed high over the center field fence.

Explanation

There are two independent thoughts. The first independent thought is underlined and separated from the second thought by the word *and*, which is circled. Boxes are drawn around the two subjects. The sentence has two subjects and two separate points of information, which are related. The relationship is between the pronoun *it* in the second part and the noun *ball* in the first part.

Investigation **A: ANALYZING COMPOUND SENTENCES**

❑ Read each of the following sentences.
  • Underline the first independent thought.
  • Circle the word or punctuation used to join the two independent thoughts.
  • Draw a box around the simple subjects of each independent thought.

1. The doctor examined the little boy's broken arm, and then she set it in a cast.

2. They are next-door neighbors, but they don't walk home together.

3. Vicki will play soccer after school, or she will go to the museum.

4. I heard a good story today; would you like to hear it?

5. The cast of the play rehearsed for weeks, and the director was proud of them for working so hard.

And, *or*, and *but* are conjunctions. You can also use a semicolon (;) to join the two independent thoughts.

INSIGHTS: Reading as Thinking ©
Charlesbridge Publishing • (800) 225-3214

❑ COMPOUND SENTENCES

Have the students read the introductory paragraph. Explain that a compound sentence must contain two or more complete thoughts. A complete thought can stand on its own. Ask the students to read the Example and Explanation of a compound sentence.

Ask the students to point out the two independent thoughts, the conjunction that joins these two thoughts, and the subject of each thought.

Investigation A: ANALYZING COMPOUND SENTENCES

Have students read the instructions and paraphrase the three tasks. When they have analyzed the sentences, ask volunteers to explain their analyses. In sentence 4, the two thoughts are joined by a semicolon, but no conjunction. Provide other examples of independent thoughts joined in this manner.

Answer Key

1. Underline: The doctor . . . broken arm. Circle: and. Box: doctor, she

2. Underline: They are next door neighbors. Circle: but. Box: they, they

3. Underline: Vicki will . . . school. Circle: or. Box: Vicki, she

4. Underline: I heard a good story today. Circle: semicolon. Box: I, you

5. Underline: The cast . . . for weeks. Circle: and. Box: cast, director

❑ COMPLEX SENTENCES

Have the students read the paragraph defining complex sentences and the Example and Explanation that follow. Emphasize that although a complex sentence has two or more thoughts, only one is complete and can stand on its own.

Ask volunteers to read each Example sentence aloud. Have the class identify the two thoughts and which thought can stand alone. Point out how dependent clauses add information about the 5W's plus How.

Investigation A: ANALYZING COMPLEX SENTENCES

Have a student read aloud the first sentence. Ask students to identify the dependent clause. (that you borrowed from Mary) Point out that the clause describes the book. Ask students which of the 5W's plus How that would be. (What) When they have analyzed all five sentences, discuss the answers.

Answer Key

1. Underline: that you borrowed from Mary. The clause tells you what book.
2. Underline: so he could see into the cookie jar. The clause tells you why.
3. Underline: before you go to bed. The clause tells you when.
4. Underline: who lives in Canada. The clause tells you who.
5. Underline: where she could reach it easily. The clause tells you where.

❑ COMPLEX SENTENCES

Another type of sentence that you will find when reading detailed information is the **complex sentence**. A complex sentence has two or more thoughts, but only one of them is complete and can stand alone. The part that cannot stand alone is called a **dependent clause**. The dependent clause has a subject and a verb but it is not a complete thought.

Example

Complex Sentences

(when) <u>When the year began</u>, business was better than it is now.

(who) The girls, <u>who often practiced together</u>, played the game well.

(why) The seedlings wilted <u>because they had not been watered</u>.

(how) Ricardo gave the speech <u>as if he had been practicing for years</u>.

Explanation

Each complex sentence has one underlined dependent clause. Notice that a dependent clause can come at the beginning, middle, or end of a sentence.

Investigation : **ANALYZING COMPLEX SENTENCES**

❑ Read each of the following sentences and underline each dependent clause.
• Write the kind of *5W's + How* information each dependent clause gives.

1. Is this the book that you borrowed from Mary? _____

2. He stood on tiptoe so he could see into the cookie jar._____

_____

3. Put the cat out before you go to bed. _____

_____

4. My aunt, who lives in Canada, is coming for a visit._____

_____

5. She put the telephone down on the table where she could reach it easily. _____

_____

Writing **Writing Connection**

Compound and Complex Sentences: Have students write a paragraph of at least five sentences on a topic of their choice, using only compound and complex sentences. After they are done, ask them to exchange papers, and underline the compound sentences and bracket [ ] the complex sentences.

---

2 Analyzing A Sequence of Events

ANALYZING A SEQUENCE OF EVENTS

In Strategy Lesson 1, you found that the structure of a sentence can help you to understand complex information. In this lesson, you will learn strategies for organizing complex information. Your knowledge of sentence structure will help you to do this.

: REVIEWING SENTENCE STRUCTURE

❏ Circle the letter of the phrase that tells what each sentence is.

1. The Egyptians in Egypt and the Incas in South America had highly advanced civilizations.

   a. simple sentence with a compound subject   b. compound sentence

2. As soon as the game began, the home team took an early lead.

   a. complex sentence   b. compound sentence

3. Mark finished his term paper, and he made sure it was handed in early.

   a. complex sentence   b. compound sentence

4. In the sixteenth century, the Incas in South America had surgeons who knew about disinfectants and burned flour in the "operating room" to kill germs before operating.

   a. simple sentence with a compound predicate   b. compound sentence

5. Thomas Edison was a brilliant inventor, and his inventions were a wonder for his time.

   a. complex sentence   b. compound sentence

◼ THREE TYPES OF COMPLEX DESCRIPTION

Now the focus will be on sentences and paragraphs which contain complex information. To comprehend complex information fully, it is useful to identify different types of information because each type requires a different reading strategy.

146 UNIT 5 – Comprehending Complex Information

INSIGHTS: Reading as Thinking ©
Charlesbridge Publishing • (800) 225-3214

Have students read the introductory paragraph. Ask volunteers to review the definitions of simple sentences, compound sentences, and complex sentences.

Investigation A: REVIEWING SENTENCE STRUCTURE

Have students read the instructions and identify each kind of sentence. Have them discuss why each sentence represents a particular type.

Answer Key

1. a. simple sentence with a compound subject
2. a. complex sentence
3. b. compound sentence
4. a. simple sentence with a compound predicate
5. b. compound sentence

❏ THREE TYPES OF COMPLEX DESCRIPTION

Have the students read the paragraph describing the three types of complex information.

Note: Point out that in this unit, the word *complex* is used to describe sentences with dependent clauses and to describe complicated, multi-faceted prose. The connection between complex sentences and complex information is that both have parts that depend on other parts to create meaning.

❏ THREE TYPES OF COMPLEX DESCRIPTION *continued*

Have three more volunteers read the three types of complex information, pausing after each student has read to elicit examples. Ask the class where they might find such information and discuss their responses.

Investigation A: DEFINING TERMS

Tell the class to re-read the descriptions of the three types of complex information before defining them.

Answer Key
1. Complex sequential information
2. places, things, features
3. included all or most of the 5W's plus How information in a single sentence containing a compound subject and predicate

❏ WHAT IS A SEQUENCE?

Have a student read aloud the paragraph defining *sequence*. Ask volunteers to give an example of sequence, such as the order in which they attend classes on a given day. List the sequence on the board and have students put them in a compound sentence and in a simple sentence with a compound predicate.

Three common types of complex information are:

1. <u>Complex Sequential Information</u>
   This is a description of a sequence of events in which the order of events described is not the order in which they really happened.

2. <u>Comparative Information</u>
   This is information in which two or more persons, places, or things are compared in terms of several features.

3. <u>Condensed 5W's Plus How Information</u>
   This is information in which an author has included all or most of the 5W's plus How information in a single sentence containing compound subjects and predicates.

Investigation **A**: **DEFINING TERMS**

❏ Complete the sentences below about the three types of complex information.

1. _____ is information

   in which the sequence of events is presented out of order.

2. Comparative information compares two or more persons, _____ ,

   or _____ in terms of two or more _____ .

3. Condensed 5W's plus How information refers to sentences in which the author has

   _____

   _____ .

It is helpful to develop specific thinking strategies to comprehend these three types of complex information. You will learn these strategies in this unit.

▣ WHAT IS A SEQUENCE?

In this unit, **sequence** means the order of events in time. A series of events is usually expressed in a compound sentence, or in a simple sentence with a compound predicate.

INSIGHTS: Reading as Thinking ©
Charlesbridge Publishing • (800) 225-3214

UNIT 5 – Comprehending Complex Information **147**

THE IMPORTANCE OF SEQUENCE OF EVENTS: TWO TYPES

Usually, the order of events is important. Recipes, for example, call for a specific sequence of events, which must be followed exactly. Similarly, in building things, in filling out forms, even in creating works of art, certain activities must be done before others. Imagine trying to paint a portrait without first looking at the person.

Understanding the order in which events happened is especially crucial in reading fiction and history. There are two types of events:

1. **Chronological**: Events that occur one after the other are called *sequential* or *chronological* events. Putting your shoe on and then tying the laces are chronological events. Running for an office, being elected, and then being sworn in are sequential events.

2. **Simultaneous**: Events that occur at the same time are called *simultaneous* events. You can walk and talk simultaneously. A person can ride a bicycle, sing, and enjoy the scenery at the same time.

Investigation A: DEFINING TERMS AND WRITING EXAMPLES

❏ Complete the sentences.

1. Events that take place one after the other are called _____

   events or _____ events.

2. Make up your own example in which one event must take place after another.

   _____

   _____

3. Events that take place at the same time are called _____ events.

4. Think of an example of two or more events that take place at the same time.

   _____

   _____

❏ THE IMPORTANCE OF SEQUENCE OF EVENTS: TWO TYPES

Have a student define *sequence* (the order of events in time). Ask volunteers to read the paragraph and the definitions of the two types of sequence. Ask the class to distinguish between chronological and simultaneous events. It may help to have them envision chronological events as a time line, and simultaneous events occurring at one point on this time line.

Investigation A: DEFINING TERMS AND WRITING EXAMPLES

Students complete the sentences and write their own examples of chronological and simultaneous events. Discuss several of their examples for each type of sequence.

Answer Key

1. sequential, chronological
2. Accept all reasonable examples.
3. simultaneous
4. Accept all reasonable examples.

❏ SIGNAL WORDS SHOWING SIMULTANEOUS EVENTS

Have the students read the introductory paragraph and the simultaneous events signals. Have volunteers read the Example sentences. Read aloud the Explanation and have the class suggest the words to complete the sentences. Explain that the underlined signal words in the Example can be replaced with other signal words. Ask the class to suggest alternatives from the list.

Investigation A: SIMULTANEOUS EVENT SIGNALS

After students write as many of the signal words as they can remember, have them check their list and add any that they left out.

 Curriculum Connection

Charting Historical Events: Divide the class into groups. Have each group choose a time period they want to research. It could be as broad as the Industrial Revolution or as specific as the Cuban Missile Crisis. Ask them to research the event in the library, then present the important dates and their descriptions in a sequence chart.

▣ SIGNAL WORDS SHOWING SIMULTANEOUS EVENTS

Sequence is often indicated by a **signal word**. Here are signal words that tell you that one or more events are or were taking place at the same time. Simultaneous events are usually expressed in complex sentences.

Simultaneous Event Signals

and (in addition to)	meanwhile
during	when/whenever (meaning during)
as	simultaneously
while	at the same time

Read the Example below and complete the Explanation.

 Example

1. <u>As</u> you add the milk, continue to beat the mixture vigorously.
2. Josh and Sam heard the news <u>simultaneously,</u> even though they were playing in different rooms.

 Explanation

In the first sentence, the writer of the recipe clearly wants the cook to do two things at once: add the milk *and* beat the mixture. The signal word is *as*. In the second sentence, two events that happen at the same time are:

_____

and _____ .

The signal word is_____ .

Investigation **: SIMULTANEOUS EVENT SIGNALS**

❏ Take out a separate sheet of paper.
  • Write "Simultaneous Event Signals" at the top of the page.
  • Without looking at this page, list as many of the signal words as you can.
  • Check your list and add any signal words that you left out.

INSIGHTS: Reading as Thinking ©
Charlesbridge Publishing • (800) 225-3214

Investigation **B**: COMPREHENDING SIMULTANEOUS EVENTS

❏ Read the following sentences.
  - Circle the signal word that tells you that the events are simultaneous. Underline one event with a solid line (_____) and the other with a broken line (_ _ _ _ _ _).
  - *Remember*: In most instances, the punctuation (comma) also signals each event.

1. While the children picked strawberries, the teenagers weighed the boxes.

2. The press releases for the opera were being distributed (sent around) during the opening night.
   Hint—**During** tells you that while opening night was taking place, the press releases were being distributed.

3. As the survivors neared the ship, the crew threw them a rope.

4. In addition to keeping notes for each meeting, the secretary had to keep the speakers on schedule.

5. The security guards for the president had to observe everyone near him and simultaneously be alert to any unusual sounds.

6. When reporters are interviewing someone, they often help themselves remember what is said by paraphrasing or summarizing each point.

SIGNAL WORDS SHOWING CHRONOLOGICAL ORDER

Chronological order is often indicated by a **signal word**. Signal words are listed below in groups so that you will think of them in terms of what they have in common.

Chronological Order Signal Words

Beginning Events	Middle Events	Ending Events
first, former	second, third . . .	last, latter
begin, beginning	next	end, ending
initial, initially (means first)	in the middle	final, finale, finally
before	after, afterwards	later
precedes (means comes first)	followed by	
prior to (means before)	subsequently (means after)	
now	then	
	and	

INSIGHTS: Reading as Thinking © Charlesbridge Publishing • (800) 225-3214

Investigation B: COMPREHENDING SIMULTANEOUS EVENTS

Have students read and paraphrase the instructions. Write the first sentence on the board to demonstrate the instructions.

Answer Key

1. Circle: While. Solid line: the children picked strawberries. Broken line: the teenagers weighed the boxes

2. Circle: during. Solid line: The press releases . . . being distributed. Broken line: the opening night

3. Circle: As. Solid line: the survivors neared the ship. Broken line: the crew threw them a rope

4. Circle: In addition to. Solid line: keeping notes for each meeting. Broken line: the secretary . . . speakers on schedule

5. Circle: and simultaneously. Solid line: The security guards . . . near him. Broken line: be alert to any unusual sounds

6. Circle: When. Solid line: reporters are interviewing someone. Broken line: they often help . . . each point

❏ SIGNAL WORDS

Read aloud the paragraph about chronological order signals. Have the class read the signal words. Discuss the three types of events indicated by chronological order signal words. Ask the class to suggest sentences using signal words for beginning, middle, and ending events.

❏ SIGNAL WORDS SHOWING CHRONOLOGICAL ORDER
continued

Have volunteers read the three sentences in the Example. Ask the class which event occurs first in each sentence. Then have them write a sentence using each of the following signal words: *followed by* and *precedes*. Discuss the Explanation, identifying the first and second events in the three sentences from the Example as well as the two sentences they wrote.

Sometimes, time signals can indicate the event sequence. Have volunteers read the time signals aloud and have the class read the Example and Explanation. Ask students to discuss how the time signals indicate the order of events.

 Example

1. <u>First</u>, you mix the eggs and flour, and then you gradually stir in the milk.
2. <u>After</u> a lengthy discussion with parents and school officials, the schools were reopened.
3. Mrs. Harris voted for the closing, but she <u>subsequently</u> changed her mind.

Explanation

The sequence signal words are underlined. Note that in the first sentence, *and then* means *next*. Event 1 is mixing the eggs and flour. Event 2 is stirring in the milk.

In the second sentence, event 1 is the lengthy discussion. What is event 2?

_____ .

In the third sentence, event 1 is Mrs. Harris's vote for the closing; event 2 is her subsequent change of mind (after) she voted.

Sometimes, **time signal words** are used to indicate the sequence of events.

Time Signals

hours of the day (3:00 PM)	seasons (spring, summer, etc.)
dates (February 3, 1987)	time of day (morning, afternoon, etc.)

 Example

1. At 3:00 PM Liz washed her hair; at 4:00 PM she vacuumed the rug.
2. On January 1, 1997, Liz made a New Year's Day resolution; she decided to spend more time studying. Her spring semester grades were greatly improved.

 Explanation

In the first sentence, you know that washing hair and vacuuming are sequential events because of the times given: 4:00 PM comes after 3:00 PM. Therefore, you know that the 3:00 PM event was first, and the 4:00 PM event was second. Similarly, in the second sentence, the dates and season establish the order of events.

INSIGHTS: Reading as Thinking ©
Charlesbridge Publishing • (800) 225-3214

UNIT 5 – Comprehending Complex Information **151**

Investigation A: CHRONOLOGICAL SIGNALS

❑ Use a separate sheet of paper.
- Write "Chronological Order Signal Words" at the top of the page. Make column headings for signal words showing Beginning, Middle, and End events.
- Without looking back at the list of signal words, write as many signal words in each column as you can.
- When you have listed all that you can, check your list and add any signal words that you have left out.

Investigation B: TIME SIGNALS

❑ Use a separate sheet of paper.
- Write "Time Signals" at the top of the page.
- Without looking back at the list of time signals, write as many of the signal words as you can.
- Check your list and add any signal words that you have left out.

Investigation C: SHOWING THE SEQUENCE OF EVENTS

❑ Read the following sentences.
- Circle the signal word(s) showing order of events.
- Underline event 1 with a solid line (_____)
- Underline events 2 and 3 with a broken line (_ _ _ _ _ _).

1. Juanita received her paycheck on Wednesday and deposited half of it in the bank that afternoon.

2. First, Marlene put the worm on the hook, and then she cast the line in the water.

3. Initially, Takashi thought he would not go camping with his uncle, but subsequently he changed his mind.

4. In the beginning of the book *The Diary of Anne Frank*, you learn that "Kitty" is the name that Anne gave to her diary; later, you find out why.

5. You should put on sunscreen before you go out in the sun.

6. Looking through the telescope, Peter first saw the moon; next, he saw the long tail of a comet; finally, he saw the Big Dipper.

INSIGHTS: Reading as Thinking ©
Charlesbridge Publishing • (800) 225-3214

Investigation A: CHRONOLOGICAL SIGNALS

Have a student read aloud the instructions. Tell students to write as many signal words as they can think of for each type of event (beginning, middle, and end). Have them check their completed list with the student book and add any words that they left out.

Investigation B: TIME SIGNALS

Have students follow the same process to list time signals.

Investigation C: SHOWING THE SEQUENCE OF EVENTS

Write the first sentence on the chalkboard and demonstrate the process. Circle the signal words, draw a solid line under the first event and a broken line under the second event.

When students have completed all six sentences, discuss the signal words and the sequence of events in each sentence.

Answer Key

1. Circle: Wednesday, that afternoon. Solid line: Juanita received . . . Wednesday. Broken line: and deposited . . . the bank

2. Circle: First, and then. Solid line: Marlene put the worm on the hook. Broken line: she cast the line in the water

3. Circle: Initially, but subsequently. Solid line: Takashi thought . . . his uncle. Broken line: he changed his mind

4. Circle: In the beginning, later Solid line: you learn that "Kitty" . . . her diary. Broken line: you find out why

5. Circle: before. Solid line: You should put on sunscreen. Broken line: you go out in the sun

6. Circle: first, next, finally. Solid line: saw the moon. Broken line: he saw . . . a comet, he saw the Big Dipper

 Strategy Lesson

Making Sequence Charts

At this time, answer any questions students may have about sequence of events. Tell students that in this lesson, they will be using sequence charts to organize complex sequential passages.

Investigation A: REVIEW

Have students complete the three sentences. Ask volunteers to read their sentences aloud.

Answer Key
1. the order of events in time
2. occur one after the other
3. occur at the same time

❏ SEQUENCE OF EVENTS OUT OF ORDER

Ask the students to read the paragraph describing events out of order. You may wish to show them an example of out-of-order sequence taken from a textbook or a work of fiction the class has read.

 Strategy Lesson

MAKING SEQUENCE CHARTS

In previous strategy lessons, you used sentence structure to figure out the sequence of events in a passage. Now you will learn a strategy for reorganizing the information you find in complex sequential passages.

 Investigation **A**: REVIEW

❏ Complete the sentences.

1. A sequence of events means _____ .

2. Sequential or chronological events refer to events that _____ .

3. Simultaneous events are events that _____ .

▢ SEQUENCE OF EVENTS OUT OF ORDER

So far, you have considered only sequences of events that are given in the order in which they happen. However, reporters, textbook writers, and fiction writers frequently give the sequence of events, or steps, out of order so that they can emphasize the points they consider important. To comprehend fully what happened, you must put together the information from the different parts of the sentence so that you have a clear picture in your mind of the chronological order. Consider the Example on the following page.

Example

1. You gradually stir in the milk <u>after</u> you have beaten together the eggs and flour.
2. The decision to reopen the schools was <u>preceded</u> by lengthy discussions with parents and school officials.
3. Although Mrs. Harris <u>subsequently</u> changed her mind, she voted for the closing.

Explanation

These sentences have the same meanings as they did when you read them on page 151. There, they gave the sequence of events in chronological order.

Here the sequences are given out of order. To comprehend sequences out of order, first change them to the chronological sequence of events. This can be done by asking yourself which event came first, second, third, and so on. It is very helpful to underline the signal words. Another strategy for more complicated and lengthy passages is to construct a sequence chart.

Each of the sentences in the Example above involves a sequence presented out of order. To comprehend the true sequence of events as it occurs in reality, you must put the events in order.

1. Event 1 is mixing the eggs and flour.   Event 2 is <u>stirring in the milk.</u>

2. Event 1 is discussions with parents and school officials.   Event 2 is _____

   _____

   _____ .

3. Event 1 is _____   Event 2 is _____

   _____   _____

   _____ .   _____ .

INSIGHTS: Reading as Thinking ©
Charlesbridge Publishing • (800) 225-3214

❏ SEQUENCE OF EVENTS OUT OF ORDER *continued*

Have volunteers read aloud the three Example sentences and the first two paragraphs of the Explanation. Have the class compare the sentences with their counterparts written in chronological order on page 151. Explain that when events are presented out of order, it is useful to ask which event came first, second, third, etc. Tell students that in this strategy lesson, they will construct charts to show the sequence of events.

Read the sequence of events aloud for the first sentence. Have volunteers suggest the sequence for sentences 2 and 3.

Answer Key

1. Event 2 is stirring in the milk.
2. Event 2 is the decision to reopen the schools.
3. Event 1 is Mrs. Harris voting for the closing.
   Event 2 is Mrs. Harris changing her mind.

Investigation A: PUTTING EVENTS IN SEQUENCE

Read the instructions and demonstrate what students are to do. Write the first sentence on the board, circle the signal word (Before), and discuss the sequence of events. You may want to write them on the board to give students a model to follow. When everyone has put all the events in sequence, discuss their answers.

Answer Key

1. Circle: Before
   a. rechecked her equipment
   b. started up the mountain
   c. reached the top
   d. breathed a sigh of relief
2. Circle: after
   a. Louis watched a video about computers.
   b. Louis took a quiz.
3. Circle: before, first
   a. save documents
   b. quit applications
   c. turn off the computer
4. Circle: Before
   a. Congress voted to accept the proposal.
   b. Congress adjourned the summer session.
5. Circle: prior to
   a. Stavros was ahead of Shirley.
   b. Shirley was elected president of the class.
6. Circle: preceded first, then, lastly
   a. worldwide economic depression
   b. Hitler's rise to power
   c. Hitler's decision to invade Poland
   d. World War II

Investigation **A**: PUTTING EVENTS IN SEQUENCE

❏ Read the following sentences.
   • Circle the signal word or words showing the order of events.
   • Write the sequence of events in the order that they occurred.

1. Before starting up the side of Mt. McKinley, the mountain climber rechecked all of her equipment; when she reached the top, she breathed a sigh of relief.
   a. _____
   b. _____
   c. _____
   d. _____
2. Louis took a quiz after he watched a video about computers.
   a. _____
   b. _____
3. Quit all applications before you turn off the computer, but be sure to save your documents first.
   a. _____
   b. _____
   c. _____
4. Before it adjourned the summer session, Congress voted to accept the proposal.
   a. _____
   b. _____
5. Shirley was elected president of the class even though Stavros was ahead of her prior to the election.
   a. _____
   b. _____
6. World War II was preceded first by worldwide economic depression, then by Hitler's rise to power in Germany, and, lastly, by Hitler's invasion of Poland.
   a. _____
   b. _____
   c. _____
   d. _____

INSIGHTS: Reading as Thinking ©
Charlesbridge Publishing • (800) 225-3214

❏ CHARTING COMPLEX SEQUENTIAL INFORMATION

❏ CHARTING COMPLEX SEQUENTIAL INFORMATION

Frequently, you have to read sequential information in passages that contain many events or steps. To understand clearly what the events or steps are, it is useful to list them in the order that they occur. This listing of events is called a **sequence chart**. Sequence charts can be quite simple. Consider the passage and sequence chart in the following example.

 Example

Stir together 2 cups of warm water, honey, and dry yeast in large mixing bowl. When the yeast is bubbly, add oil, salt, 2 cups of flour, then beat the mixture well. Next, add 2 to 3 cups more flour, a little at a time, while mixing.

Knead the dough on a floured surface until it is smooth and elastic. After the dough rises and doubles in size, shape it into a loaf. Preheat the oven to 375°F as you let the dough sit in a loaf pan. Place in oven and bake for 25-30 minutes.

Sequence Chart

1. Stir together water, honey, and dry yeast.
2. Add oil, salt, and flour, then beat well.
3. Add more flour, a little at a time, while mixing.
4. Knead the dough.
5. Let the dough rise.
6. Shape it into a loaf.
7. Preheat oven to 375°F.
8. Bake for 25-30 minutes.

Explanation

Note that a few of the separate parts of the process have been combined because they are done together. Step 2, for example, involves adding oil, salt, and flour, then beating the mixture, because adding ingredients and mixing them are parts of one process.

Have students read the introductory paragraph and the bread recipe in the Example. Ask them to identify each step in the process of making bread. When they reach the second step, have them read the Explanation. Ask them to identify the signal words that helped them to sequence the steps.

INSIGHTS: Reading as Thinking ©
Charlesbridge Publishing • (800) 225-3214

Have students read aloud the paragraph and compare the recipe and the sequence chart. Discuss why the sequence chart is easier to read than the passage.

Have a volunteer read step 1 aloud. Tell the students to try to visualize each event or step as it occurs in time. Point out that this is especially important for sequential information given out of order.

Ask another volunteer to read step 2. Ask students to suggest examples of events occurring on a time schedule (seasons in a year), or in chronological order (years in a person's lifetime or decades in a country's history).

Investigation A: WRITING THE STRATEGY

Ask students to cover the top half of the page and complete the steps for comprehending complex sequential passages.

Investigation B: CHRONOLOGY SIGNAL WORDS

Give students a few minutes to look over the three lists of signal words, then ask them to close their books. Draw three columns on the chalkboard, labeled Simultaneous Events, Chronological Order, and Time Signals. You may wish to divide the Chronological Order column into three sub-columns for beginning, middle, and ending events. Call on students to write the signal words in the appropriate column.

Look back at the passage and the sequence chart. Which one is easier to read? Clearly, the sequence chart is easier. You will appreciate the usefulness of the sequence chart when you read complex passages which are long, have sequences out of order, and involve unfamiliar content.

> To comprehend complex sequential passages, you need to follow two steps.
>
> Step 1: Underline or note mentally all of the signal words that tell the order of steps or events.
>
> Step 2: Outline the steps in a sequence chart.

Investigation **A**: WRITING THE STRATEGY

❑ Cover the top half of the page.
  • Without looking back, complete the steps that tell how to chart the events in a complex sequential passage.

Step 1: Underline or note mentally _____

_____ .

Step 2: Outline _____

_____ .

Investigation **B**: CHRONOLOGY SIGNAL WORDS

❑ Reread the signal words for simultaneous events, chronological order, and time signals on pages 149, 150, and 151.
  • After doing this, your teacher will ask you to close your book.
  • Then your teacher will call on students to write the signal words on the board.

Investigation C: COMPREHENDING CHRONOLOGICAL ORDER

❑ Read the numbered sentences in the following paragraph.
• Circle the signal words that tell you the chronological order.
• Complete the sequence chart.

(1) The initial task in cultivating rice among the Kpelle tribe in Africa involves cutting down the trees and brush at the end of the dry season, about February or March. Then, in April, the members of the tribe set fire to the trees and brush that they have cut. (2) During the rainy season, the rains gradually pound the ashes into the soil, and by June, the soil is wet enough for the families to plant the rice seeds. (3) After the planting period, the men, women, and children must guard against birds and wild animals that eat the seeds. (4) The rice can finally be cut in November; subsequently, it is dried in the sun, because now the dry season has returned. (5) The next and last stage of cultivating rice is storing the grain in storage buildings; after that, the villagers may enjoy the fruits of their harvest.

Sequence Chart

Month	Season	Task	Labor Force
February* March April	end of dry season (_____)	cutting trees and brush _____	tribe members _____
May June	_____	_____	_____
July August September	(summer) _____	_____	_____
October November December January	beginning of dry season (fall-winter)	_____	_____

*This chart begins in February because that is when the process of planting rice begins. Also, the text does not tell you the name of each season. This is typical of many texts. Leave the season column blank, or figure out the season and put it in parentheses to indicate that it is not given in the text.

▣ INTEGRATING SEQUENCES OUT OF ORDER

In the previous exercise, the events were given in order. Integrating information that is given out of order is more difficult and may require an added step. What is needed is a procedure that clearly identifies the order of events in each sentence as you read.

INSIGHTS: Reading as Thinking ©
Charlesbridge Publishing • (800) 225-3214

Investigation C: COMPREHENDING CHRONOLOGICAL ORDER

Have students read the numbered sentences in the passage and circle the signal words that tell the chronological order. Before they fill in the chart, review all the signal words in each numbered sentence or group of sentences. Work with the class to complete the chart. Call students' attention to the explanatory footnote.

Answer Key
Circled words
1. initial, end (of the dry season), about February or March, April
2. During (the rainy season), June
3. After (the planting period)
4. finally, November, subsequently, dry season
5. next, last, after

Sequence Chart
February–April: Season — end of dry season; (spring). Task — cutting trees and brush; set fire to cut trees and brush. Labor Force — tribe members; tribe members
May, June: Season — rainy season. Task — plant rice. Labor Force — families
July–September: Season — (summer). Task — protect rice from wild animals and birds. Labor Force — men, women, and children.
October–January: Season — beginning of dry season; (fall-winter). Task — cut rice; dry rice in sun; store rice. Labor Force — tribe members.

Curriculum Connection

Science: Sequence charting can be used to outline the steps of an experiment. Suggest students write the procedure (steps) in one column and the purpose of each step in a parallel column. Have students present their sequence charts to the class.

❑ INTEGRATING SEQUENCES OUT OF ORDER

After students have read the strategy for integrating sequences, discuss the concept of *flashbacks*. Ask the students to suggest recent movies or books that use flashbacks. Tell students it is helpful to visualize the events and mentally note whether the events are occurring in the present or in the past.

Investigation A: IDENTIFYING THE SEQUENCE

Have volunteers read the passage. Remind students to pay attention to the signal words that tell them whether the events are occurring in the present or in the past. Check that students have circled all the words. Go over the sequence chart when they are done.

Answer Key
Paragraph 1, circle: Before, As, back, early, After, finally
Paragraph 2, circle: Suddenly, interrupted, early, Prior to, then, throughout, back to the present, final

Sequence Chart
Events in the Dressing Room
2. about her early days of competition.
3. There is a knock on her door and a warning.
4. She thinks about early days again.
6. Latisha looks in mirror; tells herself she can do it.

Events in Early Days of Training
2. with parents about grades.
3. Received consent to train intensively.
4. Latisha believed in herself.

One strategy would be to number the events in the correct order. However, this requires marking your text. If you cannot make marks in a book, you may mentally note to yourself the correct order of events.

In the following passage, two sets of events are occurring: the events in the present and the events in the past. This is a literary device called a *flashback* that you will find in books and movies.

Investigation **A: IDENTIFYING THE SEQUENCE**

❑ Read the following paragraphs and circle all the sequence signal words.
  • Complete the sequence chart that follows the passage.

Before the Match

Before Latisha could face that huge crowd of excited tennis fans, she just had to have a few moments by herself to think. As Latisha tied her hair back to keep it out of her face, her thoughts strayed back to her early days of competition. After arguments with her parents about the need to keep up her grades, she finally received their consent to go into intensive training.

Suddenly, Latisha's thoughts were interrupted by a knock on the door; a voice told her that she had only a few moments more. Latisha's thoughts traveled again to those early days. Prior to her decision to go into training, Latisha had little self-confidence, but her coach, Mrs. Chen, urged her to keep trying. There were so many mistakes then; but Mrs. Chen would always say, "The only failure is not to learn from mistakes, Latisha." That thought had kept her going throughout her training period, until she believed in herself. The two-minute warning buzzer forced her back to the present; she took one final look in the mirror and thought, "You're on, Latisha. You've got what it takes."

Sequence Chart

Events in the Dressing Room	Events in Early Days of Training
1. Latisha awaits match.	1a. Many mistakes in early training
2. She thinks_____	1b. No self-confidence
_____	1c. Mrs. Chen encouraged her.
3. _____	2. Argued_____
4. _____	3. _____
5. The last warning sounds.	_____
6. _____	4. _____
_____	_____

 ## Curriculum Connection

Language Arts: Flashbacks.
Charting the events in the flashback with a parallel chart for the current events is quite useful in grasping the concept of flashback in literature. Choose a novel involving sequences that are chronologically out of order and have the class construct a sequence chart.

COMPARING INFORMATION

You have been applying a strategy for understanding complex sequential information: making a sequence chart for events given out of chronological order. In this lesson, you will use a strategy for understanding complex comparative information and putting it into a form that is easier to understand and to remember.

❑ COMPARING SUBJECTS AND ATTRIBUTES

Have you ever compared two movies or the personalities of two friends? Have you ever compared the plots in two or more books? If you have, then you are comparing *subjects* and their *attributes*, that is, their characteristics or features. The subject may be two or more persons, two or more places, two or more things, or two or more events. Attributes are usually given in the predicate. Note that compound predicates usually mean compound attributes.

Example

Ingrid decided to work for the Park Department during the summer. The Park Department assigned her to help people put away their sailboats in special racks for storage. To do the job requires knowing the sizes and special features of each type of boat that is stored. Consequently, the Park Department gives each employee who does this job a description of each boat and a short quiz before the job begins. Here are some of the things Ingrid had to learn.

A Catamaran has no keel and only one sail. It is very heavy and is stored on the bottom shelf. The Lightning is the next heaviest and is stored on the second shelf. It has a large keel that must be raised and two sails. The Sunfish is a lightweight, single-sail boat and is stored on the top shelf. It has a medium-sized keel that can be removed for storage.

Explanation

The topic in the example above is sailboats. You know this because the subject in every sentence of the second paragraph is the name of a sailboat or a pronoun that stands for one. Thus, the passage is a description of two or more things. The subjects, which identify the names of the sailboats, are circled. The verbs are underlined because they give you a clue to the number and location of the attributes, or characteristics, of each sailboat.

INSIGHTS: Reading as Thinking ©
Charlesbridge Publishing • (800) 225-3214

Have the class read the first paragraph. Ask students to raise any questions they have about charting sequential events. Explain that in this lesson, they will use charts to organize complex comparative information. Point out that comparisons can be made for both similarities and differences.

❑ COMPARING SUBJECTS AND ATTRIBUTES

Have the students read the introductory paragraph. Give examples of two characters from a popular movie and ask students to describe several features of each character. Point out that the two characters are *subjects* and their features are *attributes*.

Ask the students to read the Example describing the attributes of different sailboats. Have the class read the Explanation. Discuss the clues regarding the number and location of the attributes that are provided by the underlined verbs.

❑ COMPARING SUBJECTS AND ATTRIBUTES *continued*

Ask a student to read the paragraph describing how to identify categories. Have the class paraphrase the two ways they can identify categories: notice which words are repeated and infer the categories from the attributes given.

Have volunteers read the seven steps for making a comparison chart. Emphasize the importance of Step 2. Have students look again at the words that are circled and underlined in the Example passage. They illustrate Step 3.

Discuss the format of the chart (Steps 4 and 5). Emphasize the importance of keeping information in a row to one category (Step 6).

Ask students to identify the purpose of the chart (comparison). Point out that organizing information in a chart is useful only when that information is used for a purpose.

Explain that students will be following all seven steps to make a chart of the sailboat passage. Tell them comparison charts are a good way to learn information that compares subjects and attributes.

When you make comparisons, you make them in specific categories. You can identify the categories in two ways. First, you notice which words are repeated. The words *keel* and *sail*, for example, are mentioned for each boat, so you know that keel and sail are two of the attribute categories. Second, you can infer the categories from the attributes that are given. When you learn that the Catamaran is very heavy, for example, you may guess that weight will be a category. This guess is proven correct by later references to weight (next heaviest and lightweight). The attribute categories in the passage are: number of sails, size, weight, the procedure for storing the keel, and the storage location.

What is the best way to learn information that compares subjects and attributes? Make a **comparison** chart using these steps.

Step 1: Establish that the information is comparative.

    Ask yourself: Is this a description of two or more persons, places, things, or events?

    Ask yourself: Are two or more characteristics given?

Step 2: Visualize each part of the subject (person, place, thing, or event) as you read about it.

Step 3: Scan the passage by circling the subjects and underlining the verbs, as in the Example on page 160.

Step 4: Make a chart with the subjects as column headings across the top.

Step 5: List the attribute categories on the left side of the chart.

Step 6: Fill in the chart with information from the text. Information in each row must be from the same category.

Step 7: Examine the chart for similarities and differences among the subjects.

    Ask yourself: How are the subjects alike? How are they different?

INSIGHTS: Reading as Thinking ©
Charlesbridge Publishing • (800) 225-3214

Investigation **A**: STEPS FOR COMPARING SUBJECTS AND ATTRIBUTES

❑ Study the steps on the previous page.
  • Then without looking back, complete the seven steps for comparing subjects and attributes.

Step 1: Establish that the information is_____ .

  Ask yourself: _____

  _____

  Ask yourself: _____

  _____

Step 2: Visualize_____

  _____ .

Step 3: Scan the passage _____

  and _____ .

Step 4: Make a chart with _____

  _____ .

Step 5: List _____

  _____ .

Step 6: Fill in _____

  _____ .

Step 7: Examine the chart for_____

  and _____ .

INSIGHTS: Reading as Thinking ©
Charlesbridge Publishing • (800) 225-3214

Investigation A: STEPS FOR COMPARING SUBJECTS AND ATTRIBUTES

Have the class reread the steps for making a comparison chart. Students may study them with a partner. Answer any questions they may have regarding the steps. Ask students to write the seven steps for comparing subjects and attributes. Have them check their steps with those in the student book and make any corrections necessary.

Answer Key
Step 1: Establish that the information is comparative.
Is this a description of two or more persons, places, or events?
Are two or more characteristics given?
Step 2: Visualize each part of the person, place, thing, or event as you read about it.
Step 3: Scan the passage by circling the subjects and underlining the verbs.
Step 4: Make a chart with the subjects as column headings across the top.
Step 5: List the attribute categories on the left side of the chart.
Step 6: Fill in the chart with information from the text.
Step 7: Examine the chart for similarities and differences among the subjects.

Ask students to study the chart in the Example. Have the students read and discuss the first two paragraphs of the Explanation. Work with the class to complete the attribute categories in the chart. Ask them to read the last paragraph of the Explanation and discuss the value of charting subjects to compare their attributes.

Answer Key

Catamaran: no keel, no procedure, stored on the bottom shelf
Lightning: two sails, large keel, keel must be raised for storing
Sunfish: one sail, lightweight, stored on the top shelf

Example

Attributes	Catamaran	Lightning	Sunfish
Number of sails	one		
Size of keel			medium-sized
Weight of boat	heavy	next heaviest	
Procedure for storing keel			remove
Storage location of boat		second shelf	

Explanation

Notice that the names of the sailboats are the *column headings* at the top. The attribute categories (number of sails, weight of boat, etc.) are the *row headings* on the left side of the chart. Look at the attribute categories. If you read across the row, you can see that each item is related to the category. Note that each item in a column is related to the category heading at the top. Reread the passage on page 160 and use it to complete the chart.

In setting up a chart of your own, you may have some difficulty figuring out what attributes to use as the row headings. Generally, these are suggested by the items themselves. First, you list the things that go together as you would in any categorizing or sorting activity. Second, you ask yourself what the items have in common. That is the category name that you use for the row heading.

Each sailboat is essentially quite different from the others. They have no features or attributes in common. However, it is clear that there is a relationship between the weight of the boat and the storage location. The heaviest boats go on the bottom shelf, the next heaviest boats go on the next shelf, and the lightest boats go on the top shelf. You might not have seen this relationship before putting the attributes in a comparison chart.

Investigation B: CHARTING

Following are sets of descriptions and charts. Each description tells you about a job or task and then tells you what information is needed to do the task.

☐ Read each description, making mental pictures as you read. As each part is listed, add it to your mental picture of the thing that is described. As each activity is described, visualize yourself doing that activity. This will help you to understand and to remember what you need to know.
  • Use the strategy to complete the chart below each description.
  • Answer the questions that follow each chart.
  • *Remember:* In comparative passages, compound predicates and compound sentences usually signal compound attributes. You may want to underline the subjects and verbs in the description of the parts and activities.

1. Identifying Officers

José worked as a waiter near a military base. José had to deal with many people in his new job. Most of them wore uniforms that he had to recognize. It was very confusing because some parts of the uniforms were alike and some were different. The Chief Petty Officer wore a cap with an anchor design and a black chin strap, carried no arms, and always arrived in a car. The Petty Officer wore a cap with a crown-shaped design and a black chin strap, carried no arms, and arrived in a car. In contrast, the Security Guard wore a cap with crossed rifles and a gold chin strap, carried arms, and arrived in a jeep.

	Chief Petty Officer		Security Guard
Hat design			
	black	black	gold
Arms	none		
Type of vehicle			jeep

What do the Chief Petty Officer and the Petty Officer have in common?

_____

_____

_____

Investigation B: CHARTING

Explain that the next four pages contain passages students will read and chart. Have them read the instructions. Ask questions such as the following to help them to chart: **What are being compared? What heading belongs on the third column? What attribute or feature do the colors represent?** Have students use the chart to answer the questions.

Answer Key
The answers in italics are those the students fill in.

	Chief Petty Officer	*Petty Officer*	Security Guard
Hat design	*anchor*	*crown*	*crossed rifles*
Chin strap	black	black	gold
Arms	none	*none*	yes
Type of vehicle	*car*	*car*	jeep

The Chief Petty Officer and the Petty Officer both have black chin straps, do not carry arms, and ride in cars.

 ## Literature Connection

Comparing Characters: Ask students to choose a book with two or more major characters. Tell them to make notes of each character's attributes as they read, and present the information in a comparison chart. They may want to choose a book from the following list:
Paterson, Katherine, *Jacob Have I Loved*, HarperCollins, 1980.
Brooks, Bruce, *The Moves Make the Man*, HarperCollins, 1984.
Moore, Martha, *Under the Mermaid Angel*, Dalacorte, 1996.

Investigation B: CHARTING
continued

Remind students to visualize as they read Passage 2. Call their attention to the note. When students have finished their charts, review them and discuss their answers to the questions.

Answer Key

	Foot Patrol	Motor Patrol
Area watched	non-military	non-military
Knowledge required	*area and people and emergency routes*	area, people, and communications system
Services	give directions	—
Responsibilities	report anything suspicious	*investigate suspicious events*
Emergency duties	*know emergency routes*	provide emergency service

Both patrols watch nonmilitary areas and know the people and workers in the area.

The patrols differ in that the foot patrol gives directions, but the motor patrol does not; the foot patrol reports suspicious events, but the motor patrol investigates them; the foot patrol only knows emergency routes, but the motor patrol provides emergency service; the motor patrol must know communication systems, but the foot patrol does not.

2. Foot and Motor Patrols

After José befriended a few security guards, he became quite interested in learning about their jobs.

The foot patrol watches nonmilitary areas used by the military: businesses, the munitions factory, and the amusement parks. They must know the patrol area thoroughly, become acquainted with those who live and work in the area, give directions, report anything suspicious during the day, and know emergency routes.

The motor patrol has some of the same tasks. They must know the area, know the people who use it, and investigate suspicious events. The motor patrol also has to know all of the available communication installations (phones, TVs), and provide emergency service.

Note — Line up the activities so that those on the same line correspond to each other. Use a dash if there is no corresponding information.

	Foot Patrol	Motor Patrol
Area watched	nonmilitary	nonmilitary
Knowledge required		area, people, and
		communications system
	give directions	—
	report anything suspicious	
		provide emergency service

How are the two patrols alike?

_____

_____

How are the two patrols different?

_____

_____

_____

_____

_____

_____

Over the summer, José found that charting was a useful strategy for learning complicated information. He decided to use charting in school. Below is a part of José's science assignment. Read the passage and chart the information that it contains.

3. José's Assignment

Broadleaf trees grow in areas where the temperature is moderate and there is plenty of rainfall. They have large, wide, flat leaves that change color and fall to the ground in autumn. In winter, the broadleaf tree is bare. Some broadleaf trees develop large, beautiful flowers in spring. The flowers turn into seed-bearing fruits such as apples, cherries, or acorns during the summer.

Needleleaf trees grow mainly in regions that have long, cold winters. The needleleaf has small, narrow, long, sharp, pointed leaves. These leaves remain on the tree throughout the entire year. Needleleaf trees have small, plain flowers that turn into seed-bearing cones.

	Broadleaf Trees	
	moderate temperature, plenty of rainfall	
Type of leaf		small, narrow, long, sharp, pointed
What happens to leaves		
		none
Cones	none	

How are broadleaf trees and needleleaf trees alike?

_____

How are broadleaf trees and needleleaf trees different?

_____

_____

_____

Investigation B: CHARTING
continued

Have students read the introductory paragraph and Passage 3. Encourage the students to visualize as they read. Tell them to reread and to mark the text if necessary. Have students fill in the chart and answer the two questions that follow it.

Answer Key

	Broadleaf Trees	*Needleleaf trees*
Climate	moderate temperature, plenty of rainfall	*long, cold winters*
Type of leaf	*large, wide, flat*	small, narrow, long, sharp, pointed
What happens to leaves	*change colors and fall to ground in autumn*	*remain on tree throughout the year*
Flowers	*large, beautiful*	*small, plain*
Fruit	*apples, cherries, or acorns*	none
Cones	none	*yes*

Both types of trees have leaves and flowers.

The broadleaf and needleleaf differ in that they need different kinds of climates for growth; they have different leaves, flowers, and kinds of seed production.

Investigation B: CHARTING
continued

Explain that students will need to complete the entire chart for Passage 4. Have them read the introductory paragraph and passage, chart the comparisons, and answer the question.

Explain the name "Moses-in-the-boat." Tell students that the baby Moses was placed in a basket and sent floating down a river because his mother wanted to protect him from Egypt's pharaoh.

Discuss the subjects and attributes the students charted. Ask them which aspects of the chart they found most difficult to complete without prompts. Ask how it helped to look back at the strategy steps when charting this passage.

Answer Key

	Dieffen-bachia	Rhoeo Spathacea
Common name	dumb cane	Moses-in-the-boat
Reason for nickname	leaf sap may para-lyze vocal cords	flowers in pod look like people in a boat
Height	6 feet	—
Stem	one	one
Leaf	large and pointed	sword-shaped
Color	dark green/ yellow/ green with markings	dark green on top, purple on bottom

Both plants usually have one stem.

Kendra asked José to teach her how to chart information. José used the passage below to teach her how to chart. Read the passage and complete the chart based on the information given in the passage.

4. Comparing Plants

<u>Dieffenbachia</u> (dē•fen•bak'•ē•ă) is commonly called "dumb cane." The name refers to the fact that the leaves are sometimes covered with a sour-tasting sap that will burn the mouth and throat and may even paralyze the vocal cords momentarily. Usually, there is a single stem that grows to six feet. The leaves are large and pointed. Color varies from dark green to yellow-green with different color markings.

<u>Rhoeo Spathacea</u> (rō'•ē•ō•spĭ•thă'•sē•ă) is usually called "Moses-in-the-boat" because the small, white flowers crowded into boat-shaped "pods" look like people in a boat. (Moses was found floating down a river in a boat.) Usually, there is a single stem containing several sword-shaped leaves. The leaves are dark green on the top and deep purple underneath.

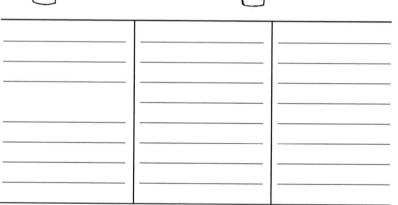

What do the plants have in common?

_____

Curriculum Connection

Comparing Places: Have students choose two or three geographic locations to compare. Remind them to choose a set of attributes (for example, temperature range, physical features, and population) as a basis for comparison. Have them use the information they find in their research to construct a comparison chart. Then, have them write two or three paragraphs comparing the locations.

Comprehending Condensed Information

Strategy
Lesson

CONDENSED INFORMATION

In this lesson, you will learn two strategies for comprehending condensed 5W's plus How information.

☐ INTEGRATING COMPLEX INFORMATION

When speaking about comprehension, the word *integration* refers to the process of combining the information in one part of what is read with information in another part. Thus, to integrate the information in a sentence, you relate the subject to the predicate. In a complex sentence there may be several parts of the subject and predicate to relate to each other.

This lesson contains sentences that are typical of history or science books and newspaper articles.

Investigation : INTEGRATING 5W'S PLUS HOW INFORMATION

☐ Read each of the following sentences, paying special attention to the subjects and verbs.
  • Answer the questions that follow each sentence. Look for clues that help you infer the required information.

1. Goat Island, which is on the dividing line between Canada and the United States, separates the two waterfalls that make up Niagara Falls.

   Is the following statement true or false? _____

   Niagara Falls are actually two falls, each of which is in a separate country.

2. Trails and steps from Whirlpool State Park lead down to the base of the cliffs, offering a dramatic close-up of the swirling waters of the whirlpool, which is 1,750 feet wide and 126 feet deep.

   Where is Whirlpool State Park located?_____

   _____

   Think: You can infer the answer by putting together the facts in the sentence.

3. From Prospect Point you can take an elevator to the base of the falls, where you can walk along a wooden catwalk underneath part of the falls; this is a particularly interesting sight.

   What is a particularly interesting sight?_____

   _____

INSIGHTS: Reading as Thinking ©
Charlesbridge Publishing • (800) 225-3214

☐ INTEGRATING COMPLEX INFORMATION

Have students read the introductory paragraphs. Ask them to state the 5W's plus How, and define what they think is meant by the phrase *Condensed 5W's + How information.*

Explain that it is often necessary to integrate the information from several sentences, paragraphs, or passages when reading complex chapters and articles. Tell them that an understanding of sentence structure can help them to integrate the information effectively.

Investigation A: INTEGRATING 5W'S PLUS HOW INFORMATION

Have students read the instructions. Have the class identify the subjects and the verbs. Help the class answer the questions.

Each sentence was constructed to illustrate a particular problem of integrating information from different parts of a sentence. Explain each integration problem as you discuss students' responses.

Answer Key

1. **It is true.**

While the sentence does not state directly that the falls are in two different countries, you know that this is true because the verb *separates* tells you that Goat Island separates the two waterfalls. *Which is* refers to Goat Island. The rest of the clause ("... on the dividing line between Canada and the United States") tells you where.

(Answers continue on next page.)

Investigation A: INTEGRATING 5W'S PLUS HOW INFORMATION
continued

Answer Key

The reader must reason that if Goat Island separates the two falls *and also* separates the two countries, the two falls must be in different countries. Explain that the words *that, whom, which,* and *whose* always refer to the person, place, thing, or event preceding them.

2. **It is at the top of the cliffs above the whirlpool.**

In this sentence the reader has to reason that trails and steps leading *down* from the park to the base of the cliffs must also lead *up* to the park at the top of the cliffs.

3. **It is the view from underneath the falls.**

This, that, these, and *those* may refer to a noun. However, the words may also refer to events and situations. The antecedents should precede these pronouns.

4. **La Salle built Old Fort Niagara.**

The pronoun *it* and the noun to which it refers (*Old Fort Niagara*) are separated by two other nouns (*mouth* and *Niagara River*). Since the mouth and the river could not have been built by La Salle, it was the fort he built in 1678. The punctuation is also a clue here; it marks off the introductory clause.

(Answers continue on next page.)

---

4. Old Fort Niagara, at the mouth of the Niagara River, is beautifully restored; it was built by La Salle in 1678.

   What happened in 1678? _____

5. At the southern end of the Niagara River is the city of Buffalo, which dominates the whole eastern end of Lake Erie.

   Who or what is this sentence about?_____

   Where is Buffalo?_____

6. Initially, Niagara Falls were formed near Lake Ontario; however, the pounding, rushing water of the falls continuously cuts away the rock underneath so that the falls inch slowly southward.

   What is causing the Niagara Falls to move southward? _____

7. When the Erie Canal was built in 1825, it brought trade, tourism, and industry, and the village of Buffalo soon expanded into a city.

   Why did Buffalo expand?_____

   _____

   _____

8. Glacial ice created the Niagara River, the gorge through which it flows, the roaring falls, and the rapids below them.

   What did the glacial ice create? _____

   _____

   _____

9. Both the New York and Ontario governments have provided a number of points of interest. These include bridges, scenic drives, restaurants with magnificent views of the falls, boat trips, and helicopter views of the falls.

   Who or what is the second sentence about? _____

10. About one mile from Whirlpool Bridge, there is a huge dam with a series of generators that produce more power than any other generators in the Western world; it cost about 720 million dollars to build.

    Who or what is this sentence about?_____

    Think: The subject of a verb is usually a noun or pronoun and may come *after* the verb.

    What cost 720 million dollars? _____

INSIGHTS: Reading as Thinking ©
Charlesbridge Publishing • (800) 225-3214

Investigation A: INTEGRATING 5W'S PLUS HOW INFORMATION
continued

Answer Key for Student Page 169 *continued*

5. **Buffalo. It is at the southern end of the Niagara River.**
In this sentence, the subject comes after the verb. The reader could say that Buffalo was at the eastern end of Lake Erie as all or part of the answer. However, the reader should know that the response "at the southern end of the Niagara River" is the *best* answer to the "where" question because the author uses the word *at* to tell you the most specific location of Buffalo.

6. **the pounding, rushing water of the falls**
Here is a signal that suggests a causal relationship. The words *so that* tell you that one event causes another.

7. **Buffalo expanded because of the trade, tourism, and industry brought by the Erie Canal.**
Frequently there are no signal words such as *because* to indicate cause and effect relationships. Social studies texts often *imply* that when one event follows another, the second event is caused by the first.

8. **Glacial ice created the Niagara River, the gorge, the falls, and the rapids below them.**
Here the reader might be tempted to refer only to the Niagara River, since it is mentioned first and since the falls and rapids are part of the river. Questions such as this one usually require a complete listing of the information given rather than integration of information.

9. **points of interest**
This, that, these, and *those* are demonstrative pronouns that refer to the person, place, thing, or event immediately preceding them. *These* stands for the points of interest listed in the second sentence.

10. **A huge dam, the dam**
This sentence typifies the many sentences in which the subject comes *after* the verb. You may want to give other examples. *It* looks as though it should refer to *Western world,* which is the noun immediately preceding it; however, other nouns often come between the pronoun and the noun to which they refer. In these instances, the reader must reason what the pronoun refers to, using the meaning of the sentence. In this case, *it* refers to the dam.

❏ COMPREHENDING CONDENSED 5W'S PLUS HOW INFORMATION

Have the class read the first two paragraphs. Write a complex sentence on the board and have them identify the dependent clause. Remind students that a dependent clause has its own subject and verb yet cannot stand alone because its meaning *depends* on the meaning of the sentence to which it is attached. Explain that such a clause usually adds 5W's plus How information to a sentence.

Have the class read the two sentences in the Example. Ask a volunteer to read the sentences aloud. Discuss why the first sentence is harder to read.

❏ COMPREHENDING CONDENSED 5W'S PLUS HOW INFORMATION

Textbook writers and reporters often use a style of writing that packs a great deal of information into each sentence. An individual sentence in a text or newspaper article may be very complicated. It may contain compound subjects and predicates as well as dependent clauses.

One reason for this compact, complicated writing style is that reporters and other writers often have limited writing space. Consequently, they try to cram most or all of the 5W's plus How information into a single sentence or two. Such a sentence can be difficult to understand even when it is well written. Consider the two sentences in the following Example.

Example

1. Winston Churchill, Prime Minister of Great Britain; Franklin D. Roosevelt, President of the United States; and Joseph Stalin, Premier of the Soviet Union, met at the Yalta Conference in 1945; their purpose was to decide how power would be divided after World War II.

2. Prime Minister Winston Churchill of Great Britain, President Franklin D. Roosevelt of the United States, and Premier Joseph Stalin of the Soviet Union met at the Yalta Conference in 1945; their purpose was to decide how power would be divided after World War II.

Explanation

Obviously, these two compound sentences say the same thing. Yet the first is more difficult to read than the second. In sentence 2, the information that identifies each person is attached to the name of each person so that it does not get in the way of understanding the sentence. In sentence 1, each name is followed by a phrase that gives the title of that person; for example, Winston Churchill, Prime Minister of Great Britain. Phrases such as these sometimes interrupt the flow of thought and make a sentence difficult to understand.

Condensed 5W's plus How information creates a special problem of comprehension. How do you understand and remember sentence after sentence of this type of information when much or all of the subject matter is unfamiliar? You can use a *5W's plus How chart*, which clearly identifies each of the 5W's plus How in a form that is easy to understand and remember.

INSIGHTS: Reading as Thinking ©
Charlesbridge Publishing • (800) 225-3214

STRATEGY FOR A CONDENSED 5W'S PLUS HOW CHART

> Step 1: Determine whether the text you are reading contains condensed 5W's plus How information. This type of information will usually be found in social studies texts or newspapers.
>
> Step 2: Underline the person, place, thing, or event that the sentence is about and underline all the verbs in the sentence. Usually, the person, place, thing, or event will be the subject of the first simple sentence.
>
> Step 3: Write the information in columns in a 5W's plus How information chart, as shown below.

Investigation  **A: USING A CONDENSED 5W'S PLUS HOW CHART**

❑ Reread the example on the previous page, then complete the chart.

Who (What) sentence is about	What Happened	Why/How	Where/When
1. Churchill (Prime Minister/Great Britain)	had a conference	to divide power after WWII	_____
2. Roosevelt (_____ / _____)			_____
3. _____ (_____ / _____)			

Notes on note taking: You have to reduce the number of words used to the absolute minimum. You may also need to use abbreviations — some of which you may need to make up yourself. In some cases, you may need to infer or figure out *why*.

❑ STRATEGY FOR A CONDENSED 5W'S PLUS HOW CHART

Ask a volunteer to read the three steps in the strategy. Have students look again at the Example. Show them how to apply each step to Sentence 2.

Investigation A: USING A CONDENSED 5W'S PLUS HOW CHART

Encourage students to think of alternate wording to shorten entries in the chart. Tell them they can use abbreviations. Remind them to infer *why* to complete their charts.

Answer Key
2. President/U.S.
3. Stalin
Premier/Soviet Union
Where/When: Yalta/1945

After the class has completed the chart, review the strategy. Have students write the three steps on a separate sheet of paper, then check their answers with the student book.

Investigation B: CHARTING THE 5W'S PLUS HOW

Tell students they will use the 5W's plus How charts to organize complicated information. Have them read the instructions. Help the class fill in the chart for the first sentence. Point out that the numbers in parentheses are clues to the number of items they should list under each heading. Have them complete the remaining charts independently.

Answer Key

1. Who (What): (1) Sitting Bull
   What happened: (1) had been pardoned; (2) performed in Wild West Show; (3) became center of Native American resistance
   Why/How: (1) not given
   Where/When: (1) Standing Rock Reservation; no date given

2. Who (What): (1) mining of copper
   Why/How: (1) copper needed for wires for electrical industries
   Where/When: (1) Lake Superior's shores during the 1860s

3. What happened: (3) ships turned off course; (4) coastal boats worked way around South America
   Why/How: (1) not given, but can infer desperate journey means people were willing to sacrifice all to get rich
   Where/When: (1) California in January, 1849

Investigation **B**: CHARTING THE 5W'S PLUS HOW

❏ Underline the person, place, or thing that the sentence is about and all the verbs in the sentence.
   • Write the 5W's plus How in the chart.

1. Sitting Bull, who had been pardoned after his return from Canada, performed in Buffalo Bill's Wild West Show for a while, but eventually made himself the center of the Native American resistance on the Standing Rock Reservation.

Who (What)	What Happened	Why/How	Where/When
(1)	(1)	(1)	(1)
	(2)		
	(3)		

2. The mining of copper from Lake Superior's shores grew in importance during the 1860s with the rise of the new electrical industries; this happened because thousands of miles of copper wires were needed for electrical circuits.

Who (What)	What Happened	Why/How	Where/When
(1)	(1) grew in importance	(1)	(1)

3. The discovery of gold in California in January of 1849 brought on the mad "Gold Rush"; jobs and families were abandoned, ships turned off course to go to California, and even coastal boats worked their way around the dangerous waters of South America (Cape Horn) in a desperate journey to reach the gold fields.

Who (What)	What Happened	Why/How	Where/When
(1) discovery of gold	(1) brought on "Gold Rush"	(1)	(1)
	(2) jobs/families deserted		
	(3)		
	(4)		

INSIGHTS: Reading as Thinking ©
Charlesbridge Publishing • (800) 225-3214

---

4. The anti-Hitler movement in Nazi Germany during World War II was not strong enough to hurt the Nazis, but it did keep alive the idea that not all Germans were Nazis.

Who (What)	What Happened	Why/How	Where/When
(1)	(1) (2)	(1)	(1)

5. The Lincoln penny was minted in 1909, the centennial of Abraham Lincoln's birth; it was the first American coin to have a portrait engraved on it.

Who (What)	What Happened	Why/How	Where/When
(1)	(1) (2)	(1)	(1)

6. The Chicago builder A.D. Taylor made cheaper wooden housing possible in the United States by perfecting the balloon-frame house; this new frame replaced the heavy timbers of older houses by using cheap, mass-produced nails to hold the timbers together.

Who (What)	What Happened	Why/How	Where/When
(1)	(1) (2)	(1)	(1)

Investigation B: CHARTING THE 5W'S PLUS HOW *continued*

Have students continue making 5W's plus How charts.

Answer Key

4. Who (What): (1) anti-Hitler movement
   What happened: (1) not strong enough to hurt Nazis; (2) kept alive idea not all Germans were Nazis
   Why/How: (1) not given
   Where/When: (1) Nazi Germany during W.W. II

5. Who (What): (1) the Lincoln penny
   What happened: (1) was minted; (2) first American coin to have a portrait
   Why/How: (1) not given
   Where/When: (1) place not given; (2) 1909

6. Who (What): (1) builder A. D. Tyler
   What happened: (1) made cheaper wooden housing possible; (2) perfected balloon-frame house
   Why/How: (1) frame used cheap mass-produced nails to hold timbers together
   Where/When: (1) Chicago; (2) date not given

 **Curriculum Connection**

Reading Current Events: Ask students to bring in current event articles from a newspaper or news magazine. Have them choose a few sentences that contain 5W's plus How information and use it to make a 5W's Plus How Chart to share with the class.

Investigation B: CHARTING THE 5W'S PLUS HOW *continued*

Ask volunteers to describe how each step of the strategy was used to complete the chart.

Answer Key

7. Who (What): (1) Nellie Bly
What happened: (1) earned fame as a female investigative reporter
Why/How: (1) by exposing corruption in business and government
Where/When: (1) late 1800s; (2) place not given

❏ THREE TYPES OF COMPLEX INFORMATION

Have the students read the definitions of the three types of complex information. Discuss the strategies they have used in this unit to understand each type of information. Ask for examples of when each strategy would be useful.

Investigation A: DEFINITIONS

After students complete the definitions, have them check their work.

Answer Key

1. included all or most of the 5W's plus How information in a single sentence containing compound subjects and predicates
2. is information in which the order of events described is not the order in which they occurred
3. places, things, events in terms of two or more features or attributes

---

7. In the late 1800s Nellie Bly earned fame as one of the first female investigative reporters by exposing corruption in business and government.

Who (What)	What Happened	Why/How	Where/When
(1)	(1)	(1)	(1)

▣ THREE TYPES OF COMPLEX INFORMATION

You have charted condensed 5W's plus How information. Different types of detailed information require different strategies. As you will recall, three types of information are:

1. <u>Condensed 5W's plus How information</u>. This is information in which an author has included all or most of the 5W's plus How information in a single sentence containing compound subjects and predicates.

2. <u>Complex sequential information</u>. This is information in which the order of events described is not the order in which the events really happened.

3. <u>Comparative information</u>. This is information in which two or more persons, places, things, or events are compared in terms of several features (attributes).

Investigation A: DEFINITIONS

❏ Complete these definitions.

1. Condensed 5W's plus How information refers to sentences in which the author has

_____.

_____.

2. Complex sequential information _____

_____.

3. Comparative information compares two or more persons, _____ , or

_____ in terms of two or more_____ .

Remember: Charting complex information is a good way to clarify and remember it whenever you are reading or studying complicated text.

Self-evaluation

elf-evaluation

Have students complete the Self-evaluation. Suggest that they use the Self-evaluation to identify the areas in which they need further preparation. Discuss any questions or areas of concern students may have before conducting the unit assessment.

1. What strategies did you learn?

_____

_____

2. What part of the unit was the easiest?

_____

_____

3. What part of the unit was the most difficult? Why?

_____

_____

4. When can you use the unit strategy?

_____

_____

_____

5. Write one question you think should be on a test of this unit.

_____

_____

_____

6. Circle the number that shows how much you learned in this unit.

1	2	3	4	5	6	7	8	9	10

DIDN'T LEARN   LEARNED A LITTLE   LEARNED SOME   LEARNED MOST   LEARNED ALL

Assessment

The Assessment is used to provide feedback on the student's progress. Students are rated on a predetermined target performance level.

Blackline Master Pages 258-260

Hand out copies of Blackline Master Pages 258-260 to each student. Have them read the instructions carefully. Answer any questions about what they are to do. Point out that in two charts they need to write some of the column heads.

Collect, score, and record the Assessments before returning them to the students and discussing their responses.

Answers for Blackline Master Page 258
Sentence 1
Who (What): (1) the Persians
What happened: (1) established pharmacies; (2) opened medical clinics
Why/How: (1) because they did medical research
Where/When: (1) Persia; (2) first century AD

The Persians were able to make so many contributions to the field of medicine because they did medical research.

Sentence 2
Who (What): (1) Lang; (2) Morton
What Happened: (1) advanced field of medicine; (2) discovered that ether could be used safely
Why/How: (1) because of their experiments to find an effective painkiller
Where/When (1) 1840s

Lang and Morton advanced the field of medicine by discovering a safe and effective painkiller, ether.

Answers for Blackline Master Page 259

Time	Events
1. 862	Russian settlement
2. 880s	Danish Vikings invade/settle in France
3. 986	settlement in Greenland and, later, in North America
4. 1016	Viking Canute became King of England and made it part of his North Sea Empire.
5. 1035	death of Canute
6. after 1035	Vikings live peacefully in isolated settlements

The Vikings established settlements in five locations: Russia, France, Greenland, North America, and England.

Answers for Blackline Master Page 260

Name of Insect	Description	Plant Damage	Controls
Aphids	soft, round, bodies with wings	suck plant juices	wipe off with soapy water
Spider mites	flat, oval bodies	cover leaves with web	lime, sulfur, oil, and soap
Scale insects	round bodies covered with hard shells	suck plant juices and secrete oil	scrape off

1. They all damage plants, and they can all be controlled.
2. Insects can damage plants by sucking plant juice, covering the leaves with a web, or secreting harmful oils.

❏ SCORING

Score 1 point for each correctly completed chart entry and each correctly answered question. Accept alternate wordings and other logical answers. Complete sentences are not required.

Mastery Level: 34 out of 42 points.

 Conditional Knowledge

Ask the students to discuss situations when they might use a chart to organize information. They might suggest academic applications such as researching a science project or writing a book report. Ask them to think of situations outside of school when a chart would help to organize information, such as planning a party, comparing brands of products before an important purchase, planning for a garden, or starting a business.

Assessment

❏ Read the following sentences and complete the chart that follows each one.
  • Answer the question under each chart.

1. As early as the first century AD, the Persians had established
   pharmacies and opened medical clinics; they were outstanding
   doctors because they did medical research.

Who (What)	What Happened	Why/How	Where/When
(1)	(1)	(1)	(1)
	(2)		(2)
	(3) were outstanding doctors		

Why were the Persians able to make so many contributions to the field of medicine?

_____

_____

2. In the 1840s, two Americans, Crawford Lang and William
   Morton, advanced the field of medicine with experiments to find
   an effective painkiller; they discovered that ether (ē'•thər) gas
   could be used safely to put people to sleep
   during surgery.

(1)	(1)	(1)	(1)
(2)	(2)		

How did Lang and Morton advance the field of medicine?

_____

INSIGHTS: Reading as Thinking ©
Charlesbridge Publishing • (800) 225-3214

Read the following passages.
- Complete the charts. You do not have to write in complete sentences.
- Answer the questions following the charts.

The Vikings

The Vikings came from an area that is known today as Scandinavia. Overpopulation of their land led the Vikings to exploration and colonization. In 862 the Vikings established a large settlement in the area now called Russia, and in the 880s the Vikings, led by a Danish warrior called Rollo, invaded France and established settlements there.

Other settlements were founded in Greenland in 986 and, a few years later, in North America. Interestingly, the Vikings settled in England as well. In fact, a Viking named Canute became King of England in 1016. He made England part of his North Sea Empire until his death in 1035. After that, the Vikings in England, like the Vikings elsewhere, tended to live peacefully in isolated settlements.

Time	Events
1. _862_	_____
2. _____	_____
3. _____	_____
	_____
4. _____	_____
	_____
	_____
5. _____	_____
6. _____	_____

7. In how many geographic locations did the Vikings establish settlements?

_____

_____

INSIGHTS: *Reading as Thinking* ©
Charlesbridge Publishing • (800) 225-3214

BLACKLINE MASTER

UNIT 5 – Complex Information
Assessment

259

Harmful Insects

There are many insects that can damage plants. Aphids have soft, round bodies with wings. They damage plants by sucking plant juices. It is possible to control aphids by wiping the plants with warm, soapy water.

Spider mites have flat, oval bodies. They damage plants by covering leaves with a fine web like a spider's web. It is important to control their growth immediately since spider mites spread rapidly. Lime, sulfur, oil, and soap are all effective controls.

Scale insects have round bodies covered by hard shells. Scale insects suck plant juices and secrete an oil that causes mold to grow. Scale insects may be controlled by scraping them off the plants.

Name of Insect			Controls
Aphids			wipe off with soapy water
	flat, oval bodies		
		suck plant juices and secrete oil	

1. What do all of the insects have in common?

_____

2. Name two different ways in which insects cause plant damage.

_____

_____

BLACKLINE MASTER *INSIGHTS: Reading as Thinking* © Charlesbridge Publishing • (800) 225-3214

Extension

At this point in the unit you may read a book of your choice or do the writing activity below. Before you make a choice, read the instructions and the story below.

▣ COMPARING CHARACTERS

1. Read the short story below. It is followed by several comparison questions and a chart.
2. Choose a partner and discuss the questions that follow the story.
3. Complete the chart.
4. Write a paragraph in which you compare the two girls.

A Tale of Two Twins

Mary and Carrie were looking through their photo album and recalling the years when they dressed exactly alike, from their barrettes down to their shoes. Now, it was hard to tell they were identical twins from the way they dressed; Carrie lived in jeans and sweatshirts while Mary preferred long skirts and flower prints. You had to look closely to notice the same friendly heart-shaped face. When Carrie wasn't wearing a baseball cap, you could see that her curly, shoulder-length hair matched her sister's too.

The twins' differences went beyond their choices of clothing. Carrie was the school's basketball star, and when she wasn't playing basketball, she enjoyed hiking and going to the beach. She was on the debate team and wanted to be a high school English teacher. Mary, on the other hand, spent her free time practicing cello or browsing through museums and art galleries. She had been playing the cello since she was seven, and she wanted to play professionally. She dreamed of traveling all over the world and playing in beautiful concert halls.

Although their interests were different, Mary and Carrie were very supportive of each other. Mary could be found at every one of Carrie's games, cheering, "Go number 14! All right Carrie!" Carrie had chosen the number 14 because she was born 14 minutes after Mary. Carrie didn't really like classical music, but she went to Mary's recitals. Carrie joked that this was her payment for all the free tickets she would get to Mary's performances when she became famous. Mary gladly promised her sister front row seats.

Mary and Carrie both understood that just because they were twins, they didn't have to like the same things. They also knew that being twins meant that they would have a best friend in each other. They never got tired of hanging out together. They loved to go window-shopping and to play catch with their little brother. That they weren't mirror images of each other didn't distance them. In fact, their differences have made them appreciate and respect each other even more.

INSIGHTS: Reading as Thinking ©
Charlesbridge Publishing • (800) 225-3214

❏ COMPARING CHARACTERS

The students may read a book of their choice or do the Extension activity, which involves organizing comparative information from a story in a chart and then using the chart to write a comparison paragraph. Have them read the story before they make a decision.

❏ COMPARING CHARACTERS
continued

The questions that follow the story will help students extract the necessary information from the passage. This method of taking notes and organizing information in a chart form is very useful for preparing research reports and comprehending complex texts.

Allow students to discuss the questions and compare the attributes they have written in the chart.

1. In what ways are Mary and Carrie similar in physical appearance?

2. In what ways do they have similar feelings about each other?

3. In what ways do they show how they feel about each other?

4. How are their future goals different?

5. How are they different in terms of activities they enjoy?

6. How have they changed since they were younger?

	Mary	Carrie
Physical appearance and dress		
Feelings about each other		
Future goals		
Activities enjoyed		

INSIGHTS: Reading as Thinking ©
Charlesbridge Publishing • (800) 225-3214

UNIT 5 – Comprehending Complex Information   **177**

Additional Activities

The Additional Activities are designed as the remediation for those students who did not achieve mastery on the Assessment. In the Additional Activities, students will write passages to accompany charts. You may wish to assign some of the Additional Activities as homework.

❏ COMPLEX INFORMATION: THREE TYPES

Blackline Master Page 269

Hand out copies of Blackline Master Page 269. Have students read the opening paragraphs. Discuss classroom assignments for which sequence charts would help organize the information.

❏ SIGNAL WORDS FOR CHRONOLOGICAL ORDER

Have the students read the instructions. Encourage them to write as many chronological order signal words as they can before turning back to page 150.

Answers for Blackline Master Page 269

1. first	8. second	17. ending
2. begin	12. after	18. final, finally
3. initially	16. last	

❏ SIGNAL WORDS FOR SIMULTANEOUS ORDER

Blackline Master Page 270

Discuss the meaning of *simultaneous*. Hand out copies of Blackline Master Page 270. Ask students to write signal words that show simultaneous events. Have them look back at page 149 if necessary.

Answers for Blackline Master Page 270

4. while	7. simultaneously
5. meanwhile	8. at the same time
6. when, whenever	

❏ WRITING SEQUENCES IN ORDER

Ask students to use the chart to write a description of the storm on a separate sheet of paper. You may wish to have the students work together to describe the events for each time period, noting when simultaneous events occurred.

❏ COMPREHENDING SEQUENCES IN ORDER

Blackline Master Page 271

Hand out copies of Blackline Master Page 271. Explain that students will need to visualize the events described to decide what omitted event might logically occur in the sequence. Work with the group to complete the first two sentences and provide help as needed for sentences 3-5.

Answers for Blackline Master Page 271
(suggested answers only – accept all reasonable responses)
1. bandaged it
2. leaned back with his hands behind his head
3. a first-aid course at the neighborhood YMCA
4. by a rainbow
5. she crossed the finish line

❑ COMPREHENDING SEQUENCES OUT OF ORDER

Demonstrate how to use logic to put the events in each sentence in chronological order.

Answers for Blackline Master Page 271
6. Event 1: Jana cut her finger.
   Event 2: She pressed the wound.
7. Event 1: Brendan peeled off his shoes.
   Event 2: He wiggled his toes in the grass.
   Event 3: He leaned against a tree.
   Event 4: He watched the clouds.
8. Event 1: Leo did not know how to save a person's life.
   Event 2: He took a first aid course.
9. Event 1: Rain fell.
   Event 2: A rainbow appeared.
10. Event 1: The sprinter crossed the finish line.
    Event 2: She raised her hands in victory.

❑ SEQUENCE CHART OF EVENTS

Blackline Master Page 272

Hand out copies of Blackline Master Page 272. Ask three volunteers to read aloud two sentences from the passage and help the group identify the signal words to underline. Help them to outline the sequence of events in the chart.

Answers for Blackline Master Page 272
Underlined words: 1895, Two years later, 1898, 1900, 1901, 1904

Time	Events
1895:	Roosevelt gained national attention as reformer.
1897:	appointed McKinley's Assistant Secretary of the Navy
1897:	organized Rough Riders
1898:	elected Governor of New York
1900:	became McKinley's Vice President
1901:	McKinley assassinated; Roosevelt becomes President
1904:	re-elected

❑ COMPARISON CHARTS

Blackline
Master Page
273

Hand out copies of Blackline Master Page 273. Ask students to read the opening paragraphs. Help them use the comparison chart in the Example to complete the questions. Then ask them to write three of their own questions. Discuss their questions with the group.

Answers for Blackline Master Page 273
1. red   5. small   9. large
2. green   6. small   10.-12. Accept all reasonable sentences.
3. circle   7. square
4. large   8. green

❑ COMPARISON CHART AS OUTLINES

Blackline
Master Page
274

Have students read the instructions at the top of Blackline Master Page 274. Explain that students will use the comparison chart as an outline to construct six sentences. Provide help as needed and discuss students' responses.

Answers for Blackline Master Page 274
Accept all sentences that use the information given in the chart.
1. The Great Northern Railroad, built by James J. Hill, had 10,000 miles of track.
2. The Santa Fe linked Kansas, New Mexico, and Arizona.
3. The Northern Pacific was built by Henry Villard at a cost of eight million dollars.
4. The Great Northern ran between the Dakotas and Maryland.
5. The Santa Fe Railroad had 7,000 miles of track.
6. The Northern Pacific linked Lake Superior to Portland, Oregon.

❏ CONSTRUCTING COMPARISON CHARTS

Hand out copies of Blackline Master Page 275. Ask students to read the passage about the Great Lakes. Tell students to visualize each lake as it is described. Help them complete the comparison chart using the information in the passage.

Answers for Blackline Master Page 275

	Lake Superior	Lake Huron	Lake Erie
waters	coldest and deepest	receives water from two other lakes	shallowest waters
length	350 miles	206 miles	241 miles
location	between Duluth, MN, and Sault Sainte Marie	between Ontario and Michigan	surrounded by Pennsylvania, Ohio, New York, Michigan, and Canada
unusual features	Mt. Royal Island	no large cities and few harbors	cluster of islands on southern shore

❏ 5W'S PLUS HOW CHARTS

Hand out Blackline Master Pages 276-277. Ask students to name each of the 5W's plus How. Have students read the introductory paragraph.

❏ WRITING THE 5W'S PLUS HOW

Have students read the directions for writing the 5W's Plus How chart. Explain that they are to write sentences that describe the person, place, or thing in each chart. As a group, write sentences to describe the first chart. Have students use the remaining charts independently, asking for help when necessary. Discuss their responses, pointing out why they are complete sentences. Encourage students to notice the variety of acceptable phrasings their classmates have used.

Answers for Blackline Master Pages 276-277

Accept all reasonable sentences that use the information in the chart.

1. The Vikings lived in the northern part of Europe, called Scandinavia, during the tenth century. They built ships and traded goods to make a living.

2. The Arabian Peninsula, which lies between the northeast coast of Africa and India, is the world's largest peninsula.

3. The Arabs, who were descended mostly from a group called Bedouins, herded camels, goats, and sheep. They wandered across the desert of the Arabian Peninsula, searching for grass and water.

4. The Sugar Act was passed by the British Parliament in 1764. The act, which taxed sugar and other goods brought into Britain's colonies, was passed to make money for Britain.

5. The South American leader, Simón Bolívar, was called "The Liberator" because he defeated the Spanish in New Granada in 1819.

❑ CHARTING THE 5W'S PLUS HOW

Blackline
Master Pages
278-280

Hand out copies of Blackline Master Pages 278-280. Help them to answer each of the *Ask yourself* questions and complete the first chart. Have students work as independently as possible to complete the remaining charts. Ask volunteers to share their charts with the group. Discuss how students were able to shorten their responses to simplify the charts.

Answers for Blackline Master Pages 278-280

1. Who (What): French fur traders
   What Happened: gave Native Americans blankets and guns
   Why/How: in exchange for beaver and other animal skins
   Where/When: in the New World; no date

2. Who (What): Iron
   What Happened: was produced in large amounts
   Why/How: because it was needed to build machine parts, bridges, and ships
   Where/When: during the Industrial Revolution
   c. *Ask yourself:* Why was the iron produced? Because it was needed to build machine parts, bridges, and ships.
   d. *Ask yourself:* Is there any information about where or when in the sentence? "During the Industrial Revolution" tells you when.

3. Who (What): coal
   What Happened: was needed
   Why/How: to run steam engines
   Where/When: during the Industrial Revolution
   a. *Ask yourself:* What was this sentence about? Coal.
   b. *Ask yourself:* What happened? Coal was needed.
   c. *Ask yourself:* Why was coal needed? Coal was needed to run steam engines.
   d. *Ask yourself:* Is there any information in the sentence that tells where or when? "During the Industrial Revolution" tells when.

4. Why/How: by blasting air under great pressure through melted iron to burn out extra carbon and other impurities
   Where/When: 1856
5. Who (What): the British
   What Happened: made rivers wider and deeper, built canals
   Why/How: to connect cities and rivers
   Where/When: England; during the Industrial Revolution
6. Who (What): Industrial Revolution
   What Happened: produced a new way of life
   Why/How: thousands of people moved to the cities to work for wages in factories
   Where/When: Britain

Additional Activities

▪ COMPLEX INFORMATION: THREE TYPES

This unit has dealt with three types of complex information: *sequential*, *comparative*, and *condensed*. In the previous lessons you were given passages to read. In this activity it will be the other way around: you will write the passages. First, you need to review some basic terms.

Sequence charts are charts that outline the time periods and events for a series of events. Sequence charts are most useful for outlining historical events, the steps in an experiment, and the events in a person's life. Many historians and novelists construct sequence charts as a form of note taking. Then they use the sequence chart as an outline for what they write. This is what you will do next.

▪ SIGNAL WORDS FOR CHRONOLOGICAL ORDER

❑ Here are the signal words showing chronological order. Complete the lists.
  • Try to recall as many as you can before looking back to Strategy Lesson 2.

Beginning Events	Middle Events	Ending Events
1. _____ , former	8. _____ , third	16. _____ , latter
2. _____ , beginning	9. next	17. end, _____
3. initial, _____	10. then	18. _____ , finale
4. before	11. and	_____
5. precedes	12. _____ , afterward	19. later
6. prior to	13. subsequently	
7. now	14. followed by	
	15. in the middle	

INSIGHTS: Reading as Thinking ©
Charlesbridge Publishing • (800) 225-3214

BLACKLINE MASTER

UNIT 5 – Complex Information
Additional Activity

269

▣ SIGNAL WORDS FOR SIMULTANEOUS ORDER

❑ List all the words that show simultaneous events.
Try to recall as many as you can before looking back to Strategy Lesson 2.

1. __and__   4. _____   7. _____

2. __during__   5. _____   8. _____

3. __as__   6. _____   _____

▣ WRITING SEQUENCES IN ORDER

Here is the sequence chart of the events in a story about a storm.

❑ Read the chart.
  • On a separate sheet of paper, write a brief description of the storm, using the information in the sequence chart as an outline.
  • Use as many signal words as you can that show chronological order and simultaneous events. Describe the events in the order that they occur in the sequence chart.

TIME	EVENTS
7:30 PM	news announcement of storm warning; man sits in a chair reading
8:00 PM	low, distant thundering, distant lightning, some light rain
9:15 PM	loud claps of thunder, rapid flashes of lightning, heavy rains with winds whistling past the window; man huddles near the radio
9:40 PM	an electric wire smashes against a window, breaking it; lights, telephone, and radio go out; water pours in from broken window; man frantically tries to fix window, but winds are too strong
9:50 PM	winds roar, water pushes in through broken window, causing flooding on the ground floor; man retreats upstairs
11:00 PM	A car drives up.
11:01 PM	You invent what happens next.

UNIT 5 – Complex Information
Additional Activity   BLACKLINE MASTER   INSIGHTS: *Reading as Thinking* ©
Charlesbridge Publishing • (800) 225-3214

■ COMPREHENDING SEQUENCES IN ORDER

❑ Read and complete the following sentences.

1. When Jana (1) cut her finger, she (2) applied pressure to the wound to make it

   stop bleeding, (3) washed it, and (4) _____ .

2. Brendan (1) peeled off his shoes, (2) wiggled his toes in the grass, (3) _____

   _____ , and (4) watched the clouds.

3. Leo did not know how to save a person's life until he took _____

   _____ .

4. The rain was followed_____ .

5. The sprinter raised her hands in victory after _____

   _____ .

■ COMPREHENDING SEQUENCES OUT OF ORDER

❑ Read the following sentences and write the events in the order in which they occur.

6. Jana pressed the wound after she cut her finger.

   Event 1:_____   Event 2: _____

7. Before Brendan leaned against the tree and watched the clouds, he peeled off his
   shoes and wiggled his toes in the grass.

   Event 1: _____

   Event 2: _____

   Event 3: _____

   Event 4: _____

8. Prior to taking the first aid course, Leo did not know how to save a person's life.

   Event 1:_____   Event 2: _____

9. A beautiful rainbow followed the heavy rain.

   Event 1:_____   Event 2: _____

10. The sprinter raised her hands in victory after she crossed the finish line.

   Event 1:_____   Event 2: _____

INSIGHTS: *Reading as Thinking* ©
Charlesbridge Publishing • (800) 225-3214

BLACKLINE MASTER

UNIT 5 – Complex Information
Additional Activity

271

◼ SEQUENCE CHART OF EVENTS

❏ Read the following passage and underline the signal words.

• Outline the sequence of events in the sequence chart that follows.

 Theodore Roosevelt's Career

Theodore Roosevelt's political career was an unusual one. In 1895, while head of the New York City police board, Roosevelt gained national attention as a reformer. Two years later he was appointed President McKinley's Assistant Secretary of the Navy. He resigned from that position to organize the "Rough Riders," a volunteer regiment. This regiment won fame fighting in Cuba in the Spanish-American War. When Roosevelt returned as a hero in 1898, he was elected Governor of New York. He became McKinley's vice president in 1900, but in 1901, McKinley was assassinated and Roosevelt became President. His vitality and enthusiasm, as well as his reforms, made him so popular that he won re-election easily in 1904.

Time	Events
_____	
	Think: The first date mentioned is 1895. Write 1895 on the line under Time.
	Ask Yourself: What happened in 1895? Write what happened on the line for Events.
_____	
	Think: "Two years later" is the signal for a new event. Add two to 1895 (1895 + 2 = 1897) and write the answer under Time.
	Ask Yourself: What happened two years later? Write what happened under Events.
_____	_____
_____	_____
_____	_____
_____	_____

Remember: A sequence chart helps clarify the order of events when the text has a lot of complex sentences that describe a sequence.

 UNIT 5 – Complex Information
Additional Activity   BLACKLINE MASTER   *INSIGHTS: Reading as Thinking* ©
Charlesbridge Publishing • (800) 225-3214

☐ COMPARISON CHARTS

You use comparison charts whenever you compare the characteristics of two or more persons, places, or things. Most often, you use comparison charts to compare characters in a story, real people, the duties of a job, or the features of plants, animals, and things.

An author may use a comparison chart as an outline for writing a book. In the exercise below, however, you will use the comparison chart to construct sentences.

Example

Comparison Chart

	Square	Triangle	Circle	Rectangle
color	red 1	green 2	blue 3	yellow 4
size	large 5	small 6	large 7	small 8

Explanation

You can construct many sentences by using the information in this chart. Complete the first nine sentences below, then write three more.

1. The square is _____ . (box 1 in chart)

2. The triangle is _____ . (box 2 in chart)

3. The _____ is blue. (box 3 in chart)

4. The square is _____ . (box 5 in chart)

5. The triangle is _____ . (box 6 in chart)

6. The rectangle is _____ . (box 8 in chart)

7. The red _____ is large. (boxes 1 and 5)

8. The triangle is small and _____ . (boxes 6 and 2)

9. The circle is _____ and blue. (boxes 7 and 3)

10. _____

11. _____

12. _____

INSIGHTS: Reading as Thinking ©
Charlesbridge Publishing • (800) 225-3214

BLACKLINE MASTER

UNIT 5 – Complex Information
Additional Activity

273

COMPARISON CHARTS AS OUTLINES

❏ Read the following comparison chart.
  • Use it as an outline to construct six sentences about railroads.

The Railroads

	Great Northern	Santa Fe	Northern Pacific
location	ran from the Dakotas to Maryland	linked Kansas, New Mexico, Arizona	linked Lake Superior to Portland, Oregon
built by	James J. Hill	Cyrus Holliday	Henry Villard
details	10,000 miles of track	7,000 miles of track	cost $8 million

1. _____

_____

2. _____

_____

3. _____

_____

4. _____

_____

5. _____

_____

6. _____

_____

UNIT 5 – Complex Information
Additional Activity

BLACKLINE MASTER

INSIGHTS: Reading as Thinking ©
Charlesbridge Publishing • (800) 225-3214

■ CONSTRUCTING COMPARISON CHARTS

❏ Read the following passage and construct a comparison chart.

The Great Lakes

Lake Superior has the coldest and deepest waters of all the Great Lakes. It stretches 350 miles from Duluth, Minnesota, to Sault Ste. Marie. The unique natural feature of Lake Superior is the island of Mt. Royal, where visitors can watch wild moose.

Lake Huron receives its waters from two other lakes. It is 206 miles long, stretching from Ontario to Michigan. Lake Huron has no large cities and few harbors.

Lake Erie has the shallowest waters of the Great Lakes. It is 241 miles long. Lake Erie is surrounded by Ohio, Pennsylvania, New York, Michigan, and Canada. The only unusual feature of Lake Erie is a cluster of islands on its southern shore.

	Lake Superior		
waters			
length			
location			

INSIGHTS: Reading as Thinking ©
Charlesbridge Publishing • (800) 225-3214

BLACKLINE MASTER

UNIT 5 – Complex Information
Additional Activity

275

5W'S PLUS HOW CHARTS

5W's plus How charts are charts that have the 5W's plus How in the column headings. These charts are for sentences that contain a great deal of information about a person, place, or thing: who, what, where, when, why, and how. You find such sentences mainly in newspapers and social studies texts. You will write the sentences to describe the information in the charts on the following pages.

WRITING THE 5W'S PLUS HOW

❑ Read the information in each of the 5W's plus How charts below. Each chart is about a person, place, or thing.

• Describe the person, place, or thing in one to three sentences on the lines below each chart.

Who (What)	What Happened	Why/How	Where/When
Vikings	built ships and traded	to make a living	northern part of Europe called Scandinavia; 10th century

1. _____

_____

_____

Who (What)	What Happened	Why/How	Where/When
Arabian Peninsula	world's largest peninsula	to make a living	between northeast coast of Africa and India

2. _____

_____

_____

Who (What)	What Happened	Why/How	Where/When
Arabs, descended mostly from group called Bedouins	1. herded camels, goats, and sheep 2. wandered across the desert	searching for grass and water	(Arabian) Peninsula

3. _____

_____

_____

_____

Who (What)	What Happened	Why/How	Where/When
Sugar Act	1. passed by British Parliament 2. taxed sugar and other goods brought into Britain's colonies	to make money for Britain	1764

4. _____

_____

_____

Who (What)	What Happened	Why/How	Where/When
South American leader, Simón Bolívar	called "The Liberator"	defeated the Spanish	New Granada, 1819

5. _____

_____

INSIGHTS: Reading as Thinking ©
Charlesbridge Publishing • (800) 225-3214

BLACKLINE MASTER

UNIT 5 – Complex Information
Additional Activity

277

■ CHARTING THE 5W'S PLUS HOW

❏ Read the following sentences.
  • Complete the 5W's plus How charts for each sentence.

1. The French fur traders in the New World gave the Native Americans blankets and guns in exchange for beaver and other animal skins.

Who (What) (1)	What Happened (2)	Why/How (3)	Where/When (4)

a. *Ask yourself:* Who or what is the sentence about?

   The French fur traders. Write the answer in column 1.

b. *Ask yourself:* What happened?

   The French fur traders gave the Native Americans blankets and guns. Write this answer in column 2.

c. *Ask yourself:* Why did the French fur traders do this?

   In exchange for beaver and other animal skins.
   Write this answer in column 3.

d. *Ask yourself:* Is there any information about where or when in the sentence?

   "In the New World" tells you where, but there is no information about when. Write this answer in column 4.

UNIT 5 – Complex Information
Additional Activity   BLACKLINE MASTER   *INSIGHTS: Reading as Thinking* ©
Charlesbridge Publishing • (800) 225-3214

2. During the Industrial Revolution, iron was produced in large amounts because it was needed to build machine parts, bridges, and ships.

Who (What) (1)	What Happened (2)	Why/How (3)	Where/When (4)

a. *Ask yourself*: Who or what is the sentence about?
Iron. Write "iron" in column 1.

b. *Ask yourself*: What happened? Iron was produced in large amounts.
Write your answer in column 2.

c. *Ask yourself*: (You write the questions and answers.) _____

_____

_____

d. *Ask yourself*: _____

_____

_____

3. Coal was also needed during the Industrial Revolution; without coal it would not have been possible to run all of the steam engines.

Who (What) (1)	What Happened (2)	Why/How (3)	Where/When (4)

a. *Ask yourself*: _____

b. *Ask yourself*: _____

c. *Ask yourself*: _____

Paraphrasing will help you fit the answer into the space in column 3.

d. *Ask yourself*: _____

_____

INSIGHTS: Reading as Thinking ©
Charlesbridge Publishing • (800) 225-3214

BLACKLINE MASTER

UNIT 5 – Complex Information
Additional Activity

279

4. In 1856, an Englishman named Henry Bessemer found a way to make steel from iron. Called the Bessemer Process, it consisted of blasting air under great pressure through melted iron to burn out the extra carbon and other impurities.

Who (What)	What Happened	Why/How	Where/When
Henry Bessemer	found a way to make steel from iron: the Bessemer Process		

5. During the Industrial Revolution, the British also made their rivers wider and deeper, and built canals to connect cities and rivers.

Who (What)	What Happened	Why/How	Where/When

6. The Industrial Revolution produced a new way of life in Britain; thousands of people moved to the cities to work for wages in factories.

Who (What)	What Happened	Why/How	Where/When

Re-assessment

The Re-assessment uses the same format as the Assessment and asks students to demonstrate the same understanding and strategies.

Blackline Master Pages 283-285 Hand out copies of Blackline Master Pages 283-285 and ask the students to read the instructions carefully. Have them look over the pages and ask any questions they might have before they begin.

Answers for Blackline Master Page 283
  Who (What):
    1. Egyptians
  What Happened:
    1. built dams and ditches
    2. dug basins
  Why/How
    1. to control the flood waters of the Nile
  Where/When
    1. Egypt
    2. first century B.C.
The Egyptians needed to control the flood waters of the Nile.

  Who(What):
    1. Mrs. Rosa Parks
  What Happened:
    1. advanced civil rights movement
    2. led to Supreme Court decision in favor of civil rights
  Why/How:
    1. because she refused to give up her bus seat
  Where/When
    1. Alabama
    2. 1957

Mrs. Parks advanced the civil rights movement because her refusal to give up her bus seat led to a Supreme Court decision in favor of civil rights.

Answers for Blackline Master Page 284

Time	Events
1. 1876	ruled by dictator, Porfirio Díaz
2. 1910	Díaz overthrown, civil war begins
3. 1917	war ends – new constitution
4. 1938	government took control of oil industry
5. 1939-1945	made war supplies for U.S. and other friendly nations
6. 1953	women receive right to vote

7. After the war, Mexican women received the right to vote.

Answers for Blackline Master Page 285

Name of Tool	Description	Used by Whom	Purpose
flint chips or choppers	*sharpened by striking with heavy bones*	*Cro-Magnon cave dwellers*	to cut food and plants
machete	made from iron by village blacksmith	*Kpelles*	*to cut brush*
scythe	*curved sword-like blade attached to long handle*	several groups of modern people	*to cut brush and high grass*

1. the machete and the scythe
2. The Kpelles used a machete to cut trees and brush. Some people still use a scythe to cut brush and high grass.

❏ SCORING

Score 1 point for each correctly completed chart entry and each correctly answered question. Accept alternate wordings and other logical answers.

Mastery Level: 34 out of 42 points.

Re-assessment

❏ Read the following sentences and complete the chart that follows each one.
  • Then, answer the question under each chart.

By the first century B.C., the Egyptians had built dams and ditches and had dug basins or bowl-shaped holes; they became expert architects because they needed to control the flood waters of the Nile.

Who (What)	What Happened	Why/How	Where/When
(1)	(1)	(1)	(1)
	(2)		(2)
	(3) became expert architects		

Why did the Egyptians build dams, ditches, and basins? _____

_____

Mrs. Rosa Parks, remarkable for her bravery, advanced the civil rights movement when she refused to give up her bus seat in Alabama in 1957; her actions led to a Supreme Court decision in favor of civil rights.

(1) (1)		(1)	(1)
(2)			(2)

How did Mrs. Parks advance the civil rights movement? _____

_____

INSIGHTS: Reading as Thinking ©
Charlesbridge Publishing • (800) 225-3214

BLACKLINE MASTER

UNIT 5 – Complex Information
Re-assessment

283

❏ Read the following passages.

• Complete the charts. You do not have to write in complete sentences. Answer the questions following the charts.

In 1876, Mexico came under the rule of Porfirio Díaz, a dictator who did little to help his people. He was overthrown in 1910 and a civil war swept over the country. In 1917 the war ended and a new constitution brought many reforms — land for the farmers, more schools, and better working conditions. In 1938 the government took control of the large oil industry, which had been built mostly by foreign companies. This angered many people. However, during World War II (1939-1945), Mexican industry grew rapidly and was able to supply the United States and other friendly nations with war goods. This helped build stronger relations with these countries. Finally, in 1953, women received the right to vote. Mexico has come a long way since the dictatorship of Díaz.

Time	Events
1. _____1876_____	_____
2. _____	_____
	_____
3. _____	_____
4. _____	_____
	_____
5. _____	_____
	_____
6. _____	_____

7. What happened after World War II? _____

_____

Different groups of people use different hand tools. One group of early cave dwellers, the Cro-Magnons, used flint chips as knives and choppers. These cave dwellers sharpened the flint and made it into different shapes by striking it with heavy bones. These chips had many uses, but they were used mainly to cut food and plants. The Kpelles, an African people, used the machete as their main tool. A machete is a long, heavy, sword-like tool, made from iron by the village blacksmith. The machete is used for cutting trees and brush to clear the land before planting rice. Several other groups have used the scythe. This tool has a long, curved, sword-like blade attached to a long handle. The sword is made of metal, but the handle can be metal or wood. The scythe is still used to cut brush and high grass.

Name of Tool			Purpose
flint chips or choppers			to cut food and plants
	made from iron by village blacksmith		
		several groups of modern people	

1. Which tools are most alike?_____

2. Who used them and for what are they used today?_____

_____

_____

INSIGHTS: *Reading as Thinking* ©
Charlesbridge Publishing • (800) 225-3214

BLACKLINE MASTER

UNIT 5 – Complex Information
Re-assessment

285